THE VIOLENT AFTERMATH OF THE KOSOVO CONFLICT

**Diary
of an**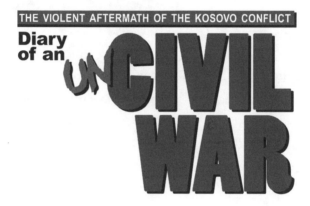

ABOUT THE AUTHOR

Scott Taylor, a former soldier, is the editor and publisher of *Esprit de Corps**, an Ottawa-based magazine celebrated for its unflinching scrutiny of the Canadian military. Research for this book was compiled first-hand from inside Yugoslavia and Macedonia following NATO s occupation of Kosovo.

PHOTO COURTESY DAVE CHAN, THE OTTAWA *CITIZEN*

Taylor appears regularly in the Canadian media as a military analyst, and is the recipient of the **1996 Quill Award** for outstanding work in the field of Canadian communications. That same year, he won the **Alexander MacKenzie Award** for journalistic excellence.

A columnist for the *Halifax Herald* and the host of *Situation Report,* Taylor has been a contributor to *Maclean's*, the *Globe and Mail*, *The Financial Post*, *Media Magazine* and *Reader's Digest*. Some of the on-site reporting that appears in this book was produced on freelance assignment for the *Ottawa Citizen.*

OTHER WORKS BY SCOTT TAYLOR

- ♦ *Tarnished Brass: Crime and Corruption in the Canadian Military*
    (co-author with Brian Nolan), 1996 (reprinted 1997)
- ♦ *Tested Mettle: Canada's Peacekeepers at War*
    (co-author with Brian Nolan), 1998
- ♦ *Inat: Images of Serbia and the Kosovo Conflict*
    (author), 2000
- ♦ *Canada at War and Peace, II: A Millennium of Military Heritage*
    (editor-in-chief), 2001

* *Esprit de Corps* magazine is a monthly publication focusing on the news and history of the Canadian military. A 12-issue subscription costs $29.95. For additional information, contact 1-800-361-2791 (in Canada) or visit the *Esprit de Corps* website at www.espritdecorps.on.ca.

THE VIOLENT AFTERMATH OF THE KOSOVO CONFLICT

Diary of an unCIVIL WAR

"Never, never, never believe any war
will be smooth and easy, or that anyone
who embarks on that strange voyage
can measure the tides and
hurricanes he will encounter."

SIR WINSTON CHURCHILL

Canadian Cataloguing in Publication Data

Taylor, Scott, 1960 -
Diary of an uncivil war: the violent aftermath of the Kosovo conflict

Includes index.

ISBN 1-895896-20-7

1. Taylor, Scott, 1960-
2. Kosovo (Serbia)--History--Civil War, 1998-
--Personal narratives, Canadian.
3. North Atlantic Treatry Organization--
Armed Forces--Yugoslavia--Serbia.
4. Kosovo (Serbia)--History--Civil War,1998-
--Participation, Foreign.
5. Macedonia (Republic)–History–1992-
I. Title. II. Title: Uncivil war.

DR1316.T385 2002   949.7103   C2002-900693-7

Printed and bound in Canada

Esprit de Corps Books
1066 Somerset St. West, Suite 204
Ottawa, Ontario
K1Y 4T3
1-800-361-2791

From outside Canada
Tel: (613) 725-5060 / Fax: (613) 725-1019

CONTENTS

ACKNOWLEDGEMENTS

The author wishes to acknowledge the contributions of those individuals whose generous assistance made this project possible. At the top of the list (again) is Bora Dragasevich and his wife Draga. Since backing my efforts to gain access to Yugoslavia during the NATO bombing, the Dragasevichs have provided the support necessary to make the research for this project possible.

Special thanks are due to the staff at the Yugoslavian and Macedonian embassies for arranging key interviews and providing me with a wealth of background information.

As for administrative support while in the Balkans, I wish to thank Mario Predrag and Mira, as well as the families Kopric, Brujic and Kocevski.

For supporting my ventures I wish to credit editors Bruce Garvey at the *Ottawa Citizen* and Terry O'Neil at the *Halifax Herald*. Dr. Bill Twatio also deserves a "mention-in-despatches" for bulldozing the bumps (and adding verbs) to the final product.

The production efforts of Cathy Hingley and Julie Simoneau in helping to bring this book to fruition are greatly appreciated as are the numerous hours volunteered by both Anne Trinneer and Jennifer Gearey.

Brian Nolan and Peter Worthington remain role models and mentors and deserve much credit for their guidance and insight.

Special thanks are due also to Miriam, Kirk, Fred, Mary, Raymond, Vlado, Rad, Natasha, Boba, Petar, Milos and the Kirkness family for their support.

Dedicated to Katherine and Kirk

ABOUT THIS BOOK

The June 1999 entry of NATO troops was hailed as the "Liberation of Kosovo" by the western media – most of whom promptly packed up and headed home from the Balkans.

The declaration of victory was naive and premature given the Alliance's stated objectives of deposing Yugoslav President Slobodan Milosevic and creating a safe multi-ethnic environment in Kosovo.

Rather than ending the civil strife, NATO's intervention set in motion a series of events which would have violent repercussions throughout Serbia, Kosovo and Macedonia over the next two years.

This book, consisting primarily of Scott Taylor's first-hand observations and interviews with the people and players, is a very personal account of war and its aftermath in Serbia and Macedonia.

As such, the journal portion has been deliberately limited to information available to the author, in the Balkans, at the time.

PHOTOGRAPHY

Unless otherwise credited, all photos appearing in this book were taken by the author. Special thanks is due to James Phillips for the provision of photographs and assistance during the author's various visits to Macedonia.
Cover photo: Paramilitary Lion inside Tetovo, Macedonia, August 2001.
Back cover photo: Albanian nationalism in Tetovo, Macedonia, May 2001.

ABOUT THE TITLE

In addition to the wordplay on any war's *civility*, the various conflicts and uprisings triggered throughout the Balkans since NATO's intervention in Kosovo have not been categorized as "civil wars." The ouster of Yugoslav President Slobodan Milosevic was a virtually bloodless "uprising" – while the fighting and ethnic cleanings in Kosovo, south Serbia and Macedonia remained too localized to be described as anything but inter-ethnic "conflicts" or "clashes."

YUGOSLAVIA AND MACEDONIA: *Map showing the major Balkan cities which the author visited or reported on following NATO's 1999 occupation of Kosovo. (MAP BY KATHERINE TAYLOR)*

ABOVE: *On June 16, 1999, British troops watched as hundreds of cheering Albanians formed a guantlet on the streets of Pristina. (SCOTT TAYLOR) As Serbian refugees (**OPPOSITE PAGE**) fled their homes, their departure from Kosovo was hastened by angry mobs of Albanian civilians. The Western media largely ignored this reversal in ethnic cleansing. (REUTERS)*

chapter one:
THE OTHER SIDE

PRISTINA, KOSOVO – 15 JUNE 1999 (Tuesday)

Queuing up at 6:00 a.m., I was lucky to get a ticket on the last Belgrade-bound bus. It was standing room only as I boarded with 67 Serb refugees carrying all their worldly possessions. The 78-day bombing campaign had reduced the Pristina bus station to little more than a pile of rubble. (The first NATO ground troops had arrived in the capital of Kosovo two days earlier, and it was now serving as a major logistics point for the British 5th Brigade.) As our over-loaded bus backed away from the platform, British soldiers came out of their tents to laugh at the spectacle.

Since Sunday, the streets of Pristina had been clogged with dusty columns of retreating Yugoslav Army units. British tanks and armoured vehicles were overseeing their progress at every major intersection. Under the terms of the Technical Agreement, signed June 9 in Kumanovo, Macedonia, the Yugoslav security forces still had 48 hours to withdraw from Kosovo. The presence of 4800 NATO peacekeepers had done little to reassure Serbian civilians of their continued safety. Televised statements by U.S. State Department officials fuelled their fears by warning, "Kosovo will not be a very healthy place for Serbs in the coming days."

The Albanian Kosovo Liberation Army wasted little time in making that prophecy a reality. As the first NATO vehicles rolled into the embattled province, several off-duty Serbian soldiers waiting for withdrawal orders were gunned down in Pristina while dozens of farmers were brutally murdered outside Prizren. The outbreak of violence sparked the exodus of hundreds of thousands of terrified Serbian civilians.

Although I had been offered safe passage back to Belgrade with a NATO-escorted convoy of foreign journalists, I felt the major news story was the reverse ethnic-cleansing. What better way to cover it than as a participant.

Just before noon our bus reached the northern city limits of Pristina. There to greet us were 600 or so rock-throwing Albanians. British soldiers were on hand, but they made no attempt to disperse the crowd. As our driver accelerated, the bus was pelted with rocks. It was a terrifying experience, particularly for the young children and elderly.

The gauntlet had been established coincidentally with the arrival of the NATO vanguard on Sunday. For two days and nights groups of Albanians manned this checkpoint to "see off" their Serbian neighbours. Several vehicles had been disabled and their Serbian occupants hauled out and beaten.

Here too, British troops stood by, laughed and did nothing. Except for me, no reporter was there to record the incident, despite the fact that 2700 foreign journalists had been accredited by NATO to report from Kosovo.

Apparently, this gauntlet was not considered newsworthy enough. Journalists were distracted by the victory celebrations following NATO's "liberation" of Kosovo, and images of terrified Serbs being taunted and stoned by Kosovars might have also altered the cultivated image of Albanians as "innocent victims of an oppressive regime."

Of course, it was largely these same journalists, through their one-sided reporting on the war, who had created this simplified picture of a complex situation. When the NATO campaign began, only a handful of Western journalists had been allowed to remain inside Serbia and Kosovo. The Serbs had great difficulty in presenting their side of the story as television studios and transmitters were bombed. As a result, most of the daily news coverage came from either the NATO press center in Brussels or from unconfirmed witness statements collected from refugee camps in neighbouring Macedonia. Although the exodus of Albanians from Kosovo started two days *after* the air strikes began, this humanitarian crisis and allegations of genocide were accepted as justification for the Alliance's military intervention.

As the bombing campaign dragged on and the Serbs showed no sign of surrender, the prospect of NATO launching a ground assault loomed larger.

In order to strengthen support for such a risky escalation of the conflict, NATO spokesman Jamie Shea simply upped his numbers. Overnight, the figure of Albanians presumed murdered by the Serbs was multiplied tenfold to 100,000.

Similarly, NATO's tactical successes were wildly exaggerated by Shea, and dutifully reported by the Western media.

When the horde of journalists finally descended upon Kosovo, reporters weren't interested in Albanian revenge killings of Serbs – they were on a collective race to uncover the first "mass graves," discover the "rape camps," and the shattered remains of the Serbian army.

What they found was evidence of a very different war from the one they had just spent the past three months reporting. The mass grave sites proved to be elusive. Despite much-repeated eyewitness accounts of the execution of 700 Albanians at the Trepca mines for example, not a single body was found. The biggest find was seven corpses exhumed at Ljubenic – a site which had purportedly been the burial ground of over 350 Kosovars. After five months of searching, UN forensic teams had uncovered only 670 bodies: Keeping in mind that this tally included Albanian, Serbian and Gypsy civilians plus suspected combatants, the numbers did not justify the careless use of the word *genocide*, and was a far cry from Jamie Shea's wildly exaggerated claims.

As the last of the Yugoslav Army and police columns withdrew, journalists were equally hard-pressed to locate the burnt-out hulks of vehicles promised them by Jamie Shea. In his daily press briefings, Shea had kept a running tally of destroyed Serbian weapon systems, boasting that NATO air power had effectively created "a ring of death around Kosovo."

The truth was sobering. Despite dropping over $15 billion (U.S.) worth of ordnance, only 13 Serbian tanks were destroyed in 78 days of bombing, and five of these were credited to UCK land mines.

Claims of mass rape also failed to stand up to scrutiny.

At the height of the fighting, the Canadian Broadcasting Corporation produced a short documentary profiling a female fighter in the Kosovo Liberation Army. Her heart-rending story was that she had taken up arms after being forced to watch as Serbian police raped, then killed, her sister When a television news crew tracked her down for a follow-up homecoming piece, they found her sister very much alive – and unmolested. When the CBC aired what amounted to a retraction of the original story, she was unrepentant. "We did what we had to do," she said. "We could not beat the Serbs ourselves."

As journalists are loathe to admit they've been duped, retractions or corrections rarely receive the same prominence as the original stories – and once public opinion has been shaped, it is difficult to shift. Since news reports are considered the first rough draft of history, books based on this one-sided coverage of the conflict exacerbate the original distortions.

In *Virtual War: Kosovo and Beyond*, Canadian author and Balkan analyst Michael Ignatieff perpetuated many of the falsehoods generated to justify NATO's intervention. Although it can be gleaned from the anecdotes he uses that only one side of the conflict is being presented, Ignatieff gives the impression that he is telling the whole story. His interviews with U.S. envoy Richard Holbrooke, The Hague War Crimes chief prosecutor Louise Arbour, and General Wesley Clark are not offset with the views of the Serbian leadership. Much of *Virtual War* was written during the air campaign and was based only on information available at the time. Consequently, Ignatieff's supporting arguments for the campaign are based on the same two "galvanizing incidents" used by NATO spokesmen to justify their actions: the January 1999 massacre of Albanian civilians by Serbian police at Racak, and *Operation Horseshoe*, the plan for Yugoslavia to ethnically-cleanse Kosovo.

By the time *Virtual War* was published in 2000, German intelligence confessed to having fabricated the *Operation Horseshoe* documents, and a UN forensic team had concluded that "no massacre" had taken place at Racak. Despite the importance of these findings, Ignatieff chose to ignore them rather than rethink his basic premise.

Likewise, veteran CBC journalist Carol Off failed to note that Racak was a hoax in *The Lion, The Fox and The Eagle: A story of generals and justice in Rwanda and Yugoslavia*. Although Off devoted one-third of her book to Hague prosecutor Louise Arbour (the Eagle), no mention was made of this new evidence.

Arbour's indictment of Yugoslav President Slobodan Milosevic as a war criminal on the basis of the Racak massacre during the NATO air campaign had served the U.S. State Department's propaganda interests. However, by proceeding with this indictment without corroborating forensic evidence, Arbour undermined not only the credibility of The Hague Tribunal, but also her professional reputation as an impartial prosecutor.

In her book, and her subsequent defence of it, Carol Off displays a marked anti-Serbian bias, which is echoed by many of the Western journalists who ventured into the Balkans from time to time over the past decade to size up the situation. Their stories were often misleading. Conditions in the "besieged" Muslim enclave of Sarajevo, for example, were deemed representative of the overall situation in Bosnia.

A dumbed-down version of 'Serbs as aggressors' became the media-accepted template for coverage, even when it completely ignored the complexity behind the multi-factional violence taking place in the former Yugoslavia.

In reporting the civil wars in Croatia and Bosnia, journalists often described the Serbs as invaders and whatever territory they occupied was referred to as captured.

Such simplistic interpretations ignore history. Most of the ethnic Serbian inhabitants of disputed areas have been living there for over 250 years. Forced from Kosovo, their religious heartland, by the Turks in 1737 during the Great Migration, thousands of displaced Serbs resettled in the Austro-Hungarian Empire and formed a buffer zone against further Turkish expansion.

In addition to ignoring past population shifts, the Western media also chose to rewrite modern history. Inspired by Croatian- and Muslim-funded U.S. public relations firms, the Serbs were often compared to Nazi stormtroopers. For the Serbian people to be depicted in this fashion is particularly puzzling. In World War II, when the Germans invaded Yugoslavia, Hitler had exploited underlying ethnic hatreds to divide and conquer. Croatia was recognized as an independent state and its *Ustasha* pledged allegiance to the Nazis. Albanians in Kosovo were recruited in great numbers into an SS Division, *Skenderberg*, while the Bosnian Muslims joined another SS Division, *Handschar*, noted for its brutality. As they had in World War I, the Serbs supported the Allied cause and fiercely resisted German occupation. As Communist partisans, or Royalist Chetniks, the Serbs were dogged fighters, much admired in the West. But they paid a hefty price for their defiance. As part of the Nazi policy of retribution, the death of every German soldier was avenged with the execution of 100

Serbian civilians. At concentration camps in Croatia, the *Ustasha* exterminated Serbs, Jews and Gypsys with such savagery that even the German SS commanders were compelled to protest.

The media continued to refer to the Serbian military as a Nazi-like juggernaut throughout the various Balkan wars of the past decade. Some juggernaut. By the time the Dayton Peace Accord was signed in December 1995, it had been defeated on all fronts and over 750,000 Serb civilians had been expelled from lost territory in western Slovonia, the Krajina, eastern Croatia and Bosnia.

Despite military setbacks and widespread suffering in Yugoslavia after a decade of economic sanctions, the media stereotype remained unchanged. In March 1999, on the eve of the Kosovo conflict, U.S. Secretary of State Madeleine Albright likened Slobodan Milosevic to "Adolf Hitler in 1938."

Milosevic was the very man who, in 1996, Albright had praised as a "man of peace," in recognition of the part he played in securing the Dayton agreement. When hundreds of thousands of Serbs took to the streets of Belgrade later that same year to protest his manipulation of municipal elections, the U.S. refused to intervene. With a U.S.-led NATO stabilization force maintaining a shaky cease-fire in Bosnia, the Americans needed Milosevic.

While the American media chose to ignore Albright's flip-flop, the Serbs did not forget. As NATO bombs rained down on Belgrade, so did U.S. propaganda leaflets urging Yugoslavs to rise up and overthrow Milosevic. Despite their hatred for the president, they were not about to do America's bidding while in the cross-hairs of a bombsight.

In the end, NATO had been forced to back down and negotiate the Kosovo peace deal with indicted war criminal Slobodan Milosevic.

In return for allowing NATO ground troops to enter the province (under a United Nations mandate), Kosovo was to remain the sovereign territory of Yugoslavia, the Albanian Kosovo Liberation Army was to be disbanded, and Serbian security forces were to remain in control of the border crossings.

The neighbouring Republic of Macedonia expected its own reward for having provided emergency assistance to the flood of Albanian refugees and for allowing NATO troops to use its territory as a staging ground for the Kosovo operation. Bankrupt and militarily unprepared, the Macedonians believed that they would be accepted as partners in NATO and the European Union, and that they would not be caught up in the escalating regional violence.

Events would prove them wrong.

ABOVE: *Pristina, June 1999. Despite the presence of NATO troops, not all Serbian refugees passed through the Albanian gauntlets unharmed. When vehicles were disabled by the stone-throwing mobs, the occupants would often be dragged into the streets and beaten.* (*SCOTT TAYLOR*)

October 5, 2000. Police **(TOP)** *attempt to disperse the massive crowds of Serbian protesters converging on Yugoslavia's Parliament buildings in Belgrade* **(ABOVE)**. *(BOTH PHOTOS THIS PAGE COURTESY KNJIGA KOMMERZ.) However, by early evening the mob ruled supreme and the end for President Slobodan Milosevic* **(OPPOSITE PAGE)** *was at hand. The following morning Milosevic ceded power to Vojislav Kostunica. (AP PHOTO)*

chapter two:
DEPOSING A DICTATOR

BELGRADE – 29 MAY 2000 (Monday evening)

This was the first time that I had ever flown into Belgrade. On previous trips to the Yugoslav capital, I had been forced to endure a six-hour minibus shuttle from Budapest, Hungary, as a result of the NATO air campaign and economic sanctions. Restrictions on international air travel had just been lifted and, after 15 months, Yugoslav Airlines (JAT) was back in business. Just barely.

A five-hour delay at Charles de Gaulle airport in Paris had been blamed on technical difficulties and the in-flight service left much to be desired. The steward had chain-smoked as he served beverages – a choice of water or blueberry nectar. No meal was served.

The Boeing 737 was half full and we were the only flight to arrive at the nearly deserted Belgrade air terminal that evening. Nevertheless, immigration and customs clearance took a long time. There were a few other foreign reporters in the queue and we were pulled aside to be registered by the police.

Waiting for us at the baggage claim counter was a harried-looking woman with a clipboard wearing a card identifying her as one of the organizers of the Conference for Journalists. There were 55 reporters from 34 countries scheduled to attend this four-day seminar.

The delay in Paris had thrown off our schedule and our little group was late for the planned meet-and-greet dinner at the Hotel Intercontinental where we were to stay as guests of the Yugoslav government, which was sponsoring the conference.

Despite the organizers' encouragement that we mingle, the natural tendency was to clique together by culture and language.

There were no Americans in the group, and the only other Canadian delegate was Serbian-channel TV host Ljiljana Lomic from Montreal. As a result, I found myself included in the Western European crowd. A few, like Stefan Blommaert from Belgium, had been in Belgrade during the NATO air campaign. For most, however, this was their first trip to Milosevic's Yugoslavia, and attending the conference was the only way they could obtain entry visas.

At dinner, as wine loosened tongues, my tablemates began discussing their plans to escape from the formal events in order to research and write stories. Given the hospitality being extended to us by the Yugoslav authorities, it seemed rather duplicitous, but I also intended to skip some of the proceedings in order to file reports for the *Ottawa Citizen*.

The first anniversary of the Kosovo peace deal was approaching, and NATO spokesmen were still trying to justify the air campaign. I felt it was important to remind people that, for Yugoslavia, the suffering hadn't stopped.

BELGRADE – 31 MAY 2000 (Tuesday afternoon)

I was up at 6:00 a.m. to jog across the Sava River into Old Belgrade and my first appointment of the day. Before leaving Canada, I had met with Alexandre 'Sasha' Trudeau (Pierre Elliott's son) to discuss his plans to produce a television documentary about Serbia. Bruce Garvey, my editor at the *Ottawa Citizen*, had been keen on the idea of profiling Sasha and his project. As I knew there would be only a couple of days when we would both be in Belgrade, I contacted his hotel as soon as I arrived. When he did not return my call, I decided to pay him a visit.

Having been out researching Belgrade nightclubs until the wee hours, Sasha was a little worse for wear when he came to his door at the Hotel Tourist. We talked for some time in the lobby before he realized that it was not yet 7:00 a.m. I let him get back to bed and then jogged back to the Hotel International for the opening session of the conference.

During the morning presentations, the various speakers undoubtedly presumed I was dutifully scribbling down their every utterance, when in fact I was writing up my interview with Sasha.

Young Trudeau among the Serbs (Ottawa Citizen)

BELGRADE, Yugoslavia. After spending the past five weeks investigating the current situation in the Balkans, Alexandre 'Sasha' Trudeau returned to Canada today, to put the finishing touches to a new television documentary. Tentatively titled *Amongst the Serbs*, the project was funded in part by the CBC and is slotted to air on The National newsmagazine sometime in late June. Billed as a one-year-later retrospective on Canada's participation in the bombing campaign and its social and political impact on the region, Trudeau's film is bound to add to the growing controversy over NATO's intervention.

In recent weeks, Defence department officials have admitted to the likelihood of Canadian pilots causing civilian deaths among the Yugoslav populace. In addition, the circumstances surrounding the alleged Serb massacre of Albanian civilians in Racak – the "galvanizing event" which prompted the NATO air strikes – have now been called into serious question.

Convinced by the maxim *truth is the first casualty of war*, Trudeau was drawn to investigate the use of propaganda in international conflicts. The break-up of Yugoslavia and the ensuing civil wars were a magnet for him. "From the outset I realized that the Western media were covering the Serbian side with anything but objectivity," he told me.

His original intention had been to profile several of the notorious figures in the Serbian paramilitary, but following a string of brutal gangster-style slayings in Serbia this winter, he altered his course. "As far as I'm concerned, the death of indicted war criminal Arkan marked the closure on a 10-year period of war and bloodshed. It provided me with a real impetus to set this film in motion because it is such an important time for the future of the Serbian people," Trudeau said. He stresses that his film is not intended to whitewash or glorify the regime of Slobodan Milosevic. In fact, since acquiring his (very hard to obtain) media visa, the Yugoslav authorities have provided him with no real access to senior officials. Even the leaders of the Serbian opposition parties have so far chosen not to grant interviews.

"It is an unfortunate circumstance that these individuals have come to believe even their very existence will be used against them by the Western press," he said. As a result, Trudeau's efforts have been aimed primarily at capturing the experiences of average citizens.

Working with a limited budget, Trudeau chose to maximize his travel research by lodging at a no-star hotel in the heart of Belgrade rather than at the (very) expensive western-style hotels frequented by most foreign journalists. In his travels throughout Kosovo, Montenegro, and Serbia, Trudeau spoke with hundreds of individuals and recorded some 35 interviews. The subjects are drawn from all ethnic backgrounds – and will also include the perspective of several Canadian peacekeepers – but the documentary is centered on the fate of the Serbians. "They are warm, highly intelligent, extremely literate, and *very attractive* people," said Trudeau. "That image is something which is not being regularly conveyed by the Western media."

Trudeau was also perplexed by the blatant hypocrisy that surrounds the NATO-imposed sanctions against Yugoslavia. "The Serbs are being denied a large number of essential items yet, at the same time, U.S.-owned McDonald's restaurants, obviously unaffected, are doing a booming business," he said.

During his stay in Belgrade, Trudeau was given cordial assistance by the Canadian embassy's chargé d'affaires, Angela Bogdan. This is in stark contrast to the treatment received in January by former ambassador to Yugoslavia, James Bissett. Having been an outspoken opponent of the bombing campaign, Canada's Foreign Affairs ministry ordered Bissett out of the embassy compound during his visit to Belgrade.

While Sasha Trudeau's documentary is not an indictment of NATO's bombing, it will be critical of our U.S.-dominated foreign affairs policies. "It's time for the West to alter its approach," he said.

JASTROBAC – 1 JUNE 2000 (Wednesday evening)

The second day of the conference included visits to several towns outside of Belgrade. Confined to buses, it was difficult to escape, but two British journalists proved themselves equal to the task when, at the first stop, they hired a taxi and sped back to the Hotel Intercontinental. The excursion was a steady succession of factory tours, culminating with a "cultural night" at a mountain resort. Once the private retreat of former Yugoslav President Josip Broz Tito, Jastrobac has since been converted into a luxury hotel. Despite the picturesque surroundings, hungry journalists became increasingly irritable as dinner was repeatedly delayed by lengthy speeches from local officials. Spirits lifted when wine was finally served and our Serbian handlers announced a major surprise was planned for midnight. The rumour began to circulate that President Milosevic himself was going to address us. Some reporters were so convinced that he would they phoned their editors to hold space in the next day's newspaper.

At midnight we were ushered out into the cold mountain air to watch a third-rate fireworks display – our hosts' major surprise. Fom the back of the crowd, Rory O'Carroll, an Irish reporter, asked the Serbs, "So this is your new air defence system?"

I headed off to file my report.

Truth is, Serbia is still hurting (Ottawa Citizen)
BELGRADE, Yugoslavia. It has been 12 months since the bombs rained down on Yugoslavia, but the regime of President Slobodan Milosevic, is still reeling.

With the treasury virtually bankrupt and NATO-imposed economic sanctions still in place, the country is enduring a financial crisis, the effects of which have sparked widespread political unrest.

At an international conference of journalists in Belgrade, Yugoslav officials tried to put a brave face on the steadily worsening situation.

Inside the impressive halls of the Sava Convention Center, the foreign media was shown several films portraying a vibrant, dynamic Serbia emerging from the ashes of destruction. The propaganda was reminiscent of those British home-front morale-boosters produced during the darkest hours of the Second World War. Shirtless workers toil happily away rebuilding a bridge while pretty young girls harvest bountiful crops.

The reality is much more grim. Mihailo Milojevic, president of the Yugoslavia Chamber of Commerce, admitted that the bombing had crippled the country's infrastructure beyond the capacity to recover without outside assistance.

"We are asking the foreign media to let the world know that we need the NATO sanctions lifted, and we need to establish industrial investment partnerships if we are to recover," Mr. Milojevic said.

He noted that even he could not venture into foreign countries without risking arrest for war crimes. The stark reality of Yugoslavia's current plight is all too evident just meters away from the sprawling conference center.

Two long lines of cars wait for hours to fuel up at the government-subsidized gas pumps. For those who can afford it, black-market diesel is sold in plastic tubs by roadside vendors. On May 30, escalating fuel prices, due to the constant devaluation of the dinar, prompted private bus companies to go on strike. With more than 1000 vehicles off the roads, the remaining 300 public buses could not cope with the massive flow of commuters. The government has refused to allow the independent bus companies to increase passenger fares from three to five dinars and, at the same time, refused to pay out any further subsidies. The buses remain parked. In addition, most people realize that government rebuilding projects are only temporary – Band-Aids aimed at shoring up Mr. Milosevic's ruling party prior to this year's elections.

There are now two bridges replacing those destroyed by bombs at Novi Sad: a crudely-constructed pontoon structure (which prohibits ship transport on the Danube), and a newly-christened railway bridge. To get maximum political mileage out of the event, Slobodan Milosevic made a rare public appearance to open the bridge.

Both bridges were completed ahead of schedule and under budget. Much attention was drawn to this, without mentioning that the workers had received civic-duty medals in exchange for involuntarily forfeiting a sizeable percentage of their wages.

While some Serbian citizens are working without full pay, many others are unemployed and being paid subsistence allowances from a depleted treasury.

Part of this problem stems from the 120,000 refugees who fled Kosovo following NATO's arrival. They joined the nearly 600,000 displaced persons already in Serbia – those ethnically-cleansed from Bosnia and Croatia during the civil war. Another major contributor to the swelling social-assistance rolls has been the destruction of industrial workplaces.

For instance, at the Zastava (Yugo) automobile plant in Kragujevac, two separate missile attacks completely destroyed the assembly lines, leaving 35,000 workers without jobs. Over the past year, the Yugoslav government has assisted Zastava to restore limited production at the plant. Yet, with an estimated one billion dollars in damage to the plant, only $20 million has been set aside to replace machinery.

As a result, the factory is producing a mere 18,500 cars a year compared with a pre-war production capacity of 225,000. Fewer than one-third of the employees have been retained; the rest are on subsistence.

With the dinar's buying power reduced by more than 60 per cent, even gainfully-employed Serbs are struggling to make ends meet. The black market economy is thriving, and there has been a tremendous increase in organized crime. Gangster-style slayings are becoming commonplace as rival factions fight for control of valuable turf.

There is also a tremendous amount of frustration, which has recently spilled into the streets in a series of large and often violent demonstrations.

While these demonstrations are aimed primarily at the ouster of Slobodan Milosevic, it is important to note that they are not being staged in support of any particular opposition party. After ten years of Milosevic rule, and with the same opponents ensconced in the Serbian parliament, people now view all politicians with the same measure of distrust and contempt.

Coordinating the latest round of demonstrations is a new movement called OTPOR (Resistance). OTPOR's symbol of a raised, clenched fist has become a favourite at student rallies.

"We're just using the protests as an outlet for our displeasure until we can vote Slobo and his gang out in the elections," said one student demonstrator. In response, Milosevic has clamped down on the independent media and ordered an early end to the university school year.

Yugoslavia's Foreign Affairs deputy minister, Nebojsa Vujovic said these demonstrations are simply "a reality that one can expect in a tolerant democracy."

ZEMUN – 2 JUNE 2000 (Thursday evening)

The conference concluded with a farewell dinner at the press club. The reporters who had made token appearances at the dinners (and the brewery tour) were surprised to learn that a collective resolution had been voted on during their absence. This news sparked a heated exchange between British and Iraqi delegates that almost came to blows. In the end, the statement "We condemn NATO," was replaced by the innocuous, "We shall endeavor to seek the truth."

Milosevic's attempt to win over the international media had failed miserably. The evidence of economic ruin was visible to every reporter, as were signs of growing political unrest.

In November 1999, I had been introduced to the proprietor of a small, private, club, which had become the center of political opposition in Serbia. During the previous week, I had not been able to discover much about the OTPOR movement, but knew that I could learn more about it by talking to Jovan Mandic.

Anti-Milosevic factions move closer to action (Ottawa Citizen)
BELGRADE, Yugoslavia – Atop a private terrace overlooking the Danube River and the picturesque Belgrade skyline, the leaders of Serbia's heretofore-splintered opposition movements gather regularly to discuss a collective strategy.

The serene atmosphere of the club is a surreal setting for the civil disobedience and violence that are discussed over wine, slivovitz and barbecued pork. Although the factions propose divergent policies, they share the same goal: the rousting of President Slobodan Milosevic and his regime.

The owner of this establishment is Jovan Mandic, a former power company executive who has already paid a heavy price for challenging the government.

In 1992, Mandic assisted anti-Milosevic demonstrators by ordering a power blackout of Belgrade during a 200,000-strong candlelight procession. For his actions, Mandic lost his top-level job and was severely beaten by the police.

Undeterred, Mandic has since dedicated his efforts to the "removal of the communists," and has worked tirelessly to unite the various opponents to Milosevic's regime. Only invited political activists frequent his private club. At their meetings, they developed the strategies that have culminated in student demonstrations and widespread general strikes.

Until recently, Mandic's club had put its support behind various registered political parties, but that is no longer the case. "Among the population, these so-called opposition parties have lost all credibility," said Mandic. "It is time for a new movement and an entirely fresh leader."

In pursuit of this objective, the club has openly embraced the creation of the new OTPOR (Resistance) movement and helped to organize the recent mass demonstrations. As for a new leader, the club has thrown its support behind political neophyte Milan Protic, a charismatic 45-year-old university professor. Last week, Protic and 100 influential signatories registered as an official political party, thereby creating the 16th such organization currently seeking a measure of popular support in Serbia. In an effort to gain the higher moral ground, the club has successfully enlisted the support of orthodox priests from Halkidiki, the Serbian religious centre in Greece.

At the other end of the spectrum, the club intends to establish Protic and his party as a "serious resistance force" in the forthcoming weeks. "There will probably be a rash of executions in the next 10-14 days," said one club member. "Killing people is the only way to get the regime's attention."

With the opposition showing the first signs of establishing a united front, Slobodan Milosevic's ruling Socialist party could be facing a very rough time. The Yugoslav president is currently embattled on several fronts that are beyond his control and damaging to what is left of his popular support. One year after it was signed, several of the key provisions of the Kosovo peace agreement with NATO have yet to even be partially adopted, making a mockery of Milosevic's claims of victory.

So far, NATO officials have refused to allow the Serbs any of the rights to enforce sovereignty over Kosovo as outlined and agreed to in the peace deal. The Kosovo Liberation Army has nominally been disarmed, albeit reconstituted as the Kosovo Protection Corps. Yet, Serbian military and border guards have still not been allowed back into what is still officially recognized as the Yugoslavian sovereign territory of Kosovo.

The second major problem plaguing Milosevic is the tremendous strain put on his already bankrupt treasury by the ongoing NATO sanctions.

In addition to problems with the economy and political unrest, the Milosevic regime was dealt another blow last week when Bulgaria announced that it would open a separate diplomatic mission in Kosovo.

Despite the mounting pressure, it will be necessary for an opposition movement to create the climate required for fundamental change. At this point, the option of an armed insurrection is no longer being discounted. Members of the club believe that the army (excluding the senior brass) would support a coup. When asked about the tragedy of Serbs killing Serbs in a civil war, Mandic replied, "We would consider it to be Serbs versus Communists."

PARIS – 3 JUNE 2000 (Friday morning)
It was an early morning flight out of Belgrade but Ludwig, a Polish reporter,

insisted they open the bar. Throughout the entire conference he had been in various stages of inebriation, but today, he claimed that it was his fear of flying which triggered his thirst. Stefan Bloemmart and Françoise Wallemacq, two Belgian reporters, were on the same flight and, out of "conference camaraderie," we agreed to join Ludwig for a drink.

Ludwig caused a commotion when he discovered that JAT offered no bar service. After a screaming match with the flight steward, he purchased a 40-ounce bottle of duty-free cognac. The arrangement with the flight crew was that it had to be emptied before we landed. As no one, not even Ludwig, could realistically expect to down the entire bottle alone, he enlisted our help.

By the time we reached Paris, the mission was accomplished and we had all overcome our "fear of flying." As we parted company, Bloemmart said, "It's strange, but somehow I know we'll be back in Belgrade soon. You can just sense something big is about to happen."

OTTAWA – 21 SEPTEMBER 2000 (Thursday)

From the news coming in from Yugoslavia it seemed that a major political showdown was brewing. In the past, Slobodan Milosevic and his Socialist party had been able to hold on to power by dividing the opposition. However, with the September 24 federal election imminent, the anti-Milosevic movement successfully united 18 political parties under the banner of the Democratic Opposition of Serbia (DOS) and a single leader. The little-known Vojislav Kostunica was new to the scene, but had quickly captured the hearts of the disillusioned Serbian majority. Milan Protic had failed to achieve the same level of public support but, despite being cast out of the figurehead role, remained a key figure within the DOS coalition.

There have been numerous stories about the U.S. State Department's funding of the DOS campaign as part of their ongoing effort to oust Milosevic. In addition, the U.S. continued to encourage Milo Djukanovic, Montenegro's separatist-minded President, to boycott the federal Yugoslav elections. As relations between Milosevic and Djukanovic soured, the U.S. offered economic incentives for Montenegro's eventual succession. The Republic of Yugoslavia is fast becoming nothing more than Serbia proper. In anticipation of Milosevic using military force to rein in Djukanovic, it was reported that British and U.S. Special Forces were training Montenegrin police. While denying intimidation,

NATO announced that it will be conducting major naval and air exercises off the Dalmatian coast.

Inside Serbia, Milosevic had begun another crackdown on local media outlets opposed to his regime, and a number of foreign reporters suddenly had their visas revoked.

In August, Yugoslav police at a Kosovo border post arrested two Canadians. Shaun Going and his nephew, Trevor Glass, were caught returning from Montenegro with a pair of British policemen, no entry visas and a trunkful of detonators. As a construction contractor, Going claimed that the explosives were "job-related" but his association with senior Albanian guerillas and U.S. officials had aroused suspicions.

Foreign Affairs Minister Lloyd Axworthy had immediately decried the Canadians' detention as nothing more than a pre-election, anti-NATO propaganda stunt by Milosevic.

Despite rumblings of unrest, the editors at the *Ottawa Citizen* remained unconvinced that the Yugoslav elections would prove newsworthy enough to warrant an assignment. Nevertheless, I had obtained a media visa and reserved a flight, but the final word had been passed. "We'll pick up whatever happens on the newswire," said editor Bruce Garvey. "Cancel your plans."

BELGRADE – 24 SEPTEMBER 2000 (Sunday)

The voter turnout was larger than expected, and the international monitors did not report any major incidents of violence across Serbia. There were a number of reports of ballot-box stuffing and other irregularities, but all in all the election proceeded rather smoothly. In the early evening, Milosevic's Socialist party headquarters held a press conference to announce their initial exit poll results. Security had been tight, with armed bodyguards searching reporters and their gear.

Kostunica's DOS coalition appeared to be leading the Socialists, but Milosevic's spokesman claimed otherwise. On the basis of partial results from villages in Kosovo (where the Albanians were boycotting the election), the Socialists predicted they would win a sweeping victory.

By 11:00 p.m. things were much clearer. At DOS headquarters, Kostunica's people proclaimed a victory which was confirmed by independent observers. When reporters rushed back to cover Milosevic's announcement, they encountered a scene of abject despair. The few remaining bodyguards appeared to be in shock and nobody even bothered to conduct security checks. Several hardcore Socialist party members were crying openly while once optimistic spokesmen started talked about the need for a second, run-off vote.

Milosevic admitted that he had lost, but not by enough of a margin to relinquish power without a fight.

BELGRADE – 3 OCTOBER 2000 (Tuesday afternoon)

At a midday press conference, Zoran Djindjic, the Democratic Opposition of Serbia campaign director, set the stage for the final battle by calling for a "country-wide demonstration" and the resignation of President Slobodan Milosevic by 3:00 p.m. on October 5. In the nine days since the disputed election, Yugoslavia had been plunged into chaos.

On Wednesday, September 28, the federal Yugoslav electoral committee had tabled the final vote results – which purportedly showed that no clear winner had emerged. Milosevic then declared that a second election would take place on October 8.

While Vojislav Kostunica denounced the official results, he did not immediately reject the idea of participating in the second ballot. Opinion within DOS varied, and it appeared as though Milosevic's "divide and conquer" strategy might yet prevail. A step ahead of Kostunica, Zoran Djindjic rejected the results and the need for another vote and called for a general strike on October 2.

Many chose not to wait. On Friday evening, September 29, 7500 coal miners barricaded themselves in the coal mines at Kolubara. Until then, the working class, particularly in that region, had been loyal to Milosevic's Socialist regime. The miners' revolt started a chain reaction across the country.

The next day, oil refinery workers in Pancevo announced that they would join the strike, and work ceased at the copper refinery in Sevojno. On Sunday, October 1, another 4500 miners in Kostolac refused to leave the mines. On Monday afternoon, Kostunica visited the defiant miners to offer them support. Milosevic could no longer ignore the deepening crisis.

He had sent the commander-in-chief of the army, General Pavkovic, to negotiate a settlement. Pavkovic had commanded the Third Army during the Kosovo crisis, and was a national hero for bringing his forces home virtually intact. However, even this desperate attempt to play to Serbian nationalism fell on deaf ears. Discussions lasted until 3:00 a.m. but Pavkovic left Kolubara without a deal. The strike continued to spread. A public prosecutor in Belgrade was fired when he refused Milosevic's request to issue arrest warrants for eleven of the Kolubara ringleaders. Nearly 3000 copper miners joined the strike in Majdanpek, and traffic controllers in Belgrade walked off their jobs. Garbage collection had also been halted and Belgrade's traffic-congested streets were becoming filthy. The people were suffering the brunt of their own actions, but this *inat* – or stubbornly defiant spirit – has long been a characteristic of the Serbian people.

BELGRADE – 4 OCTOBER 2000 (Wednesday)

The Kolubara miners had become a symbol of defiance, and Milosevic grasped the importance of extinguishing the spark they had struck before it became a flame. Following Pavkovic's failure to end the strikes, armoured police vehicles rolled into the mining compounds. Although the police were able to gain control over some of the Kolubara mines, the OTPOR student organization rallied to the cause and thousands of student protesters appeared on the scene to join the miners. The police were forced to withdraw.

Although the situation looked desperate for Milosevic, DOS party oganizers were not sure whether they had the momentum to force the president to resign.

With a general strike scheduled for the next day, a secret meeting was arranged at Jovan Mandic's club. Senior officials from the army and police attended along with Kostunica's inner circle. The security forces still remained loyal to Milosevic, but even the most ardent Socialist supporters were beginning to have their doubts. The police representative told the DOS delegation that his forces were prepared to concede to the public will – povided that will could be clearly demonstrated. "If you put 100,000 people on the streets tomorrow, my men will not resort to lethal force," he told the gathering. Jovan Mandic asked the obvious, "What if we have less than that number?"

"Then the police will fire on the crowd," was the answer.

BELGRADE – 5 OCTOBER 2000 (Thursday)

The uprising against Milosevic began in the early morning with columns of cars and trucks converging on Belgrade from all over Serbia. In the vanguard was a 20-kilometre long convoy from the town of Cacak. Velimir Ilic, the mayor and an anti-Milosevic activist, had organized his townsfolk into a formidable force. With over 200 trucks and 40 pieces of construction equipment, the Cacak contingent easily broke through the lightly-manned police barricades.

Belgraders left their homes and offices to join the swelling crowds. With the streets clogged, people began moving towards the city center on foot.

By 3:00 p.m., the time of Zoran Djindjic's ultimatum, it was estimated that nearly 800,000 people had converged around the Yugoslav Parliament building.

Since the first of the anti-war demonstrations in 1991, Serbs had taken to the streets, often in numbers exceeding 100,000, yet they had not managed to topple Milosevic. Today they were determined to succeed.

At 3:35 a number of students slipped past the police barricade and entered through a window of the Parliament building. When they later appeared at a second-floor window the crowd let out a triumphant cheer. The police saw this as a signal to disperse the crowd and unleashed a barrage of tear gas canisters before charging. The sheer crush of humanity made it difficult to clear the square, but the front ranks of the crowd gave way to the phalanx of baton-wielding police and were pushed back into side streets. However, for a generation seasoned to the toxic cigarette-smoke clouds of the Belgrade discos, tear gas did not prove to be particularly disabling. By 4:00 p.m. the crowds had stormed back towards Parliament and the police retreated.

Windows were smashed and part of the Parliament building was set on fire. In nearby streets, police cars were overturned and gunfire could be heard when the crowd cornered fleeing policemen. At the height of the rioting, it was rumored that the army was poised to enter Belgrade to restore order. Instead, the commander-in-chief issued a public statement that his troops were "joining the people."

Less than an hour later, Belgrade's chief of police met with DOS party officials to negotiate terms. By 6:00 p.m. the major police stations were empty as policemen put their weapons away and ventured out to join the crowd.

In addition to Milosevic's resignation, one of Zoran Djindjic's key demands was for Radio-Television Serbia (RTS) to cease broadcasting. This government-controlled agency was the propaganda arm of Milosevic's regime and had long been hated by the people. As anarchy reigned, the people took it upon themselves to take RTS off the air.

RTS's headquarters was stormed around 5:00 p.m. and set ablaze. Outside on Takovsk Street, several RTS news-anchors were beaten by the crowd.

Early in the evening, President-elect Vojislav Kostunica appeared to address the crowd in front of the Parliament building. He congratulated them for their courage and determination and urged them to remain on the streets "throughout the night." Despite the day's events, Milosevic still had not conceded to what now appeared to be inevitable.

OTTAWA – 5 OCTOBER 2000 (Thursday afternoon)

Given the time difference, the first word of the Yugoslav uprising had been reported on the Ottawa lunch-hour news shows. A strange, empty feeling had overtaken me, as I was relegated to observer rather than participant. To make matters worse, Bruce Garvey called my office to ask if my Yugoslav visa was till valid and find out "How fast can you be on a plane?" Although I was sorely tempted to jump on a flight that night, even with the best of connections I could not be in Belgrade until late the following afternoon. And that was too late.

New York-based documentary filmmaker George Bogdanich was familiar with my reporting on the Balkans and he had recommended me as an analyst for Fox Television news. All the major U.S. networks were covering the developing situation in Yugoslavia live and interspersing their coverage with colour commentary. I was kept on hold to give a military perspective. Altogether I spent several hours on standby without getting any airtime, it allowed me to hear the analysis and predictions being offered. To put it kindly, it was not a good day for American punditry.

One U.S. military expert went on at length about how the Yugoslav Army was fanatically loyal to Milosevic. Likening the Serb dictator to Napoleon, he claimed that Milosevic had "led his soldiers to victory over the past decade."

He also predicted that the Serbian military would crush the revolt, regardless of civilian casualties, within 48 hours.

An American senator was asked what, if anything, the U.S. military could do to provide assistance to the Yugoslav opposition. His answer was that America had already done its part by bringing the situation to a head. The rationale was that the decade-long economic sanctions and the NATO bombardment had weakened Milosevic's "iron grip on Yugoslavia."

"We have been instrumental in bringing democracy to this country. Now it's up to the Serbs to recognize what we've given them," he said.

Following Kostunica's speech and the capitulation of the security forces, speculation turned to Slobodan Milosevic's future. Fox's Balkan analyst stated that the ousted Yugoslav President would never give up power willingly.

Pointing out that both of Milosevic's parents had committed suicide, he predicted that "Slobo" would be dead by his own hand before daybreak.

BELGRADE – 6 OCTOBER 2000 (Friday)

A very much alive Slobodan Milosevic met with Vojislav Kostunica to formally cede the Yugoslav presidency.

BELGRADE – 25 OCTOBER 2000 (Wednesday afternoon)

A contract to publish a Serbian-language edition of my book *Inat: Images of Serbia and the Kosovo Conflict*, included a promise to attend the Belgrade Book Fair. A very literate society, this is a major annual event for the Serbs. During the recent political unrest, organizers had considered postponing the fair but, in the end, had decided that the show must go on.

Promoting a book about the 1999 NATO air campaign seemed a little out of date, particularly when other publishers were already presenting accounts of the October uprising. One selling point was that *Inat* included a (prophetic) November 1999 prediction of how events would unfold. "By next fall, when the federal elections are held, the people will be ready to take to the streets once again to send their message to the Milosevic government." This analysis had been made by Katarina Njegovan, a then 22-year-old philosophy student and political activist.

In order to cut expenses during my stay, I had arranged through Sasha Trudeau's colleagues to stay at an apartment in New Belgrade. This turned out to be a rather unique flat on the 21st floor of the landmark Genex Kula. Built in the mid-70s, the twin-towered structure has a numer of nicknames including "Gateway to Belgrade" and "the Idiot Brothers."

I settled in and set to work on a series of articles about Milosevic's ouster.

Entering a New Era: Hopeful Serbs face tough challenges
(Voice of Canadian Serbs)

BELGRADE, Yugoslavia: Since the dramatic October 5 uprising, which forced Milosevic to concede the Yugoslav presidency to Vojislav Kostunica, the citizens of Serbia have been celebrating Slobo's fall from power. After a decade of internal suppression and international sanctions, it seems as though a cloud has lifted.

In Belgrade's cafés and bars, everyone speaks affectionately of Kostunica, often referring to him in the possessive as "my president." A much-praised private life and the fact that Kostunica continues to live in a modest apartment block without security add to the new leader's widespread popularity. By contrast, Slobodan Milosevic – who rarely made public appearances during his ten-year presidency – has now gone into hiding somewhere in Belgrade.

In the three weeks since Kostunica and his Democratic Opposition of Serbia (DOS) party swept into power, there have been a number of significant developments. The international community has lifted the "inner wall" of economic sanctions and has pledged financial aid to Yugoslavia. Domestically, Kostunica successfully dissolved the Socialist party-dominated parliament and called new elections for December 23. Despite this, Yugoslavia remains plagued with political uncertainties and its people continue to face hardships. "We know that it will take time for these changes to bring real prosperity," said Mariotta Porobic, a reporter with *Danas*, Serbia's major independent daily newspaper. "After the past ten years, we are used to suffering through hardships. The difference now is that there is finally a light at the end of the tunnel."

Milosevic's legacy does not bode well for a quick economic recovery in Yugoslavia – the country is bankrupt, the transportation and communication infrastructures are in ruins, and the power system is on the brink of collapse. "If people knew how bad the situation really is, they would be back on the streets seeking vengeance against Slobo and his Socialists," said a senior executive with the Serbian Power Company. Belgrade experiences rotating blackouts of four to six hours a day, as the over-stretched power company tries to balance its diminished generating capacity with demand. Last year's NATO bombing campaign damaged an already decrepit Yugoslav power grid, and this summer's draught, the most severe in a hundred years, has lowered the Danube's water level so much that hydroelectric plants are producing at only

50 per cent capacity.

With current output sufficient to provide for only 65 per cent of domestic demand, Yugoslavia must buy additional power from neighbouring countries. In spite of pledges of short-term economic aid from the European Union, Serbian officials forecast a difficult winter. "There will be blackouts until the spring," said Jovan Mandic, the former Power Company executive who is now an elected member of Kostunica's party. "With much of Serbia relying on electric heating, the situation could become critical in the event of a prolonged cold spell," he told me.

Yugoslavia will need to purchase over $100 million (U.S.) of electricity – in addition to the $90 million (U.S.) that it already owes – just to survive until spring. Although the amount of financial aid offered by Western countries sounds significant (Canada was one of first to donate a humanitarian relief package of some $10 million Canadian), the pressing needs of Yugoslavia far exceed the contributions. For instance, the 200 million Eurodollars pledged by the EU will merely shore up Yugoslavia's Treasury and enable it to cover overdue pension cheques and public servants' wages.

Politically, it is imperative that President Kostunica keep the public service appeased during this transitional and tumultuous time. The massive bureaucracy left behind by Milosevic is burdened with hard-line Socialists. However, while many of the key officials have already been quietly stripped of their powers (but not their jobs), Kostunica's fledgling DOS party still has to rely on the existing public service to keep the country running.

Public pressure to purge Socialists is one of the major challenges facing Kostunica. In the past week, major banks, the post office and the telephone company have all experienced strikes. In each case, the workers were not demanding higher wages; they wanted their directors fired. After meeting with the strikers, Kostunica gave assurances that changes would be made soon, but that undue haste might create a dangerous vacuum. Similarly, Yugoslav diplomatic personnel posted abroad – most of whom are political appointees of Slobodan Milosevic – have been informed that, in due time, they will be replaced.

One important change that DOS has already implemented is a drastic revision of its communications strategy. After a few embarrassing gaffes by inexperienced politicians, DOS has decided to restrict the handling of foreign media to a few qualified spokespersons and "fixers."

The Yugoslav Foreign Ministry has been equally hard-pressed to keep pace with Kostunica's agenda. After ten years of imposed isolation, relatively inexperienced bureaucrats are scrambling to organize a flood of international delegations. In some cases, the rapid pace of this "thaw" has served to heighten the divisions that exist within the Federal Republic of Yugoslavia.

On October 24, a delegation was dispatched to Bucharest, Romania, to officially join the Pact of Stability in southeast Europe. This loose-knit organization first met in 1999, following the Kosovo conflict. At that time, all Balkan countries – including Montenegro – were admitted, with the exception of Yugoslavia. However, by allowing Kostunica's government to join the pact –as the Federal Republic of Yugoslavia (FRY) –the independence movement of Montenegro's president, Milo Djukanovic, has only intensified. Although technically still a member republic of FRY, Montenegro insisted upon – and received – independent status before joining the Pact.

Even as the world continues to laud the ouster of Slobodan Milosevic, it is becoming increasingly evident that his popular successor faces enormous problems. Sitting atop a loose coalition of 18 independent political parties, President Kostunica must contend with the real possibility of Montenegro's secession. In the coming months, the remnants of the Socialist party and the nationalist Radical Party of Serbia will attempt to regain power in the republican elections. In addition, with a treasury that is entirely dependant entirely upon foreign aid, Kostunica must somehow try to rebuild a collapsed infrastructure, while simultaneously convincing the U.S. State Department to lift "the outer wall" of economic sanctions, thereby allowing Serbia to begin rebuilding in the long term.

Perhaps the largest political hurdle facing Kostunica is the question of Kosovo's independence. Under the terms of the 1999 peace agreement, the UN recognized that Kosovo would remain the sovereign territory of the Federal Republic of Yugoslavia. Events since then, including the Albanian elections and the UN's steadfast refusal to allow Yugoslav border guards back into the province, have led many Serbians to believe that Kosovo has been forever lost to them. As the religious heartland of Serbia, the secession of Kosovo would gravely undermine Kostunica's current popularity.

However, the inaugural "honeymoon" continues and most Serbs are facing the future with confidence. "Kostunica has already accomplished the impossible by giving Serbians back their spirit," said Mariotta Porobic, summing up popular opinion in Belgrade. "Why should we doubt him now?"

ABOVE: *October 5, 2000. A pall of smoke and tear gas hangs thick above the Belgrade skyline. After the police joined ranks with the protesters, President-elect Kostunica urged the crowds to stay on the streets overnight to ensure their victory. Kostunica's fledgling regime would soon face its first major challenge: an Albanian insurgency in south Serbia. (PHOTO COURTESY KNIGA KOMMERZ) In response, Yugoslav troops* **(OPPOSITE PAGE)** *were mobilized in the Presevo valley. (SCOTT TAYLOR)*

chapter three
SECTOR B

BELGRADE – 18 DECEMBER 2000 (Monday evening)

On the flight from Vienna, I recognized a few familiar faces: international reporters arriving in Yugoslavia to cover the December 23 Serbian election. While no one really expected a repeat of the October 5 uprising, this was the Balkans, and anything could happen. Having missed out on the "big one," I had convinced my editor, Bruce Garvey at the *Ottawa Citizen*, that the election was still newsworthy. From a professional perspective, the timing of the Serbian election was advantageous as, due to the holidays, it was an otherwise slow news period. However, on the personal side, it would mean spending Christmas away from home. In addition to reporting on the results of the vote, my ten-day assignment included writing an update on the escalating violence in south Serbia.

Lost in the media's preoccupation with the George W. Bush-Al Gore vote split in the U.S. presidential elections was the offensive in south Serbia by the Albanian Kosovo Liberation Army (Ushtria Clirimtare Kombetare or UCK). On November 21, from prepared positions within Kosovo they had engaged lightly-armed Yugoslav police units inside the five-kilometer Ground Security Zone (GSZ).

This demilitarized buffer zone surrounding Kosovo was established as part of the June 1999 United Nations Peace Resolution 1244. Under the terms of the Technical Agreement, the Yugoslav Army could not deploy heavy weapons or troops within the GSZ.

In the vicinity of Cacak, the UCK had launched a mortar barrage at a Yugoslav police bunker. All three Serbian policemen manning the bunker had been slightly wounded in the bombardment and, after radioing for assistance, had tried to withdraw. The UCK guerrillas had little difficulty in overtaking the wounded men. Despite pleading for their lives, the three MUPs (a nickname for the Ministry of the Interior's police force) were executed at point-blank range and their bodies mutilated.

Constables Dusko Gligoric, Cvetan Jovanov and Dusko Djukovic were the first fatalities of the Albanian offensive. Within a few days, an estimated 1500 heavily-armed UCK fighters would cross unchallenged into the GSZ through the U.S.-controlled sector of the Kosovo border. The Yugoslav police MUPs offered no resistance and withdrew their remaining units.

Following the scant media coverage of these events, it was interesting to note the belligerent tone that NATO adopted towards the Yugoslavian federal government. Although the Albanians were mildly admonished for their aggression, the message to Yugoslav President Kostunica was that no retaliatory attacks against the UCK would be tolerated.

It appeared that NATO was using their UCK "allies" to either provoke a military response from the Serbs or undermine Kostunica's tenuous domestic authority. What was even more interesting to me was that the NATO representative delivering this hard-line message was none other than Canadian Colonel Serge Labbé. Discredited by the public inquiry into the Somalia scandal, Labbé had disappeared from Canada – only to esurface as NATO's key negotiator in the Balkans.

Having reported extensively on Labbé's alleged involvement in the 1993 cover-up in Somalia, I was anxious to learn more about his new role.

BELGRADE – 20 DECEMBER 2000 (Wednesday morning)

It had taken a number of phone calls and personal interventions on my behalf, but I had finally managed to arrange an interview with General Simic. As the head of the Yugoslav Army's information directorate, Simic would be able to provide me with contacts and authorization to visit the disputed territory in the Presevo-Bujanovac region of south Serbia.

Diplomatically, the situation there was at a critical phase. For the first time since its troops occupied Kosovo, NATO was officially resuming negotiations with the Yugoslav government. President Kostunica had appointed Nebojsa Covic – a capable politician – as a special envoy for south Serbia and Kosovo. A prominent Socialist, Covic had amassed a fortune through private business. However, a last-minute decision to abandon Milosevic was much-appreciated by DOS and guarenteed Covic a high-profile presence in the new government.

Discussions between Covic and his NATO counterpart, Peter Feith, were at a very preliminary stage, and one-upmanship was the overriding tone at these meetings. However, in contrast to the Milosevic regime, it appeared that Kostunica's government understood the importance of winning over international public opinion. Thus far in the crisis, despite the provocation of the UCK, the Serbs had shown uncharacteristic restraint – overriding the natural *inat* for which Serbs are known.

General Simic explained that the troops of the Third Army were not happy with the new policy of restraint. "Of course, they do not like to see the UCK occupying Serbian territory and killing Serbs with impunity," he told me. "But when the order does come down to fight, they will do so with conviction, because they are much happier serving a president they believe in."

General Simic was particularly keen to assist me in my research on Colonel Labbé. "We have had some concerns with this Canadian," he said.

I had been put in contact with a senior officer in the Yugoslav Army's intelligence branch. Captain S. was one of the delegates who regularly met with the NATO team – including Labbé – to discuss the implementation of the UN Technical Agreement. Captain S. would become an invaluable source for providing background on both the UCK incursion and Labbé's activities. We agreed to meet informally at the Nis bus station the following morning.

BELGRADE – 20 DECEMBER 2000 (Wednesday evening)

As a registered journalist covering the election, my press credentials gave me access to the campaign wrap-up rally for the Democratic Opposition of Serbia party. Held at the 5000-seat Sava Convention Center in Novi-Belgrade, it was a surprisingly lavish affair. In contrast to the primitive propaganda efforts of

Milosevic's Socialists, the DOS pep rally had all the trappings of an American political convention. Booming rock music accompanied slick video images depicting the October uprising and set the stage for speeches and choreographed "high-fives" by the 18 party leaders who formed DOS.

The highlight of the rally was the arrival of the President-elect of Yugoslavia. Although not an official participant, Kostunica stole the show by simply showing up. The applause as he walked to his front-row seat was enough to bring the house down. DOS President Zoran Djindjic's address drew only a modest response – but then Kostunica is a hard act to follow.

BELGRADE, DECEMBER 21, 2000 (Thursday morning)

Under Yugoslavian election regulations, there can be no campaigning or media events for a full 48 hours prior to election day. The previous evening's DOS rally had ended just prior to the midnight blackout. After filing a background piece on the elections, I packed up my gear and made arrangements to head into south Serbia.

Last call for Milosevic (Ottawa Citizen)

BELGRADE, Yugoslavia: For the second time in three months, Serbs are headed back to the polls to determine their nation's destiny.

Posters across Serbia proclaim, "One more step to the finish line!" in an effort to encourage voters to rid themselves once and for all of Slobodan Milosevic and his Socialist party. Although the dramatic October 5 uprising forced Milosevic to accept defeat and concede his federal Yugoslav presidency to Vojislav Kostunica, the Socialists remained in control of Parliament. Today's election is seen as a crucial hurdle for Kostunica to clear if his fledgling coalition government (the DOS) is to consolidate its power base.

At the federal level, all that remains of Yugoslavia are the republics of Serbia and Montenegro. With economic ties between the two already partially severed and Montenegro's separatist president, Milo Djukanovic, threatening a referendum on independence, Kostunica's umbrella government could be ousted.

With so much at stake, DOS is trying to once again capitalize on the tremendous wave of anti-Milosevic sentiment that swept Kostunica to power.

The party's election slogans encourage voters to "clean out" the rot of socialism. Since taking office just 12 weeks ago, Kostunica and his coalition cabinet have embarked on a whirlwind campaign of domestic house-cleaning –

Socialists holding key government positions have been replaced by members of DOS – and international bridge-building. But despite his party's tremendous efforts, President Kostunica conceded this week that the situation he inherited was even worse than expected.

"In some cases, we knew what we were getting into; in other cases, it was either far more complex – or a complete surprise," he said. Of particular concern is the worsening situation with Montenegro's possible secession. "We had been led to believe that Milosevic was the major obstacle to a successful union, but it appears that the problem goes much deeper," said Kostunica. Even among Serbs, the prospect of breaking ties with Montenegro has become popular.

Adding to the domestic pressures has been the recent increase in violence, which has spilled out of Kosovo and into south Serbia. With Albanian terrorists escalating their activities and seizing control of several Serbian villages in the demilitarized zone, relations between Yugoslavia and NATO are once again being tested.

Until now, the Serbian military has respected the UN Technical Agreement and it has not yet deployed heavy weapons into the five-kilometer buffer zone. However, Yugoslavia is stepping up its demands for the UN Security Council to take stronger action. Without a serious UN effort to curtail Albanian aggression, Kostunica has made it clear that Serbian forces are prepared to "cleanse the region of terrorists."

NATO spokesmen have repeatedly claimed they will not tolerate any Serbian military action in the demilitarized zone.

However, a showdown with NATO would only jeopardize the flow of vital foreign aid that has been propping up the Yugoslav treasury. Throughout the election campaign, Slobodan Milosevic's Socialists and the right-wing nationalist Radical Party of Serbia described this developing situation as "NATO blackmail." Both Vojislav Seselj – leader of the Radical Party – and Milosevic have played to the voters' patriotism, urging Serbs to reject the "blood money" offered as foreign aid and thereby retain their independence.

Such sentimental appeals have in the past kept Milosevic in power, even as Yugoslavia disintegrated. But the polls here indicate that Serbs are wearying of hard-core nationalism.

"Of course we recognize that with foreign investment, we will lose some control," said Vladimir Krajnovic, a 38-year-old Belgrade-based economist. "However, if such a sacrifice means having a job and a future for my children, then I'm willing to give this up. After ten years of oppressive sanctions, costly civil wars in Bosnia and Croatia, and last year's devastating bombing campaign, many Yugoslavs are anxious for any sign of a possible economic recovery."

In Belgrade, there are some telltale signs of renewal. A new pay phone system – which has been in total disrepair for the past decade – has been installed along downtown streets. Independent banks are opening across Serbia and, with the "inner wall" of sanctions lifted, the free-falling dinar has finally been stabilized, although at one-third of its 1999 value.

Unfortunately, by freezing the dinar and removing the Socialists' subsidies for many staple products, the new DOS policies have led to severe inflation. As prices soared, Milosevic's attacks against the DOS's platform were stepped up. His election advertisements in the daily papers remind voters of rising prices, with the Socialist party slogan, "It's not too late to avoid disaster!" But rather than stirring up nostalgic yearnings, most Belgraders find the ads amusing.

"It is true that the official prices were lower, but there were never any products in the stores," said Zoran Suvakovic, a senior editor with the *Politika* newspaper. "It may cost us four times as much now, but at least we can actually purchase what we can no longer afford." Virtually overnight the black market economy, which has unofficially kept Yugoslavia functioning and created a tremendous amount of criminal activity, has been shut down.

Under Kostunica's DOS regime, the police have been prosecuting many former Socialist officials. The most prominent arrest was that of Mihalj Kertes, the former chief customs administrator. His arrest led to rampant speculation that Milosevic himself may soon face criminal charges.

As for Yugoslavia's utilities, managing the power company is a vital and challenging task, particularly as winter threatens to overload the battered power grid. NATO's bombing in 1999 only further reduced an already aged electrical production system. When coupled with a summer draught, which reduced the Danube's hydroelectric capacity by 50 per cent, Serbia will fall well short of its minimum domestic requirement. "We are already importing the maximum power and producing the maximum power," said Rade Simovic, a Serb-Canadian engineer working for the company on contract. "When the cold weather hits, there will definitely be regular blackouts."

The temporary reprieve from power outages and inclement weather has served to prolong the euphoric mood that swept over Serbia with the October 5 uprising and Kostunica's election. For many Serbs, their new president has acquired an almost "divine" status, reflected in his approval ratings – currently sitting at 91 per cent. His repeatedly strong stand against U.S. interests, and his public snubbing of U.S. Secretary of State Madeleine Albright last month, has elevated Kostunica to hero status.

The DOS has tried to capitalize on this popularity and convert it into votes for Zoran Djindjic, the party's presidential candidate in this weekend's election. But Djindjic's leadership is viewed by many Serbs as a potential liability to DOS – long associated with the Serbian Democratic Movement, Djindjic is distrusted by most Serbs and the many compromises and coalition agreements he made with Milosevic have led voters to question his true values.

"We don't fully trust him, but he is the candidate for our party," said Vesna Jukic, a DOS political organizer. "We will just have to hold our noses when we vote and tell ourselves that we're doing it for Kostunica."

While it is considered highly unlikely that Milosevic could form a majority government, none of the polls has ruled the Socialists out of finishing second. In the September elections, when Milosevic was defeated, he was still able to get more than 1.8 million presidential votes, roughly 40 per cent of the electorate. These results, though, came about through his control of the state Radio Television Service, as well as government newspapers. Since then, these outlets have switched loyalties.

In protest, Milosevic filed a formal complaint against "a prejudicial media" with the Organization for Security and Co-operation in Europe (OSCE), which is monitoring the election. It found that Milosevic had not been granted equal and objective coverage of his party's platform. However, under the complex Serbian electoral system, Milosevic stands to gain simply through the preponderance of candidates.

On Saturday's ballot there will be eight lists for voters to choose from various coalitions, representing 209 political parties and movements. Even Zeljko

Raznatovic – Arkan, the infamous Tiger warlord – has a political party (the Serbian Unity Party) entered on the ballots, despite the fact he was murdered in January 2000. Because of the sheer number of these splinter groups, many will fail to garner the minimum five per cent of the overall vote required to retain official status; their share of the votes will then be transferred proportionately to the major parties.

Under the present system, 250 parliamentary seats are allotted after each party's vote-percentage determines the number of successful candidates. Although early results will be available within hours, it is not expected that a final election result will be available until December 25. In the unlikely event that DOS fails to achieve the required 51 per cent to constitute a majority, the possibility exists that another compromise coalition would have to be struck in order to form an interim government.

Potential voter apathy due to political burn out could yet prove to be the spoiler in Kostunica's quest to consolidate power. "For many Serbs, they want to believe that they already made their choice twice: First at the ballot box on September 24 and then in the streets on October 5," said Vesna Jukic. "All DOS is asking for is for them to take that one more step."

NIS – 21 DECEMBER 2000 (Thursday night)

The late night bus from Belgrade had been delayed by a heavy snowfall and we didn't arrive in Nis until well past midnight. I had informed Captain S. of my arrival time, but without a cell phone I could not contact him to explain the delay.

There was plenty of commotion at the bus station as the entire city was experiencing a power blackout. The headlights of the buses provided the only available light and, in their blinding glare, passengers were reduced to silhouettes. I had not thought to ask S. for a description of himself and I now had serious doubts about finding him.

But as the passengers left the platform, I spotted a solitary figure leaning against a pillar. Tall, with broad shoulders, his trench coat collar pulled up around his ears and smoking a cigarette in an elegant holder, he fit the Hollywood stereotype of the intelligence officer. The dead give-away, however, were dark sunglasses worn in the poorly-lit bus station in the middle of the night. "Welcome to Nis, Mr. Taylor," he said as I approached.

We managed to find a bar that had its own generator. Smoke-filled and packed with young people, the sound system was blaring rock and roll when we entered. S. had a certain authority about him, and after a brief word with the proprietor the music was discretely lowered.

For the next three hours, S. briefed me on the situation in the Presevo valley and his talks with Labbé's NATO delegation. This small corner of the Balkans, currently occupied by UCK guerrillas, has long been part of the Albanian Mafia's heroin trafficking route, through which a lot of European-bound drugs have been smuggled through the historically lawless mountain passes into Kosovo and then up into Bosnia and Montenegro. According to S., the original Albanian incursions into south Serbia had been small-scale and drug-related and the seizure of the GSZ by the UCK could have been avoided if the Yugoslavs had acted sooner.

The first occupation occurred in January 2000, when a small group of UCK set up shop in Dobrosin. Apparently, they were able to do so as the result of a miscue on the part of the Yugoslav security forces – the police had believed the army was patrolling this section of the GSZ and vice versa. The Albanians quickly filled the vacuum.

Over the next five months, the UCK would continue to flex their muscles in the GSZ, simultaneously testing NATO's resolve to control the border. As Yugoslav casualties mounted and the UCK established a fairly extensive operations base in the Serbian territory known as Sector B, S. and his superiors lodged strong protests with NATO officials.

In June their protests paid off. Internal diplomatic pressure on Albanian Kosovar leaders had produced no results, so NATO commanders struck a secret deal with the Yugoslav Army. "We were told we had 72 hours to clean out the Sector B pocket – by whatever means necessary," said S. "The NATO delegates assured us that, for this period, they would turn a blind eye to us moving heavy weapons into the GSZ. It was believed that by the time any formal complaints were issued, the situation on the ground would have been resolved," S. said.

"Detailed plans were made by both the police and army to mount a sweep of the terrorists," S. continued. "But at the last moment, the army's high command convinced Milosevic that NATO was actually planning to spring a trap and the whole thing fell through." S. remained convinced that the NATO negotiators he'd dealt with were acting in good faith. However, he did admit that the U.S. was doing everything it could to bring about Milosevic's downfall.

In August, shortly after the Yugoslav Army rejected NATO's offer, all negotiations with the Serbs had been suspended. "When we finally began talking to them again, the players had changed and it was your Colonel Labbé we were dealing with," S. told me. "The spirit of co-operation had disappeared completely."

We discussed his role and S. provided me with Labbé's telephone number. "If you're in Velika Trnovac later today, you might get lucky and run into him," he told me.

BUJANOVAC – 22 DECEMBER 2000 (Friday morning)

I missed the 3:00 a.m. bus to south Serbia and had to endure a very cold two-hour wait at the blacked-out Nis bus station.

I arrived in Bujanovac before 7:00 a.m. The snow-covered city was already abuzz with activity and resembled an armed camp. Outside the bus depot, close to a dozen Serb soldiers were trying to keep warm beside an armoured personnel carrier. When I asked for directions to the press centre, none of them bothered to reply; a corporal simply pointed down the main street and continued talking to his mates.

It turned out to be a long, cold hike to the old school house that had been converted into a temporary media centre. Equipped with computers, Internet access and telephones, this government press facility marked a whole new approach to foreign journalists for the Serbs. Biserka Matic, one of President Kostunica's two new ministers of information, was on hand to meet me. She explained that the Bujanovac press center was intended to "finally win the media war after the Federal Republic of Yugoslavia had lost so many battles." It was Biserka's belief that the new regime could "avoid bloodshed by using the media."

The only thing missing was foreign reporters. A few Serbian journalists arrived during the morning, but other than a pair of American stringers and myself, no international reporters were present.

Matic had scheduled a press event for later that afternoon, which included a tour by U.S. chargé d'affaires William Montgomery of the disputed territory.

She was hopeful that Montgomery, upon seeing the situation first-hand, might sway U.S. foreign policy. In the meantime, I teamed up with the Americans and headed off to make contact with the UCK. Terry and James had both covered the Kosovo conflict and had very good contacts with the Albanians.

A few weeks earlier, Terry had been to the occupied south Serbian village of Malo (little) Trnovac, which now served as the UCK's headquarters. Here he had met with and interviewed Commandant Leshi, the notorious local war lord.

Terry and James felt that if we were lucky, we could hire an Albanian guide to take us to the UCK. This turned out to be much easier than we'd thought.

Leaving the Yugoslav Army checkpoint at the Bujanovac city limits, we drove a short distance to Velika (big) Trnovac. Waiting for us at the entrance to this ethnic Albanian village was an eight-man section of heavily-armed UCK guerrillas.

We could not believe how boldly the guerrillas were operating within full view of the Yugoslav forces. The edge of Velika Trnovac marked the outer perimeter of the five-kilometer Ground Safety Zone, and the UCK had pushed right up to it. Looking back towards Bujanovac, we could clearly see Yugoslav tanks on the hillsides.

Only one of the Albanians who approached our car was wearing a crest which displayed the letters UCMBP (Liberation Army of Medvedja, Bujanovac and Presevo) – the acronym in use by NATO and the Western media to identify the guerrillas in this south Serbia region. The rest of the squad all proudly displayed their red and black UCK (Kosovo Liberation Army) badges on American-style combat fatigues and black T-shirts.

Crossing the central square of Velika Trnovac and moving west towards the open countryside, we were stopped twice by roving UCK patrols. Estimating regular shift rotations from the sentries we encountered, we figured there had to be an entire 100-man company of UCK stationed here.

Our plan had been to push on up into the mountains to the UCK headquarters in Malo Trnovac, but this was frustrated by the sudden appearance of Commandant Leshi and his bodyguards. Cut off by a Landrover, we suddenly found ourselves staring down the barrels of several Kalashnikovs. Leshi drove up beside our car and conducted a brief conversation with us without ever getting out of his vehicle.

He recognized Terry from their previous encounter, but it was obvious from his demeanour that he and his men were on edge. They knew that the Yugoslavs were threatening a major operation against them, and Leshi was aware of William Montgomery's planned visit. In fact, this is what brought him down from his mountain stronghold. The UCK commander intended to watch the Serbian show of force from a front-row seat in Velika Trnovac. "For our own safety," we were instructed to return to Bujanovac immediately.

BUJANOVAC – 22 DECEMBER 2000 (Friday afternoon)

The first UCK checkpoint we passed was no longer manned. The reason became apparent when we turned towards Bujanovac. Straddling the road was a formidable array of Yugoslav armoured vehicles and security forces. Behind the police and army units was a large group of civilians and media, curious about the lone vehicle emerging from Velika Trnovac.

The Yugoslav column had moved to within 200 meters of the UCK positions but had not advanced farther for fear of provoking a violent response. Heavy machineguns and sniper rifles were trained on the Albanian positions and the Serbian troops were understandably nervous. William Montgomery and about 75 reporters and monitors were clustered on the exposed road. Other than the impressive-looking armoured vehicles, there was no natural cover. Should a firefight erupt, the Serbs and their civilian charges would be sitting ducks.

Yugoslav officials had obviously staged this show of force to demonstrate their troops' restraint, well aware that any violence perpetrated by the UCK would create an immediate international backlash against the Albanians. However, Commandant Leshi proved too savvy to take the bait. When four Serbian jeeps probed the outskirts of Velika Trnovac, the UCK held their fire.

BUJANOVIC – 22 DECEMBER 2000 (Friday night)

The Yugoslav Army's dog-and-pony show continued throughout the afternoon outside other Albanian-controlled villages with troops, supported by tanks, moving right up to the demarcation line of the five-kilometer Ground Security Zone. Many of the Serbian homes in these villages had been destroyed when the UCK seized control. Although there were a number of NATO officials from Kosovo accompanying the official delegation, a French captain informed me that Colonel Serge Labbé was not among them.

Back at the press center in Bujanovac, Yugoslav envoy Nebojsa Covic spoke briefly to reporters to reiterate that "terrorist provocation would not be tolerated," as NATO officials made vague promises to step up their control of the "administrative boundary" between Kosovo and Serbia proper.

The bus back to Belgrade was scheduled to leave at 6:00 p.m., but due to a heavy snowstorm and a delay at the Macedonian border, it was running over an hour late. As I waited in the tiny café at the Bujanovac depot, Marko Stefanovic, a sergeant with the Yugoslav police (MUP), joined me. Speaking excellent German, Stefanovic told me that he had just returned from a two-year assignment in Hamburg. As part of the narcotics squad, he had been attached to the Deutsche *Bundes-polezei* as part of a co-operative effort to clamp down on the Kosovo-based heroin trade. He described this corner of the Balkans as the key smuggling corridor for the Albanian Mafia. "The guns and drugs which flow through here have become a major headache for Germany and other European countries," Stefanovic said. "The Yugoslav police have been providing intelligence and personnel in exchange for money and training." I asked him what had become of this joint police effort during the NATO intervention in Kosovo. Incredibly, he replied that, even at the height of the bombing, there had been no suspension of the German-Yugoslav counter-narcotic collaboration.

BELGRADE – 23 DECEMBER 2000 (Saturday morning)

Due to snowy roads and a missed connection at Nis, my bus had not arrived in Belgrade until after 3:00 a.m. It was my second sleepless night in a row, but this being election day in Serbia, sleep was out of the question. I tried several times to reach Colonel Labbé at his NATO office in Pristina, and left messages with the duty officer for him to return my calls. Before leaving Canada, I had contacted several sources to obtain reactions to Labbé's current posting. Although I had everything necessary to complete my article, I still hoped to top it off with a comment from the Colonel himself. I made a last attempt to reach him just past noon. This time, a rather tipsy Danish captain advised me that the KFOR Christmas party had just begun and that I should "try again next Wednesday." As this was not possible, I concluded my report, filed it and left to cover the early election results.

'Failed' soldier in charge in Kosovo (Ottawa Citizen)
BELGRADE, Yugoslavia – With Yugoslav forces and Albanian guerrillas escalating their conflict in south Serbia, a controversial Canadian officer has been
appointed to handle delicate negotiations between the two factions and keep
the shaky peace in Kosovo.

Colonel Serge Labbé, who was cited by the commission of inquiry into the
notorious Somalia affair as having "failed as a commander," has emerged as
the key negotiator for a Pristina-based NATO delegation charged with implementing last year's Technical Agreement, designed to prevent a renewal of
open warfare between Serbs and Albanians.

Tensions in the region have heightened since November 21 when Kosovar
guerrillas executed four Yugoslav border guards and occupied the Ground
Security Zone, a five-kilometer-wide demilitarized area inside south Serbia.
The Yugoslav government denounced NATO forces in Kosovo (KFOR) for allowing such a large-scale incursion to occur without intervention.

Yugoslav military and police units have so far limited their actions to the
containment of the Albanian offensive, but a major "cleansing operation" of
the occupied area by police is thought to be imminent.

Since the offensive began, NATO has denounced the Albanian actions, but
maintained that it will not tolerate any Yugoslav military counter-offensive
inside the GSZ. In the days ahead, should the cleansing operation proceed
and diplomatic efforts fail, the Yugoslav military and NATO could once again
be facing a showdown.

Since 1993, Colonel Labbé has been thrust into the public spotlight on a
number of occasions and was a central figure in the Somalia affair – the torture
and murder case that led to the disbandment of the Canadian Airborne Regiment. An inquiry into the incident – it was aborted before it could investigate
any cover-up – upheld five allegations against Colonel Labbé in its 1997 report. The commission's findings read in part: "We conclude that Colonel Labbé
failed as a commander."

Colonel Labbé's promotion to brigadier-general was revoked following the
Somalia revelations. The beleaguered Canadian soldier also faced a Career
Review Board after allegations of improprieties involving an officer's mess
waitress in Kingston led to a military police investigation and a separate probe

by the Defence department's ombudsman.

Throughout the Somalia inquiry, Colonel Labbé was a pivotal witness who confronted damning allegations from fellow soldiers and officers. As commander of the Canadian contingent, Labbé was alleged to have offered a "case of champagne" to the first paratrooper to kill a Somali.

In response to a shooting incident on March 4, 1993, in which one Somali was killed and another wounded, Labbé claimed in an interview with CBC Radio that the two victims had been "armed" and were "trained saboteurs." Evidence uncovered by police investigators and revealed at the inquiry concluded the two Somalis were unarmed civilians.

Major Barry Armstrong, the unit medical officer, has maintained one victim had been executed at close range after being wounded. As one of the key witnesses to testify against Colonel Labbé at the Somalia inquiry, Dr. Armstrong (now retired) is critical of Labbé's NATO assignment.

"I'm not sure why Labbé is even still in uniform," said Dr. Armstrong. "I don't think that he's best suited to serve Canada's interests. In Somalia he failed to serve his troops, his country and the UN mandate."

The former commissioner of the Somalia inquiry, Justice Robert Rutherford, said he was not surprised Colonel Labbé was chosen as a NATO negotiator. "After the government shut down our public inquiry, nothing surprises me anymore," he said.

Although he is technically the deputy head of KFOR's Technical Agreement Implementation Committee, the Serbian commanders with whom he negotiates claim that Labbé has far more real authority than his nominal superior, French Brigadier Bruno Neveux.

"Labbé is the one who makes all of the decisions and Neveux trusts his judgement on every issue," said one Yugoslav officer who, as part of the army delegation that attends the weekly briefings with NATO, spoke only on the condition that he remain anonymous as the meetings are considered to be at a very sensitive stage.

"We have been aware of Labbé's background for some time now, and we will voice our concerns about him if and when it becomes necessary to challenge his authority," he said.

The Canadian Forces' senior commanders have always maintained their faith in Colonel Labbé. Chief of Defence Staff Maurice Baril has repeatedly stated that Labbé "remains the best colonel of the army."

In June 1996, at the time he was recommended for the sensitive intelligence post at NATO Headquarters, then-Army Commander Lieutenant General Bill Leach wrote: " I have complete and total trust that Colonel Labbé can, when selected, perform at the very highest standard and will fit into the international environment almost immediately."

Of note, there is no mention made in General Leach's assessment of Labbé about the events in Somalia, subsequent police and ombudsman investigations, nor why his promotion to brigadier general has been on hold since 1993. It is also unclear whether his NATO superiors are aware of his past.

Colonel Serge Labbé could not be reached for comment.

BELGRADE – 23 DECEMBER 2000 (Saturday evening)

The Yugoslav election committee had established a media center in the offices of the federal parliament. Journalists were advised in advance that no interim announcements of the election results would be released and that an official announcement would be made only after all votes were tallied – and this was not expected to be completed until Monday morning. To file my story in time for the *Citizen*'s deadline meant racing around various political party headquarters to record their unofficial, independent results.

To assist me in the course of the evening, I contacted Vladimir Kopric, a 24-year-old university student whom I had first met during the 1999 bombing campaign. At that time, the Kopric family had overcome many difficulties in order to provide me with the transportation, translation and computer services necessary for me to file daily reports. Circumstances may have changed, but the pressure of racing against a deadline in Belgrade brought back a lot of memories for both of us.

Voters rout Milosevic cronies (Ottawa Citizen)

BELGRADE, Yugoslavia – The democratic coalition allied with new Yugoslav President Vojislav Kostunica swept to an easy victory clearing the way for the exorcism of the last vestiges of Slobodan Milosevic's rule.

According to the first unofficial results, which were released just hours after the polls closed, the Democratic Opposition Party of Serbia (DOS), an 18-party coalition, won 65 per cent of the overall vote and will form a majority government.

According to exit polls, Slobodan Milosevic's Socialist party was second, but trailed badly with 14 per cent, according to exit polls. The path has now been cleared for Kostunica to consolidate domestic political power and hasten the economic recovery of this war-weary country.

Newly elected, Serbian President Zoran Djindjic stated that his first priority would be "to work together with Kostunica towards improving living conditions for the average Serbian."

Long into the night, hundreds of DOS supporters celebrated their apparent victory at Belgrade's city hall. In comparison, the streets were relatively quiet, with no repeat of the jubilation that accompanied either the October 5 uprising or the end of last year's 78-day NATO bombing campaign.

Andjelka Kopric, an 81-year-old grandmother, was among the first to cast a vote. In the past, the elderly had largely been staunch supporters of Milosevic and his Socialist party. However, Andjelka stopped believing in Milosevic long before the October uprising. "I realized how corrupt the Socialists really were; there was no way I would vote for them," she said.

Former president and prime ministerial candidate Slobodan Milosevic was also an early voter, and cast his ballot furtively in order to avoid the media. Having advised reporters he would be at the polling station at 11:00 a.m., he slipped in quietly at 8:30 with no cameras present. By contrast, Zoran Djindjic's ceremonial vote casting was attended by a massive throng of cheering DOS supporters and was covered by an impressive media entourage.

Serbian residents in the occupied province of Kosovo turned out in large numbers to vote under the watchful protection of KFOR troops. "We doubled up security and placed additional guards at the polling stations," said Captain Fulgencia, a spokesman at KFOR Headquarters in Pristina, but "there were no violent incidents."

While the UN did not support the elections being held in Kosovo, it had no mandate to prevent them. According to Article 1244 of the 1999 UN peace agreement, Kosovo remains the sovereign territory of the Federal Republic of Yugoslavia. Kosovar Albanians boycotted the vote registration, but did not interfere with the electoral process.

Throughout the autonomous region of Vojvodina, the voter turnout was proportionally much lower due to the high percentage of non-Serbian residents. Unlike the Orthodox-Christian Serbs, who celebrate Christmas on January 7, many of the Hungarians and Croats here were too busy with Christmas to get to the polls.

Although massive power blackouts across Serbia hampered the evening's vote collection and tally, there were no major incidents reported. As the polls closed, the electoral commission also reported that no official complaints had been registered with the Organization of Security and Co-operation in Europe (OSCE), which was monitoring the elections.

Now remains the complex process of calculating vote percentages and applying them to the political parties that garnered at least five per cent of the overall vote. Of the eight coalitions listed on the ballots, early results indicate that only three will gain official status. In addition to Djindjic's DOS and Milosevic's much diminished Socialists, the extreme nationalist Radical Party, under the leadership of Vojislav Seselj, seems to have gained a secure foothold with an estimated eight per cent.

The party led by Milosevic's former political opponent, pro-Western Vuk Draskovic, appeared to have been officially eliminated with only three per cent of the vote, however the first official results will not be posted until noon local time today.

At 4:00 p.m., it was estimated that only 35 per cent of registered voters had cast ballots. Under the Serbian constitution, a minimum 50 per cent of the electorate must vote or the results are considered invalid. Under such circumstances, the current interim government would remain in power until another election could be called within the next three months.

"I really hope to God that our future is not put on hold because of some technicality," said student activist Katarina Njegovan. "I really don't know if we, as a people, can keep going through this unrest and instability."

BELGRADE – 25 DECEMBER 2000 (Monday morning)

The hectic pace of the previous 72 hours had taken its toll, and I spent most of Sunday catching up on my sleep. I had made arrangements with Stefan Blommaert, a Belgian journalist, to spend Christmas Eve at a restaurant in the Skedalja district. Food, music and too much wine made for a very memorable evening, but it definitely wasn't a traditional Canadian Christmas.

As this was still a regular workday in Orthodox Serbia, I had to wake early, shake off the effects of the wine, and get back to the task at hand. Before leaving for Bujanovac last Thursday, I had been lucky enough to secure an interview with Zoran Zivkovic, Yugoslavia's charismatic new Minister of the Interior. As head of police operations and internal security, Zivkovic is at the centre of the crisis in south Serbia.

I had been told to expect no more than a 20-minute meeting, but the 40-year-old novice politician proved to be quite accommodating and surprisingly direct. We spent more than two hours discussing a wide range of topics.

When I told him that I would be leaving the next day, he suggested it would be wise for me to extend my stay for a few days as a major Serbian offensive in the Presevo valley was imminent. I explained to him that I had just missed Christmas and any further delay would test my wife's patience beyond the limit. He pointed to his own wedding band and said, "*Ja razumem* [I understand]."

Later that day, I filed my last story and prepared to head home to mend family fences.

Serbs 'ready' to cleanse terrorists (Ottawa Citizen)

BELGRADE, Yugoslavia – With the parliamentary elections now concluded, the Yugoslav government is taking a much stronger stand against the armed Albanian insurrection in south Serbia. According to Yugoslav's Minister of the Interior, Zoran Zivkovic, police forces "will launch a major operation to cleanse Albanian terrorists from Serbia" within the next 48 hours. Over the past few weeks, the Yugoslavs have mounted a massive buildup of military and police forces outside of the demilitarized zone around Kosovo.

Until now, these troops have been limited to containment operations in an attempt to halt further territorial gains by the Albanian guerrillas. The Albanians have begun digging in and reinforcing newly-seized positions in preparation for what appears to be an imminent showdown with Yugoslav security forces.

In discussing the scope of his planned cleansing operation, Zivkovic said, "Army units will not deploy into the security zone – only police forces. Yugoslavia intends to fully respect the conditions as specified in the UN Kosovo peace agreement."

While Zivkovic says the military will not be participating directly in terms of providing heavy weapons or armoured vehicles, he admitted that the "army will provide logistic and communication support to the police units involved."

On Sunday, Yugoslav police launched a preliminary attack outside the town of Vranje, recapturing a key bunker after a brief skirmish with the Albanians. There were no Serbian casualties and Albanian losses were unknown.

Despite the large number of Albanian fighters they face, the Yugoslav police are confident of a quick and successful operation. "We can push the UCK [Kosovo Liberation Army] out of the main villages in two hours and we can re-occupy the entire zone in just 24 hours," said Marko Stefanovic, a sergeant with the Ministry of the Interior police force (MUP) in the disputed town of Trnovac. "If it wasn't for politicians keeping us at bay, this whole issue would have been resolved weeks ago," he told me.

The new Yugoslav government has been uncharacteristically slow to respond to this recent aggression. "We have been steadily pursuing a peaceful solution to the problem," Zivkovic said. "However, now that all avenues have been exhausted, we will take the appropriate course of action to resolve the situation."

These statements mirror those made just days ago by President Vojislav Kostunica. "The only way for there to be peace is for the terrorists to leave ... or be cleansed out," he said.

On December 19, Yugoslavia appealed to the UN Security Council to amend Article 1244, which details the conditions set out in the 1999 peace agreement. Although the U.S. vetoed the proposed changes, particularly those which would allow Serbia to reduce the demilitarized zone to just one kilometer, the council did condemn the actions of "Albanian extremists."

It was also proposed that NATO forces occupying Kosovo (KFOR) take responsibility for the removal of Albanians from Serbian territory. Although KFOR has now stepped up patrols to prevent Albanian reinforcements and supplies coming from Kosovo, the Yugoslav government does not fully trust this arrangement. "It was through the American sector that over 1600 soldiers passed into Serbia," said Zivkovic. "How is that possible, given the U.S. army's sophisticated surveillance technology? Unless of course the KFOR troops were complicit in the action," he added.

Since the start of the recent offensive, NATO commanders have said they will not tolerate Yugoslav military activity in the security zone. The Serbs regard this as akin to tacit approval of the Albanians' actions. "They are sanctioning the terrorists through their lack of direct opposition," said Zivkovic.

The first of the Albanian incursion into the security zone began last January, and a brief outbreak of hostilities in the south Serbia region occurred in May. This area, known as the Presevo valley, encompasses three major towns: Medvedja, Bujanovac and Presevo.

The Albanian commander is a flamboyant Fidel Castro lookalike who nicknamed himself "Commandant Leshi" after a Second World War partisan hero.

During a brief interview in Trnovac, Commandant Leshi claimed his troops were "conducting large-scale military exercises in preparation to repulse the Serbians." He said his mountain headquarters at Malo Trnovac "has been evacuated of all but four civilians in anticipation of heavy fighting."

For now, however, the main streets of Velika Trnovac remain busy. Albanian residents cheerfully stroll about the marketplace while UCK-uniformed soldiers patrol the roads. "We feel that we are liberated from the Serb aggressors," said Artan Kryeziu, the village's English teacher. "We don't want to have to live under Serbian oppression again."

Only recently have UCK troops become brazen enough to enter the town of Velika Trnovac in daylight. Previously, they entered under cover of night, and were welcomed in secret.

The continued presence of Albanian civilians – in close proximity to the guerrillas – and the potential for "collateral damage" should fighting break out, have been major considerations for the new Yugoslav regime.

Serbian officials are hoping that their new policy of openness towards the media will prove to be a decisive factor in the world's judgement of their proposed actions.

In another attempt to garner international support prior to their police counter-offensive, the Yugoslav government arranged for a delegation of diplomats, most notably U.S. chargé d'affaires William Montgomery, to visit the disputed zone last Friday.

While it amounted to little more than a show of force by both sides, the exercise clearly demonstrated just how well entrenched the Albanian guerrillas are in the security zone.

By taking such precautions, the Yugoslav authorities believe that they've paved the way to conduct operations, without an international rebuke. "We've changed our approach to such affairs and we believe that it has been successful," said Zivkovic. "Now it is up to our police to restore order."

Yugoslavia's military and police forces have been re-equipped, reorganized and revitalized since the ouster of Slobodan Milosevic. New rifles, protective helmets and flak jackets have been issued and morale is high. "This is our land, and now we will be fighting for a president that we believe in," said Sergeant Marko Stefanovic. "We will defeat the terrorists because it is our duty."

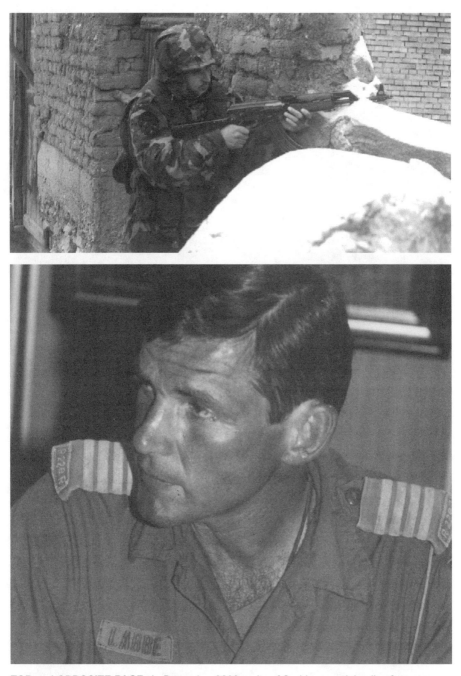

TOP and OPPOSITE PAGE: *In December 2000, units of Serbian special police forces were deployed throughout the Presevo valley to contain Albanian UCK guerrilla incursions. (SCOTT TAYLOR) Negotiating this tense standoff on behalf of NATO was Canadian Colonel Serge Labbé* **(ABOVE)** *– an officer previously cited by a public inquiry into the 1995 Somalia scandal. (DEPARTMENT OF NATIONAL DEFENCE)*

ABOVE: *As police casualties mounted, Macedonians vented their anger against Albanian shops and properties.* (BORIS GRDANOSKI, ASSOCIATED PRESS)

OPPOSITE PAGE: *In spring 2001 ethnic Albanian nationalism manifested itself into armed conflicts in northern Macedonia. Macedonian police forces suffered a number of setbacks at the hands of Albanian UCK guerrillas, veterans of Kosovo and other Balkan conflicts.*

chapter four:
BEYOND THEIR BOUNDS

BELGRADE – 27 APRIL 2001 (Friday evening)

My Austrian Airlines flight had been delayed for over three hours in Vienna and we did not touch down in Belgrade until after 5:30 p.m. As a frequent traveller, I have come to expect such inconveniences, but in this case the delay was particularly troublesome. I had hoped to hit the ground running in Yugoslavia – using the last hours of the work-week to finalize arrangements for interviews. Before starting out on this short trip to the Balkans, I had sent numerous e-mail messages to set up an appointment list. Invariably, my contacts had replied with "Welcome back – call me when you arrive." I had long since learned that few people in the Balkans like to commit themselves to a specific time, but it is nevertheless a frustrating exercise when you have a very tight, fixed schedule.

Admittedly, my plan was rather ambitious; I was trying to cover a number of Balkan-related stories as well as research some depleted uranium issues in Iraq all within a two-week timeframe.

Since my last trip to Yugoslavia in December, there had been a number of significant developments. In early February, President Vojislav Kostunica had formally ratified Yugoslavia's heretofore-disputed border with the Republic of Macedonia. Since Macedonia had peacefully seceded from the Federal Republic in 1992, then-President Slobodan Milosevic had refused to define the border. However, with Albanian guerrillas now occupying territory in south Serbia and threatening action inside northern Macedonia, Kostunica's government felt it only prudent to clearly set out areas of military responsibility. Within days of the agreement being signed, Albanian UCK guerrillas had crossed into Macedonia from Kosovo to launch a major offensive.

In March, the international media turned its attention to this latest round of inter-ethnic Balkan fighting, particularly in the northwestern Macedonian city of Tetovo, which had been the scene of several clashes between the UCK and Macedonian security forces.

This little known city was thrust into the world news spotlight with the release of some graphically-violent footage. Macedonian television crews at a security checkpoint had captured the killing of two members of the UCK on tape.

The incident began when a Macedonian policeman stopped the Albanians and one of them pulled out a hand grenade. As the startled policeman ran from the car, shouting a warning, his comrade opened fire. The Albanian with the grenade was hit, but despite his wounds, still managed to throw it. The Macedonians unleashed a deadly barrage, killing him and his companion.

Albanian media outlets claimed that the two men were innocent civilians murdered by Macedonian security forces, and that the grenade had in fact been a cell phone.

Rade Lesko, a former soldier, was one of the Macedonian cameramen who filmed the incident. In this footage, the Albanian is clearly shown tossing a grenade, which came to rest against a curb with the safety pin still attached.

At the end of March, it was reported that the UCK guerrillas had withdrawn back to their bases inside Kosovo. International envoys – Javier Solana, president of the European Union, and George Robertson, NATO's secretary-general, in particular – made several trips to Macedonia to try to hammer out a peaceful solution. Many analysts believed that further violence could be avoided and that a peace proposal might be formalized by mid-June.

On April 1, the media focus shifted back to Belgrade, when Yugoslav authorities stormed the villa of former president, Slobodan Milosevic.

A month earlier, federal prosecutors had announced that they were launching an investigation into allegations of corruption by the deposed Yugoslav dictator. On March 29, following police questioning, Milosevic had been charged and then released. This set in motion a comic-opera police raid on his home. For twenty-six hours, Milosevic's bodyguards returned fire with the police tactical squad as a herd of journalists surrounded his walled estate. At one point Milosevic issued a statement to the press that he would not be taken alive, but in the end he was—very much so.

Immediately after Milosevic's anti-climatic surrender on April 3, the United State's Secretary of State, Colin Powell, promised to provide Yugoslavia with $50 million in "reward" money. Although the country desperately needed the money, the American statement undermined political support for the new regime. To many, it appeared as if Serbian President Zoran Djindjic, and to a lesser extent federal President Vojislav Kostunica, had sold out to American interests.

Even though the original charges were for corruption within Yugoslavia, The Hague War Crimes Tribunal wasted little time in demanding Milosevic's immediate extradition. The chief prosecutor, Carla del Ponte, had submitted a warrant to the Yugoslav authorities on April 5. A few days later the U.S. State Department dangled a financial carrot of $1.3 billion in foreign aid, but the release of these funds was predicated upon the handing over of Milosevic to the tribunal.

Further destabilizing Kostunica's fledging government was the continued threat of Montenegrin secession from Yugoslavia. Under the Milosevic regime, the United States had encouraged Montenegrin President Milo Djukanovic to break away from Serbia. Although circumstances had changed dramatically since October 5, the Montenegrin separatist movement remained a formidable impediment to the consolidation of Kostunica's federal powers.

On April 29, Montenegro held a general election and it was believed that a clear separatist victory would give Djukanovic the mandate necessary to hold a quick referendum, thereby setting in motion the break-up of Yugoslavia.

It was my intention to produce three separate reports for the *Ottawa Citizen* covering the fallout from Milosevic's arrest, the results of the Montenegrin election, and the aftermath of the fighting in Macedonia. However, with the loss of Friday afternoon due to my late arrival, it appeared as though my tight schedule was already in jeopardy.

BELGRADE – 28 APRIL 2001 (Saturday morning)

I had been keeping open the option of catching a flight to Podgorica to report on the Montenegrin elections until mid-morning. However, after an interview with Captain S., my contact in the Yugoslav intelligence service, I decided the results of the election would not justify the effort.

There had been a lot of speculation in the European media that Montenegrin President Milo Djukanovic might try to use security forces to strong-arm a victory for his separatist party. If this occurred and pro-unity supporters re-acted violently, pundits predicted that Montenegro would be plunged into chaos. Over cappuccinos at the Hotel Moskva's café, S. told me that Yugoslav intelligence expected no such crisis to develop as Djukanovic was unlikely to win a convincing majority.

For the most part, my conversation with S. centered on developments in south Serbia. The UCK still occupied the area known as Sector B in the Presevo valley, however in an effort to contain further offensives, NATO had allowed the Yugoslav Army back into the five-kilometer Ground Security Zone. This demilitarized sector surrounding Kosovo had been established as part of Article 1244 of the UN peace plan signed in June 1999. Until now, NATO had reneged on virtually every major condition outlined in 1244 (i.e., disarming the UCK and the return of Yugoslav troops to border posts). On the other hand, NATO officials remained adamant that Serbs adhere to their part of the agreement.

Nebojsa Covic, the special envoy appointed by Kostunica to negotiate with NATO, seemed to be making some progress. In an effort to show good faith, Covic had conducted an investigation into allegations that the Yugoslav Army (JNA) had looted Albanian homes in the disputed territory. The official statement that Serb soldiers had done so was a first step, and demonstrated that President Kostunica wanted to keep his troops in check. Covic had also announced that the victims would be fully compensated. Contrary to what I expected to hear, S. claimed that this new policy had actually improved morale among soldiers of the Yugoslav Third Army.

Under the command of Commandant Leshi, approximately 1600 UCK soldiers were reportedly still dug into positions inside Sector B. According to S., the Yugoslav Army had submitted detailed plans to the NATO Security Council for re-entry into the contested area which they hoped to re-enter peacefully before the UCK strengthened their forces. However, if NATO denied this request, the JNA was prepared to act unilaterally.

On February 13, police forces and the JNA launched an attack on Commandant Leshi's forces. For over four hours Yugoslav artillery, mortars and tanks pounded suspected UCK positions around the villages of Bukovac and Gornje Shoshaje.

Unable to withstand a conventional assault, the UCK retaliated by launching terror attacks throughout Kosovo. One Serb civilian was killed and two others wounded in an ambush outside Pristina, despite the presence of a KFOR escort. In the village of Strpce a sniper gunned down a Serbian farmer, while in northern Kosovo three more Serbs were wounded when a landmine destroyed their tractor.

Three days later, the UCK attacked a civilian bus that was travelling between Nis and Gracanica, Kosovo. Seven passengers were killed and more than 40 wounded. The Yugoslavs suspended their offensive in south Serbia while NATO conducted an investigation into the incident.

The current fighting in Macedonia was considered to be directly linked to the UCK, and Yugoslav intelligence expected them to mount another offensive in the Kumanovo region before mid-May.

S. confirmed that the JNA was providing both emergency military aid and intelligence to its Macedonian counterparts. "We still harbor a grudge against them because of their past co-operation with NATO," he said. "However, now we have a mutual enemy."

When I inquired about Colonel Serge Labbé's activities, S. replied that the controversial NATO negotiator had been replaced. Apparently the relationship between the Canadian colonel and Yugoslav Army delegates had deteriorated to the point of impasse. "We had a number of serious disagreements with Labbé and we felt he was far too pro-Albanian – both personally and professionally – for him to continue as a mediator," said S.

One incident, which had enraged Serbian authorities, had been the capture and torture of two of their soldiers. After straying inside the Kosovo boundary during a foot patrol, the Serbs had been held for 25 days by the UCK. It was Labbé who finally negotiated their release and turned them over to the Yugoslav Army. However, when it was discovered that both soldiers had been tortured and maimed during their captivity, Yugoslav authorities insisted that

NATO prosecute those responsible. According to S., Colonel Labbé refused – without consulting his NATO superiors – to take any official action against the Albanian commanders. "The details of the torture these soldiers endured were so horrific that our troops are now demanding they be issued with suicide pills," said S. "They would rather kill themselves than suffer such pain... You can only imagine the outrage of the victims' families when we told them of Labbé's decision."

The final straw for the Serbs had been Labbé's personal relationship with Braha Gylanize, his 26-year-old Albanian translator. Using his NATO position as clout, Colonel Labbé allegedly intervened and obtained travel documents from the Yugoslav Foreign Ministry in Pristina for Ms. Gylanize and her family. "It is necessary to maintain a good relationship with your staff," conceded S., "but we felt Labbé had taken this too far."

Since Labbé's departure from the NATO negotiating team, Nebojsa Covic was able to gain a number of concessions. S. predicted that while there would still be some fighting in the short term, a peaceful solution for Kosovo and south Serbia might be possible. "We will have to give up our claims to some territory and not everyone will be happy with that, but our soldiers are tired of fighting," he said.

BELGRADE – 28 APRIL 2001 (Saturday afternoon)
Following my conversation with Captain S. at the Hotel Moskva, I arranged to meet Dr. Pavle Todorovic, former Yugoslav ambassador to Canada. He insisted we drive to his summer house, located in a small village south of Belgrade. I first met Todorovic in April 1999, when the NATO bombing campaign was in full swing. His staff had been instrumental in arranging my Yugoslavian entry visa – a rare document for a Western journalist at that time. Since then I had crossed paths with Todorovic at several official functions in Ottawa, which invariably included much alcohol. Our present meeting would prove to be no exception. Relaxed by the flowing wine, Dr. Todorovic's initial diplomacy was soon replaced with characteristic Balkan bluntness.

BELGRADE – 29 APRIL 2001 (Sunday morning)
The morning news featured reports of an incident in Macedonia yesterday which threatened to destroy the shaky six-week-old cease-fire agreement.

Outside the village of Vejce, a Macedonian patrol had been ambushed by UCK guerrillas. According to the reports, when the firing first erupted, Corporal Ilco Stojanova had swerved his NIVA jeep into a roadside ditch and leapt from the vehicle. Just 40 meters ahead of him, a Macedonian army Hummer had been hit by a rocket-propelled grenade and was already ablaze. Small-arms fire had torn up the road surface and smashed into the patrol's remaining two vehicles. Like Stojanova, his comrades had abandoned their vehicles and sought cover from the fusillade. This 16-man patrol was a mixture of elite police and army personnel whose mission had been to demonstrate a security presence up to the Kosovo border. They had driven 12 kilometers from their base in the city of Tetovo, when the UCK had opened fire. Caught by surprise, the Macedonians were outnumbered and at a tactical disadvantage along the narrow roadway.

Stojanova had used his cell phone to call headquarters and report that several of his colleagues were dead or wounded, with the remainder pinned down. Stojanova had requested the immediate support of helicopter gunships and reinforcements.

For ten minutes following the initial onslaught, Stojanova had continued to return fire and call for help. During that time, the eight surviving Macedonian troops from the rearmost vehicles had been able to withdraw on foot back down the road. Stojanova then remained the only unwounded Macedonian able to fight.

At 24 years of age, Ilco Stojanova was a six-year veteran of the police force, with most of this time spent serving with the highly trained tactical squad. He had survived several firefights with the UCK, but today he would not be so fortunate. Leaning out from behind his NIVA to take aim, he was hit in the head and the one-sided battle was over.

News of the ambush was soon broadcast by the national media. Although details were sketchy and the names of the slain were not released, Stojanova's mother feared the worst when she learned of the attack. Her son had frequently called home on his cell phone, even during tours of duty in operational sectors. Upon hearing the news reports, Mrs. Stojanova tried desperately to reach her son, and Ilco's failure to answer his phone caused her tremendous anxiety. She prayed that he was unhurt. Several hours later, Bitola's police chief and two assistants arrived to personally convey the grim news of her son's death.

Although my original plan had been to write a detailed background piece on the past fighting, it appeared as though I might now have more current news to report from Macedonia.

Also in the news were the early results from the Montenegrin election. Although not yet official, the exit polls indicated that President Milo Djukanovic's separatists would win a narrow victory, but without a clear majority there would be no immediate push for a referendum on secession from the Federal Yugoslavia Republic. As Captain S. had predicted, there had been very few incidents of intimidation or violence during the voting. Although significant, this election had not amounted to much of an international news story. I was relieved that I hadn't missed much and thankful that I had saved myself the additional travel.

Before leaving for Macedonia, I had to write and file a situation report on the political upheaval in Yugoslavia. I decided to concentrate on Milosevic's arrest and the Canadian-related issues from my earlier interview with Todorovic. I felt I would be able to better incorporate the heightened tensions in south Serbia with a feature story about the Macedonian conflict.

Sympathy for the Dictator (Ottawa Citizen)

BELGRADE, Yugoslavia – "I pity Milosevic," said Dr. Pavle Todorovic. "I used to believe in him, but ultimately he's responsible for the actions of the people with which he chose to surround himself." As Yugoslavia's former ambassador to Canada, Todorovic was recalled to Belgrade from Ottawa and is no longer working with the Yugoslav Foreign Affairs office. As a medical doctor by profession, Todorovic's diplomatic posting to Canada – from 1997 to 2001 – was a purely political appointment. Following last October's popular uprising which overthrew Slobodan Milosevic and his regime, Yugoslavia's new president, Vojislav Kostunica, has quickly acted to remove the remaining Socialist party members from their diplomatic positions around the world.

By chance, Todorovic's small Belgrade flat overlooks the nearby prison where Slobodan Milosevic is currently incarcerated. Last month, the former Yugoslav president was arrested on corruption charges following a dramatic 36-hour stand-off between his bodyguards and police. On April 27, the original 30-day pre-trial custody period for Milosevic expired, but it has now been formally extended for an additional two months. In the previous week, several senior-ranking Socialist party members were also arrested throughout Yugoslavia in a string of sudden police raids. Those charged include the former customs chief and several top military officers. The citizens of Belgrade are now speculating that Slobodan Milosevic's much-hated wife, Mira, will be the next ex-senior political official seized.

Doctor Todorovic does not believe that the Yugoslav prosecutors can prove their cases in a court of law. "These arrests are political and are being driven by the United State's influence," he said. "NATO needs to justify their aggression against Yugoslavia, with the dictatorial regime of Milosevic. Somebody has to be held responsible." Todorovic personally suspects that the circumstances surrounding Milosevic's botched arrest and the harsh conditions of his custody are deliberately aimed at humiliating the former president into taking his own life. "He knows far too much about the secret deals that were made behind the scenes for NATO to seriously want him to testify before The Hague Tribunal," said Todorovic.

A member of the Central Prison's psychiatric staff has revealed to the local media that Milosevic is "absolutely paranoid of being killed in jail," and that he will only eat food prepared and delivered by his wife. When a new heater was brought into his frigid cell, Milosevic demanded that the device be completely dismantled and reassembled in the presence of his lawyer.

Doctor Todorovic, who has known Milosevic since they attended the University of Belgrade together, regards the former president as "a very strong man" but he acknowledges that suicide remains a possibility. "Both of Slobodan's parents took their own lives; this is something which has always been a tragic reality for the Milosevic family."

As for The Hague Tribunal itself, Todorovic sees the war crime indictment as "purely political – nothing more." Todorovic insists that "Canada's participation in the tribunal should be regarded as an embarrassment to all Canadians. Louise Arbour [the former chief prosecutor who indicted Milosevic during the 1999 NATO bombing] was a party to the process and therefore played an active role in the deception and deceit orchestrated by the U.S. State Department." In particular, Todorovic cited the alleged January 1999 Racak massacre, which was widely acknowledged as the galvanizing event that led to NATO's military intervention in Kosovo, and formed the basis for Arbour's high profile war crime indictments. "Now that the final report has been issued by the Finnish pathologist and the massacre was proven to be a masquerade – a staged hoax – why aren't the Canadian media pushing Arbour to answer for her actions?" he asked.

Todorovic was appreciative of Canada's Foreign Affairs ministry for resisting U.S. pressure to shut down his embassy in Ottawa during the 1999 air campaign. Canada had closed its embassy in Belgrade when the bombing began and most NATO countries quickly expelled Yugoslav diplomats for the duration of the war. However, in April 1999, as the bombing intensified, Canada's refusal to completely break off official relations with Yugoslavia attracted the attention of America's Secretary of State. "Madeleine Albright flew to Ottawa from London to try and persuade Canada to shut down our embassy," said Todorovic. "To the credit of your ministry of Foreign Affairs, they refused her request."

While praising the senior bureaucrats with whom he often negotiated (in particular Jim Wright, who headed up the European desk at Foreign Affairs), Todorovic has little respect for the department's then-minister, Lloyd Axworthy. "He was an absolute hypocrite in his dealings with us. During the Kosovo crisis, he refused to even receive a delegation of Canadian Serbs who wished to express their concerns," said Todorovic. "Then in the fall of 2000, when two Canadians were being held in jail as suspected terrorists, this same Axworthy made an appeal to Serb-Canadians, asking them to pressure Milosevic to release them."

While Axworthy was often frustrating for Yugoslav officials to deal with, Defence Minister Art Eggleton's comments upset Todorovic even more. In March 2000, immediately following a press conference outlining the Yugoslav government's official list of bombing casualties, Eggleton dismissed Ambassador Todorovic as "Milosevic's henchman." This derogatory comment was repeatedly broadcast by the Canadian media.

"That was definitely the lowest point in my diplomatic career," said Todorovic, still visibly angered by the remark. "At the time, I was encouraged by many of the other ambassadors in Ottawa – including one NATO member – to demand a formal apology for Eggleton's startling breach of protocol," explained Todorovic. "In the end, I decided that this personal attack against me was only his inability to justify the bombing with any factual arguments."

Prior to being recalled from Ottawa, Todorovic filed a final complaint with the Canadian government about its restrictive policies directed at Yugoslav citizens requesting travel visas. His requests to relax the criteria went unheeded. As a result, Angela Bogdan, Canada's ambassador in Belgrade, has been receiving a lot of bad press throughout Serbia in recent weeks. "All male applicants are being asked a litany of questions about their previous military service (which is compulsory in Yugoslavia). Where did you serve? Who was your commander? Since these same questions are not asked of Croatians, Albanians or Muslims, the implication is that all Serbs – and only Serbs – are guilty of war crimes."

There are now over 250,000 Canadians of Serbian descent and Todorovic believes this factor alone dictates that Canada must work to improve badly-strained relations with Yugoslavia.

"One of the first priorities must be the payment of reparations for the bomb damage created by Canadian planes," said Todorovic. "Your generals are proud to claim that they dropped ten per cent of the bombs, so they should be responsible for no less than this amount of reconstruction aid." (The present estimate of destroyed infrastructure is $10 billion U.S. and Canada has so far contributed only $10 million Canadian in funding).

"We are presently in a tremendous state of transition and the political situation here is still very tenuous. Canada – and the rest of NATO – must now show in concrete terms that they are prepared to support democracy in Yugoslavia," Todorovic concluded.

SKOPJE, MACEDONIA – 30 APRIL 2001 (Monday morning)

At daybreak, as we reached Bujanovac, it was already hot. Most of the passengers – including Serbian soldiers and policemen – disembarked here, and the ominous presence of armoured vehicles and bunkers at traffic intersections reminded the rest of us that we were now proceeding into disputed territory. Crammed aboard a full bus that had no air conditioning, it had been a long and unpleasant night. Having left Belgrade's central station just after 11:00 p.m., the Skopje "milk run" had taken nearly nine hours to cover the 550 kilometers to the Macedonian border.

On the final stretch in the Presevo valley, the only other vehicles on the highway had been Yugoslav armoured personnel carriers. At the crossing itself, the Serbian border guards and their Macedonian counterparts were on full alert. Sandbagged bunkers lined the now-collapsed trenches that had been dug during 1999's Kosovo conflict. Throughout NATO's bombing campaign, Yugoslavs and Macedonians had confronted each other from these same positions across the then-closed border. Now, both sides were actively scanning the nearby hillsides for any evidence of Albanian guerrillas.

As a Western journalist, my presence attracted considerable attention from the Macedonian police. Despite having all my documentation in order, I had come to expect delays at Balkan borders – and this would prove to be no exception. After waiting nearly 45 minutes as the police searched my luggage, the sergeant in charge reluctantly returned my passport. With a grunt and dismissive wave of his hand, he welcomed me to Macedonia. Having been the cause of the delay, my fellow passengers, who were still sitting aboard the sweltering bus, were equally cordial when I clambered aboard. Angry looks, muffled insults, and several rude gestures greeted my return.

At the bus terminal in the heart of old Skopje, I was besieged by a horde of Albanian and Gypsy taxi drivers, all eager to fleece a foreigner. I had previously arranged to meet a contact at the Hotel Tourist, but without a map, I had no clue as to where I was.

The obvious leader of the cabbies was a tall, rough looking Albanian in his mid-30s. He spoke no English, but in broken German, demanded a flat rate of 30 deutsch marks for the trip to the hotel. In the depressed economy of the Balkans, such a sum for a taxi fare is substantial, if not outrageous. Having long ago realized that Balkan cab drivers prey upon hapless victims, I replied that I would gladly pay the meter rate. To my surprise, the big Albanian railed at this suggestion, shouting that it was an insult to his *stolz* (pride). More than eager to uphold their leader's honor, the other cabbies crowded around me, yelling derogatory comments in a combination of Albanian, English, and German. I desperately looked around the square for a policeman. As luck would have it, I couldn't see so much as a sympathetic bystander. However, I saw a large neon sign indicating that the Hotel Tourist was 200 meters away, just over the Vardar River's pedestrian footbridge.

Short-tempered after a sleepless night, I traded insults with the cabbies then forcibly pushed my way through the crowd. Momentarily caught off guard, they parted ranks and fell silent. Then they started shouting insults again, which escalated into the hurling of stones. Walking briskly, I did not dare glance back until I had reached the center span of the bridge. The drivers hurled a final round of catcalls before dispersing towards their parked cabs. I had just been welcomed to Skopje.

My contact, Naun Nachevski, a 60-something retired diplomat, was waiting for me at the Hotel Tourist. His well-tailored suit made me very conscious of my unkempt appearance: dressed in casual clothes, sporting two days of chin stubble, and sweating as a result of the incident at the bus terminal. It was readily apparent from Nachevski's expression that he was unimpressed with me. His son Alex, who lives in Toronto and is a director of the Center for Peace in the Balkans, had put me in touch with him. Having been told that I was an author, Nachevski bluntly admitted that he expected me to be much older. I assumed this to mean respectable, and I wished I had time to change into a shirt and tie before our meeting. Despite his misgivings, Nachevski promised to provide me with whatever assistance he could.

While making arrangements for my visa in Canada, officials in the Macedonian embassy had told me that May 1 and 2 are national holidays, and had urged me to complete all the necessary arrangements – press accreditation, interview requests, etc. – as quickly as possible upon my arrival. To facilitate this, First Secretary Dusko Uzonovski had been very helpful in providing contacts for me at the Foreign Ministry in Skopje, however, nobody had accounted for the human factor. Given the two-day midweek break, virtually every bureaucrat in Macedonia had either called in sick or booked today off in order to enjoy a very long weekend. Except for security guards, the Foreign Affairs Ministry and the press accreditation offices were empty.

It was frustrating to say the least. I had very little time to research the issues behind the February and March clashes and with the fighting threatening to escalate at any moment everyone I needed to contact was away. Although he was a former journalist, Naun Nachevski had spent most of his career working for the Yugoslav communist bureaucracy. To him, my situation was obvious. Without official authorization, there was nothing for me to do but relax, enjoy Skopje, and wait until the government offices reopened on Thursday morning.

Having run out of options, we shared a late breakfast at an outdoor café, Nachevski did his best to brief me on the causes of the impending civil war, complete with the requisite Balkan history lesson, but on several occasions the ominous roar of helicopter gunships flying low over the city center interrupted our conversation. The waiters were anxiously listening to the radio inside the kitchen and provided Nachevski and me with occasional updates. According to the news reports, fighting between UCK guerrillas and Macedonian security forces had broken out again around Tetovo. The gunships we saw had apparently been dispatched to lend support to the ground troops.

With so much action so close (Tetovo is only 45 kilometers from Skopje), it was impossible to simply accept my forced inactivity. There was one last phone number to try on the list of contacts Alex had provided me with – that of Sonja Stefanovic, a journalist with Skopje-based Skynet Television. I told Naun that while I could not officially work without proper authorization, it would be helpful for me to remain plugged in to events by moving on to Tetovo. Despite his reservations and insistence that I stay put, he made the telephone call to Ms. Stefanovic.

TETOVO, MACEDONIA – 30 APRIL 2001 (Monday afternoon)

After a brief introduction, Sonja insisted that I join her and her family for lunch, and having just eaten is not a viable excuse to refuse a meal in the Balkans. The Stefanovic family was incredibly generous, even by Macedonian standards.

The tranquility of sitting in their garden sipping white wine and eating roast lamb was disturbed by the occasional overflight of Tetovo-bound helicopter gunships and radio news bulletins on the fighting. The Stefanovics' hospitality was hard to refuse, but I insisted that I needed to get to Tetovo. As it turned out, Sonja worked Skynet's culture desk and normally had little contact with reporters. However, because it was a holiday weekend, one of her colleagues had been assigned to cover the situation in Tetovo. Making a few phone calls on my behalf, she arranged for me to not only be met by her friend at the bus station, but she also booked me a room at the Hotel Electra.

Despite the fighting, a few Skopje-Tetovo buses were still running, but Sonja warned me that I had to arrive at the hotel before the military's 9:00 p.m. curfew. The Stefanovics could not understand my eagerness to head into a war zone, but they wished me well and I was on my way.

The fatigue of a sleepless night coupled with an afternoon of sunshine and wine had taken its toll. Almost immediately after I boarded the Tetovo-bound bus, I dozed off. At a checkpoint, a burly policeman clutching a Kalashnikov automatic rifle shook me awake and demanded to see my documents. I surrendered my passport and stammered in broken Macedonian that I was a Canadian journalist. A second policeman was checking the identification cards of the other passengers, but once again it was the presence of a foreign journalist that seemed to attract the most attention.

This checkpoint consisted of a sandbagged bunker manned by half a dozen heavily-armed policemen. The two who boarded our bus were hard-looking characters. Physically fit and in their mid-thirties, these were obviously not city cops or young conscripts. I was worried that without having proper Macedonian press accreditation, I would either be turned back to Skopje or, worse still, taken into custody. When one of the policemen disembarked to confer with his colleagues, my fears were heightened. I was puzzled, but relieved when the entire group erupted into laughter and peered into the bus to get a better look at me. Although I speak a smattering of Serbian (and even less Macedonian), I have long known that my first name, *Skot*, means *jerk* or *asshole* in both languages. Evidently, the policemen who had come aboard the bus were quite amused by this and had simply wanted to share the joke with the others. They were still laughing when they handed back my passport.

A short distance beyond the checkpoint, the bus stopped at an intersection just inside the Tetovo city limits. When many of the passengers got off, I assumed that this was a courtesy stop prior to our arrival at the bus station. However, after we turned back onto the main highway and the road signs read Gostivar, I realized that something was wrong. I notified the conductor, who was gracious enough to make my error known to the rest of the passengers. The description of my plight, coupled with my unfortunate first name, caused a great deal of laughter. Pleased with his joke, the conductor then returned his attention to helping me out. Approximately 15 kilometers from Tetovo, he stopped at a roadside service center, where he explained my predicament to two amused gas jockeys. Without hesitation they proffered me a can of Coke, telephoned for a taxi, and invited me to watch their television until it arrived.

The early evening news from Skopje was on and there was a lot of footage showing the fighting around Tetovo. Naturally, the attendants were anxious to follow events so close to their premises. At one point, they used a mixture of pidgin English, Macedonian, and hand gestures to explain that one of the televised helicopter strikes had actually occurred just up the road.

Following the Tetovo stories, the newscast showed images of a massive funeral procession in the city of Bitola. I could understand enough to realize that this ceremony was being held in honour of four of the eight policemen killed in an ambush the previous Saturday in Vejce. Thousands of mourners followed the coffins in a candlelit procession. Incredibly, the next news item was a detailed account by the Macedonian coroner, complete with graphic illustrations, of how the policemen's bodies had been mutilated before and after their deaths. Even without completely understanding the commentary, the emotional impact of seeing grieving families followed by mutilated corpses was powerful. I could see that the two gas station attendants were becoming visibly upset as they watched, their comments angrily punctuated by anti-*Shqiptare* (Albanian) expletives. I could not believe that news editors would air such an irresponsibly provocative show at a time when ethnic tensions across the country were already highly charged.

TETOVO, MACEDONIA – 30 APRIL 2001 (Monday evening)

By the time the taxi dropped me at the Tetovo bus station and I met the Skynet reporter, it was already dark and fast approaching curfew. Armoured police vehicles rumbled through the nearly vacant streets. En route to the hotel, we passed heavily-armed troops moving forward to man a bunker near the sports stadium. Leaving me at the Hotel Electra's reception desk, my contact raced off into the darkness towards his home. Primarily a banquet hall and restaurant designed to host wedding receptions, Electra's owner, Vojce Stojkoski, had added five rooms to accommodate out-of-town guests who attended functions there. However, since the crisis began in February, Stojkoski's catering contracts had all but disappeared and hotel rooms were in short supply. When fighting broke out, foreign journalists and European Union monitors descended upon Tetovo and most had booked themselves into the centrally located Hotel Macedonia. A product of the old communist era, the Macedonia was overpriced and had seen better days. By contrast, Stojkoski's five large rooms were brand new and comparatively inexpensive. At just 30 Deutschmarks (about $22 Canadian per night) including breakfast, the quaint little Hotel Electra was a rare find, perfectly suited to my needs.

I arrived just in time for the evening meal and, with the curfew now in effect, I had the opportunity to dine with the staff. Vojce, the proprietor, was in attendance along with his secretary (a former Miss Tetovo) and several of the serving staff who lived in the hotel. Collectively, they were a cross-section of Slavic cultures – Croats, Serbs, and Macedonians – most of whom had in some way already experienced the hardships brought about by the previous Balkan conflicts.

German was the common language that evening as few of them spoke English, and the hotel's only other guests, Friedhelm Peel and Phillip Eisenring, were German and Swiss nationals, respectively. Both men were engineers assigned by a German foreign aid foundation to build a university in Tetovo. For the twenty-something Eisenring, this was his first field operation and the first time he'd been so close to combat. As a grizzled old veteran of numerous projects around the globe, Herr Peel was no stranger to dangerous situations. With nowhere else to go that evening, we swapped war stories and became acquainted over (too many) bottles of wine. An experienced non-partisan observer who worked daily with both Albanian and Macedonian officials and workers, Herr Peel was able to provide me with valuable insights into the Tetovo situation. Shortly after midnight we heard an exchange of machinegun fire on the outskirts of town.

TETOVO, MACEDONIA – 1 MAY 2001 (Tuesday morning)

During the previous evening's discussion, Peel had explained to me that NATO still had a "lodger" presence in Tetovo, comprised of a German transport company. This unit was part of the logistic chain necessary to supply their troops, which were located just across the Kosovo border.

I knew it would be a bit of a stretch, but since I had valid KFOR credentials (although no Macedonian authorization as yet), I clipped on my press pass and hoped for the best. My first point of contact was the Macedonian military caserne, which was located some 800 meters north of the Hotel Electra. Ramshackle and rundown, its construction predated the turn of the century. Iron gates barred the main entrance and beyond the sandbagged bunkers, tree-lined roads separated rows of barracks. My arrival caused a fair amount of commotion among the young conscripts who were at the gatehouse. It was soon evident that they believed me to be an American (*Amerikanski*) and this sparked hostility towards me. A sergeant who spoke fair German came forward to meet me with a stream of rhetorical questions. "Why do you support the *Shqiptares* and then come around here? Are you here to portray us as *ungahoya*'s (monsters)?" For a finale, he switched to heavily accented English. "Why don't you go fuck yourself!" Needless to say, the half-dozen conscripts milling about found this one-sided exchange hilarious.

Luckily for me, one of the guards had summoned an English-speaking military policeman from the headquarters buildings and he arrived just in time to prevent the bellicose little sergeant from launching into a second tirade. Naturally, the policeman's first request was to see my Macedonian press credentials. Armed only with the KFOR card plus contact numbers for the Macedonian Ministers of the Interior and Defence, I briefly explained my predicament to the MP. I would pick up the necessary papers in Skopje on Thursday I told him, but in the meantime, I needed to make the most of my time. I was relieved when he offered to make a few phone calls to his superiors. Before leaving the front gate, he took time to explain to the still smirking guards that I was a *Kanadski* not *Amerikanski*. Their attitude towards me changed immediately. The sergeant apologized for his mistake and a corporal was sent to get me a coffee while I awaited official clearance.

The MP was absent for at least 45 minutes and during that time the soldiers provided me with a wealth of information. They were eager to talk about their circumstances and the recent fighting. This particular unit had just been transferred to Tetovo from the city of Prilep in southern Macedonia. It had been sent in to replace the battalion from Bitola that was ambushed the previous Saturday. It was explained to me that the transfer had been immediate so as to prevent the Macedonians from launching retaliatory attacks to avenge their slain comrades. Using their sergeant as an interpreter, the gate guards took turns grumbling about the restrictive controls placed upon them by their government. Apparently two members of their unit had just been disciplined for using their truncheons during the arrest of a suspected Albanian terrorist. The Albanian was released with an apology, while both Macedonians were sent to detention barracks for 30 days.

"How are we supposed to fight this war?" asked Corporal Ljubica Mirev. "If we use artillery, they threaten to send our commanders to The Hague, and if we use billy clubs, our soldiers go to jail." His colleagues shook their heads in disapproval when Corporal Mirev went on to state that ex-Yugoslav President "Slobodan Milosevic had the right idea when it came to dealing with the *Shqiptares* [in Kosovo]." One sentiment that all the guards wished to express was their willingness to fight for Macedonia regardless of the consequences.

These army conscripts were all carrying out twelve months of unpaid national service. To help them financially and allow them to occasionally buy a few creature comforts (i.e., beer, cigarettes and junk food), families would often contribute small cash donations. As I chatted at the front gate, a steady stream of civilians approached the guardhouse to deposit envelopes. While most took only casual notice of me, one middle-aged man proved to be an exception. Speaking fluent English, he inquired as to my nationality and media outlet. Once that was established, he immediately began berating all Western journalists as being nothing more than "willing prostitutes of the United States." Holding out a handful of crumbled Macedonian dinars (presumably for dramatic impact on the guards) he shouted, "How much do we have to pay you to tell the truth?" He then turned to the soldiers and translated his question into Macedonian. The response was uproarious laughter.

Thankfully, the military policeman returned to the gate at this point, and with a shake of his head handed back my passport. He explained regretfully that there was nothing he or his superiors in Tetovo could do to help me. Until I received press credentials, I would not be allowed to talk to soldiers and I was strictly prohibited from taking photographs of military vehicles or installations. It was very disappointing news.

The MP, however, also told me that riots had broken out in Bitola the previous evening. After the policemen's funeral, thousands of mourners went on a rampage. Albanian shops and schools were looted and set ablaze all over the city. Extra police units were mobilized to curtail the violence and the Minister of the Interior then closed the city to outsiders. With everybody off work on this May 1 holiday, there was no shortage of Macedonians with time on their hands to vent their rage.

After leaving the caserne, I headed for the bus terminal to see whether or not buses were still running to Bitola. I was informed that under normal circumstances, buses made the three-hour trip at least five times a day. However, in light of the city's closure, service to Bitola was suspended. The option of hiring a car and driver to take me there also offered no guarantee of entry, particularly without press clearance. I resigned myself to staying in Tetovo.

When no one at the hotel could find a road map of the region, I decided to get the lay of the land by going for a long, leisurely jog. In Kosovo, prior to NATO's entry in June 1999, I had done the same thing and found it quite effective. Unlike North America, few people jog in the Balkans and the sight of a recreational runner close to the front lines tends to amuse the combatants rather than alarm them.

In covering a twelve-kilometer circuit, I was able to make a fairly detailed assessment of the Macedonian military's positions. As an ex-soldier, I was appalled at the amateurish bunkers they had constructed – usually nothing more than a pile of sandbags, with a sheet of corrugated metal overhead to protect them from the elements. There were very few trenches, and other than a couple of armoured vehicles, I could not see any shelter that would be able to provide protection against heavy weapons. I did not risk crossing over into the suburbs, which were reportedly occupied by Albanian UCK guerrillas.

TETOVO, MACEDONIA – 1 MAY 2001 (Tuesday afternoon)

During my reconnaissance run I had noticed that two major Albanian political parties had their headquarters in Tetovo's central square. Despite the holiday, and perhaps as a result of the violence in Bitola, both offices appeared to be open. I returned to the hotel, quickly showered, changed, and headed back to the square.

In order to understand the background issues and complex political intrigue behind the Macedonian conflict, I was anxious to talk to Arben Djafferi, leader of the ethnic Albanian Democratic Party (DPA). I was surprised to see a poster on the DPA's office door proclaiming that "An independent Kosovo is the only way to peace in the Balkans." The message was "paid for by the American-Albanian League." Until now, Western media coverage had carefully portrayed the Macedonian situation as being unrelated to the previous conflict in Kosovo. The major issue was purportedly the quest for increased human rights for ethnic Albanians under a revised Macedonian constitution. However, by posting the independence slogan, the DPA's leadership was making no attempt to distance their ultimate political goal from events in Kosovo.

Inside the office suite, the plush furniture and abundance of electronic devices – modern computers, big screen TVs, and a large stereo system – impressed me. The DPA was obviously well-financed. The few staff members present were very friendly and apologetic that Djafferi would not be back until Thursday. Arta Gylanize, one of his assistants, agreed to do her best to answer any of my questions. When I asked her to outline on a map the areas in which the UCK operated, Ms. Gylanize admitted she was originally from Albania and had only been in the Tetovo area since March. Her English was impeccable, and spoken with an American accent. She was very contemptuous of the Macedonian police, but when she spoke of the UCK, she did so with reverence. Naturally, the situation in Bitola was a disturbing topic and Gylanize believed the Macedonians were showing their true feelings. "They can no longer hide their hatred from the world. This is how they truly wish to treat us – by beating us and burning our houses."

When I asked her about the eight murdered policemen, Gylanize showed no pity or remorse. "There was a crowd of 200 [Macedonian] women who came to our offices to protest the Vejce killings," she said. "I don't know what they hoped to achieve. Perhaps we should protest in Skopje every time the police kill a UCK member."

It was interesting to hear her claim that the local Albanian population had actually been reduced as a result of the Kosovo crisis. Most Macedonian and Western media reports cited the ethnic cleansing conducted by Yugoslav troops as a primary cause for the current unrest. "A lot of our people actually went north into Kosovo to take advantage of the [relatively] booming economy," said Gylanize. She admitted that the economic boom in Kosovo was a direct result of massive foreign aid coupled with the large-scale presence of NATO troops and civilian aid workers.

As we were talking, a pair of Macedonian helicopters began flying menacing low-level patterns over the western suburbs of Tetovo. A young DPA party member rushed into the room to better observe the gunships as they flew overhead. "Those fucking bastards," he said. "They are doing that deliberately, constantly trying to intimidate us or to provoke the UCK into defending themselves!" Turning to me he asked, "Do you see how they treat us? How are we supposed to live with them?" I took this opportunity to ask just how I might make contact with the local UCK commanders. There was an awkward silence during which Gylanize exchanged nervous glances with the young man. Then she said, "The DPA has no contact with the UCK."

By now the two helicopters were hovering above a collection of houses well up a mountainside. The young man explained to me that the little hamlet, which the gunships were overflying, marked the overland route to Kosovo.

After leaving the DPA offices, I decided to take a walk up into the mountain villages as there was still plenty of daylight left. I presumed that if the police units were maintaining checkpoints on the Skopje-Tetovo highway, they would surely be trying to control the access route from Kosovo. As I walked up the steep incline through Tetovo's suburbs, I noted that the helicopters had departed. Children played in the schoolyards, while groups of men clustered around outside the numerous coffee bars which lined the narrow cobblestone streets. It was a hot afternoon and I was soon drenched in sweat. After clearing the outskirts and passing a deserted hamlet, I continued to climb the eerily empty, winding road. About five kilometers from the city center, I was beginning to think I was wasting my time when I came upon a Macedonian outpost manned by at least a dozen well-armed special police equipped with Kalashnikovs, body armour, and several heavy machineguns. Behind them, camouflaged in the woods, was a sandbagged bunker. Parked farther up the road was an armoured personnel carrier. My unannounced arrival did not seem to cause them any concern. In fact, they seemed rather amused to meet an out-of-breath Western journalist.

Pointing out a Macedonian army bunker about 50 meters ahead of their position, they explained that everything beyond it was under Albanian control. When I asked where the UCK were, their sergeant swept his arm in a 360-degree arc and said, "All around us."

They offered me a beer and I returned the gesture by distributing a couple of packs of smokes that I had brought along for just such an eventuality. When I asked if I could take a few pictures, it sparked quite a heated discussion among them. They eventually agreed upon a compromise. The policemen donned their black Balaclavas and instructed me not to include any background that could identify their position. It would have made a great photo session had it not been for the sudden arrival of their commanding officer. Leaping from his battered little Yugo, he began screaming at his men and demanded an explanation from a sergeant. As the policemen doffed their masks and scrambled back to their posts, I quickly gathered up my camera bag and sneaked away in the confusion.

As I walked back down towards Tetovo, I realized just how isolated those

TOP: *As the Albanian spring offensive escalated, nationalist sentiment was invoked in the Macedonian enclaves in the Tetovo valley. (JAMES PHILLIPS)*

ABOVE: *A Macedonian army patrol moves up into the front lines around the village of Ratae. (PHOTO COURTESY JAMES PHILLIPS)*

ABOVE: *Albanian UCK commanders "Mouse" (left) and "Jimmy" controlled the guerrilla units based in the village of Slatina. The 36-year-old Mouse was a locally-recruited ethnic Albanian from Macedonia, while 23-year-old Jimmy boasted of having fought in Kosovo and Chechnya.* (SCOTT TAYLOR)

TOP: *During the spring, as the fighting continued, the trickle of refugees – both Macedonian and Albanian – turned into a flood. (OLEG POPOV, REUTERS)*

ABOVE: *The Macedonian police forces were initially ill-equipped and unable to contain the UCK offensives. (COURTESY NATO)*

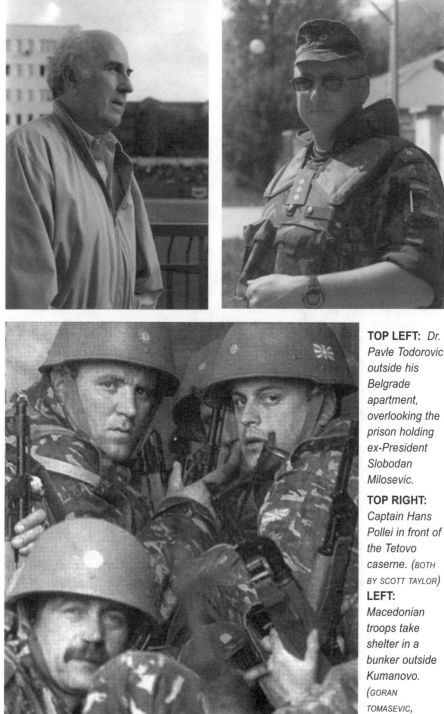

TOP LEFT: *Dr. Pavle Todorovic outside his Belgrade apartment, overlooking the prison holding ex-President Slobodan Milosevic.*

TOP RIGHT: *Captain Hans Pollei in front of the Tetovo caserne. (BOTH BY SCOTT TAYLOR)*

LEFT: *Macedonian troops take shelter in a bunker outside Kumanovo. (GORAN TOMASEVIC, REUTERS)*

Macedonian soldiers were. With or without helicopter gunships, their outpost would be indefensible in the event of a UCK offensive.

TETOVO, MACEDONIA – 1 MAY 2001 (Tuesday evening)

The suppertime discussion at the Hotel Electra was dominated by news of the continued rioting in Bitola. In Skopje and several other major cities, copycat mobs had also begun vandalizing Albanian property. The inter-ethnic violence was escalating despite the government's desperate pleas for calm. Friedhelm Peel ironically noted that his young colleague, Phillip Eisenring, had left Tetovo for the safer haven of Skopje – just in time for the riots.

TETOVO, MACEDONIA – 2 MAY 2001 (Wednesday morning)

I awoke early and ventured into the street market just in front of the Hotel Electra. The mostly Albanian vendors were still setting out their produce stalls and there was quite a bit of commotion. About 200 meters down the street I could see a pair of heavily-armed Macedonian policemen yelling at a fruit seller whose cart had overturned. The hapless Albanian was trying desperately to collect his spilled produce as they shouted insults and kicked at the upturned cart. Sporting my KFOR press pass and carrying my camera bag, I approached the scene. One of the policemen spotted me and tugged on his colleague's sleeve and hissed *novinar* (journalist) to get his attention. The pair grumbled a *dobar don* and quickly left to resume their foot patrol. The tormented fruit seller thanked me profusely for my intervention as other vendors rushed over to help him set his stall in order.

Returning to the hotel, I learned from a waiter that there had been a heavy exchange of gunfire around the village of Ratae. This Macedonian hamlet of approximately 2000 inhabitants lies approximately five kilometers north of Tetovo, at the base of the Shar Mountains. The surroundings villages along this ridgeline are largely populated by ethnic Albanians and are a major staging area for the local UCK.

Goran, the waiter's friend, introduced himself to me as I ate breakfast. Although his English was limited, he told me he was a member of a police auxiliary unit known as the Wolves. With a great deal of pride, he mentioned that he and his colleagues had been involved in the action in Ratae. Goran said he was anxious to take me on a tour of the Tetovo area, and, in particular, he wanted me to visit his home village of Brevenica. As we drove there, Goran explained to me that of the 4000 inhabitants, over 700 are Macedonian policemen and their families.

Like Ratae, Brevenica is situated on the valley floor, with Albanian villages dominating it along the hillsides. Goran boasted that every Macedonian house was a veritable arsenal and that he and his neighbors would never surrender their homes to Albanian terrorists. To dramatize his statement, he pulled a .44 caliber automatic pistol out from under his seat and opened the glove compartment to show me a couple of hand grenades.

He put the weapon back under the seat and we continued our tour. In several of the villages, Goran stopped the car and pointed out various landmarks. These were usually coffee bars that often doubled as Albanian brothels, he explained.

The girls who were visible on the streets did not wear Muslim head coverings; Goran said that most were either Ukrainian or Bulgarian prostitutes. Their unkempt appearance supported his assertion that these girls were also drug addicts. Their clientele are primarily young Albanian men who wear the trademark black T-shirts of the UCK. Whenever our presence began to attract attention, Goran quickly drove off. I could only imagine what would happen to us if the car were stopped and the weapons discovered. Needless to say, I was relieved when the tour was over and we returned to the central district of Tetovo.

My deadline for the Macedonian background piece was looming and I felt I should make one last attempt to contact the UCK. To do this, I went to the headquarters of the Albanian Democratic Prosperity Party (DPP) headquarters whose leader, Imer Imeri, was rumored to be closely linked to the guerrillas. I hoped to acquire a contact name or phone number for a DPP spokesman in order to arrange an interview, but to my amazement I was ushered into the main office and introduced to Imer Imeri himself.

Communicating in German without having had time to prepare left me a little flustered, but Imeri and his staff proved to be gracious and patient hosts. I knew that the DPP represented a much harder line of Albanian nationalism than Djafferi's DPA, and Imeri's blunt comments certainly confirmed this. He was not convinced of the Macedonian government's commitment to their own appeasement policy, and seemed anxious to bring about an armed conflict. An awkward moment arose when I asked about the DPP's links to the UCK. Imeri quietly consulted his colleagues in Albanian before responding. Admitting it was a sensitive issue, he informed me that one of his top people had just broken away from the DPP to form his own ultra-extreme political party. I was further advised that this defector, Adam Haxhirexha, and his New Democratic Party were now the political arm of the UCK. "Officially," Imeri said, his party "had no way of contacting the guerrillas."

As I left the DPP offices, a young man followed me and, catching me at the stairwell, told me that if I wanted to get in touch with the UCK leaders, I should take the bus to Prizren, Kosovo. I explained that I was on a tight schedule and such a side trip would not be possible. "It's too bad that you are leaving here so soon," he said, "You are going to miss all the action."

TETOVO, MACEDONIA – 2 MAY 2001 (Wednesday afternoon)
Following my visit to DPP headquarters I went to the NATO compound to talk to the German troops stationed there. Located at the outer edge of the Macedonian caserne I had visited earlier, the Germans had established their own internal security perimeter.

In stark contrast to the antiquated vehicles used by the Macedonian army, the German transport battalion had modern trucks and equipment. Although without any official mandate in Macedonia, NATO troops had encountered a fair amount of resentment from both Albanian and Macedonian factions.

"Each side believes that we are here to assist them," a press officer explained. "Whenever the fighting starts, everyone expects us to intervene on their behalf. However, our only function here is to protect our own troops and the supplies intended for Kosovo."

At mid-afternoon I returned to the Electra where I set up shop at a table in the back of the banquet hall. I spread out my notes and began writing my article. Friedhelm Peel arrived after work and asked how my interviews had gone. I told him that Imeri was opposed to Peel's university construction project as it would favor Macedonians and undermine the existing Albanian underground university. Imeri had even provided me with statistics to prove that the Albanian minority was subjected to systemic discrimination.

Peel became visibly perturbed. He was particularly incensed by the claim that ethnic Albanians under the current constitution could not hold any office of authority within Macedonia. To prove his point, he opened his briefcase and began laying down a stack of business cards that he had collected over the previous three months. "Look," he said. "The mayor of Tetovo, the police chief of Tetovo, the senior municipal architect… They're all Albanian. What is Imeri talking about?"

The impressive number of top-ranking Albanian bureaucrats severely undermined Imeri's claim of discrimination, and Peel was equally nonplussed by comments about Imeri's underground university. The way Imeri had described it, I was led to believe that this school was an officially outlawed, clandestine institution. Peel informed me that this Albanian university was actually a landmark, five-story building right in the center of Tetovo, complete with a neon sign on the roof.

TETOVO, MACEDONIA – 2 MAY 2001 (nearing evening)

I finished writing my Macedonian backgrounder piece just before the military's curfew. From the Electra's office suite I faxed in a situation report – a summarized version of my research.

On the Brink of War (Ottawa Citizen)

TETOVO, Macedonia – A number of violent clashes over the past week have heightened ethnic tensions and pushed Macedonia to the brink of a full-scale civil war. What had previously been limited to local skirmishes between armed extremists and Macedonian security forces has now expanded into widespread civil disturbances with the homes and shops of the Albanian minority prime targets.

The already cash-strapped Macedonian government is desperately attempting to resolve this crisis through a program of appeasement while simultaneously building up the country's tiny military in an effort to suppress the escalating insurrection. It is a race against time which senior officials admit they cannot win without rapid and substantial intervention help the international community.

The latest outbreak of violence was sparked last Saturday by a brutal ambush in the mountain village of Vejce, which is just inside Macedonia's border with Kosovo. An estimated 30 Albanian fighters from the Kosovo Liberation Army (UCK) opened fire on a security force convoy. The eight Macedonian soldiers, unable to escape, were either killed in the fusillade or executed by the UCK guerrillas, who then butchered the bodies.

Media reports of the incident had generated immediate outrage throughout Macedonia, but the fury was further intensified by television news coverage of the policemen's funerals. At the same time that hundreds of mourners were shown participating in the candlelight procession, a state coroner was publicly revealing the horrific details of how their bodies had been mutilated by the UCK.

According to these reports, the slain policemen had been carved up, with fingers, eyes and scalps removed for the purpose of providing trophies for the guerrillas. In the city of Bitola, where four of the eight policemen were buried, an emotionally-charged crowd of mourners quickly became a mob bent on revenge.

Throughout the night of April 30, more than 40 ethnic Albanian shops were ransacked. Over the next two days, riots erupted in major cities throughout Macedonia, including Skopje and Kumanovo, as the violence in Bitola continued despite a massive effort by police forces to curtail it.

The root of this tension lies in the quest by Macedonia's ethnic Albanian minority to acquire more autonomy – either under a revised constitution or through outright independence. Over the past five decades, through a disproportionate birth rate (the highest in Europe) and a tremendous influx of legal and illegal immigrants, the Albanian population in Macedonia has nearly tripled. Albanian political leaders feel this rapidly altered demographic has not been recognized by Macedonia's present constitution. Imer Imeri, leader of the radical Democratic Prosperity Party, last week issued a demand to the Macedonian government ordering them to address the Albanians' concerns, "or we will do it by force."

Although the exact percentage of the population that is Albanian remains in dispute (between 25 and 45 per cent depending on which faction you ask), Imeri believes his people's basic human rights are being violated. "In the areas where Albanians are 80 to 100 per cent of the population, we still cannot conduct any official business in anything but the Macedonian language. This is not right," Imeri said. The DPP and the recently formed New Democratic Party are considered political arms of the UCK. Therefore Imer Imeri's warning that force will be used to achieve his objectives is by no means an idle threat.

At the centre of the present conflict is the picturesque city of Tetovo, which is situated at the base of the Shar mountain range that forms the natural boundary between Macedonia and Kosovo. It was here that the first armed clashes between the UCK and Macedonian police occurred back in March. After several days of fighting, the UCK had withdrawn over the Shar Mountains into Kosovo, but to gain this limited success, the Macedonians had to use both heavy artillery and recently-leased Ukrainian helicopter gunships. Six ominous-looking Mi-24 Hind attack helicopters currently provide support to Macedonia's military, and fly regular patrols over the mountains surrounding Tetovo.

However, this limited victory by Macedonia's security forces also served to illustrate how poorly equipped and trained this fledgling army is. It is widely believed that the aborted UCK offensive was simply a probing attack to explore Macedonian weaknesses.

When Macedonia broke away from the Federal Republic of Yugoslavia in 1992, it did so peacefully. One of the conditions agreed to was that all of the heavy weapons and tanks belonging to the Yugoslav National Army would be returned to what was left of the Federal Republic of Yugoslavia. At that time, Milosevic was supported and arming Serbs fighting in Croatia and Bosnia. The Macedonians complied as they felt, quite naively, that the Balkan wars would never spread to their newly-independent country.

Bankrupt, with a population of just two million, Macedonia had made little effort to rebuild its army. As a result, military efforts to quell the Albanian insurrection have been woefully inadequate. The few tanks the Macedonians have date back to 1954, while their armored personnel carriers are a mix of second-hand castoffs from Germany and Bulgaria. There is even a shortage of modern small arms and the second line reservists carry old fashioned bolt action rifles. The officer corps of the Macedonian army is considered professional, as many were career soldiers in the former JNA. However, unlike their UCK counterparts, these officers have no combat experience and, without a professional cadre of non-commissioned officers, the Macedonians have been hard-pressed to provide adequate training to the young conscripts who comprise the bulk of the army.

Following the clashes in March, the Albanians in Tetovo hold Macedonian troops in contempt. "They are like little boys, always afraid of our UCK," said

Arta Gylanize, a 38-year-old political activist with the moderate Albanian Democratic Party. "The Macedonians will beat up our children, but you will notice they always get shot in the back because they run away in battle."

The constant taunting and baiting have provoked the troops. Tempers flare during encounters with Albanians and many of the Macedonians say their patience is wearing thin. Corporal Ljubica Mirev, a military police reservist, has been recalled to active duty in Tetovo for the duration of the crisis. His squad is tasked with guarding Albanian homes that were vacated along the confrontation line. "We are risking our lives to protect their property, yet when we drive past they throw rocks at us," said Corporal Mirev. "They call us an *occupation army* and tell us to go home, but this is our country. And we will fight for it!"

To bolster the sagging morale, the Macedonians are increasingly employing Serbian mercenaries, including former members of Arkan's infamous Tigers. In a hilltop bunker above Tetovo, 36-year-old Rade explained that he was a Serbian volunteer and anxious to settle some old scores. "I was with the Tigers in Bosnia and Kosovo, and the Mujahadeen and UCK were fighting across from me then," said Rade. Despite his bravado, he had no doubts about his own fate if he were ever to be captured. Waiving his pistol, he warned his young Macedonian comrades to "always save the last bullet for yourself."

The Macedonians have also established their own elite volunteer paramilitary force known as the Wolves, which is equipped with a wide array of modern weapons and special armoured vehicles. The UCK responded by placing a 400 deutsch mark ($300 Canadian) bounty on the head of each Wolf. After last Saturday's ambush in Vejce, when it was learned that four of the eight killed were in fact Wolves, the Albanians contemptuously cut the bounty saying that a dead Wolf "wasn't worth that much."

The six helicopter gunships piloted by Ukrainian and Bulgarian mercenaries are considered the one trump card that the Macedonians have, and there has been an order placed to secure another dozen of these aircraft along with two Russian fighter planes. The Macedonians' tactical objective in deploying this rent-an-air-force is to contain the UCK in the mountain passes as they enter from Kosovo.

The Macedonian ground forces are trying to halt this incursion and simultaneously deal with the armed Albanian extremists in their midst. To beef up its combat teams, the Macedonians desperately want to acquire a fleet of NATO-standard armoured personnel carriers.

All of this rearming and procurement of military hardware will take a fair amount of time and money; things that are both in short supply for the Macedonians. "The transition from a Communist system to the free market has not been an easy one for us," said Naun Nachevski, a retired diplomat who once served as Macedonia's consul general in Toronto.

"The Macedonian treasury is bankrupt and our current unemployment rate is over 40 per cent. These tough economic times have served to further fuel the underlying ethnic tensions with the Albanians and to delay the Macedonian government's attempts to reform," he continued. "Now every dollar we spend on bullets is one less that we can spend on appeasement programs. Each new act of violence delays the vital foreign investment that Macedonia urgently needs for it to recover. This is a vicious circle which will benefit no one."

Even those appeasement programs that are funded by the European Union (EU) are viewed with skepticism by the Albanian leaders. In Tetovo work is already underway to build a new university. Although the construction is proceeding rapidly (from the sod turning in March, the entire campus is to be completed by October 1), Imer Imeri is unimpressed. "We already have our own unofficial university here which they [the Macedonians] refuse to recognize," he told me. When I asked him if this project indicated a sincere effort to recognize and raise status of Albanians in Macedonia, Imeri scoffed. "The EU is paying for this so it is an empty gesture. They will learn this when no Albanian students register at their school."

For Phillip Eisenring, a Swiss engineer working on the Tetovo university project, this was his first experience in the Balkans. He admitted that the mutual hatred between the Macedonians and Albanians has been a major stumbling block. "It seems that no one wants this school to succeed. The Macedonian newspapers wouldn't even publish our advertisements because they contained Albanian text," he says.

An extremely partisan press on both sides of this conflict has compounded the language barrier. By not receiving opposing views or details of their own force's activities, each faction believes they are the victims of unprovoked attacks. Naturally, such reports incite the already substantial animosity that exists here. The Albanians refuse to believe any reports of UCK brutality and dismiss the Macedonian media accounts of such as "fabrications."

"It is not our custom to cut up bodies or kill wounded," said Arta Gylanize. "Since the memory of our ancient hero *Skenderberg*, who fought gloriously over two hundred years ago, Albanians only fight with honor and courage." Ms. Gylanize, like most of the UCK's political supporters, believes their guerrillas will score a quick victory in the coming weeks. One of Imeri's assistants confided that "the attack will come soon."

The UCK staging area is located just south of Prizren, and it is estimated that over 5000 fighters are currently undergoing training exercises there. With over 50,000 soldiers stationed in Kosovo, many Macedonians are furious at NATO's lack of will to either prevent UCK incursions or to simply disarm the guerrillas.

A battalion of German logistic troops has been stationed in Tetovo since the crisis in Kosovo, and many residents feel that these NATO soldiers should be doing more to protect Macedonians.

"Our role here has caused a lot of confusion, especially during the March hostilities," said Captain Hans Pollei, a German press officer. "When we brought in four Leopard tanks, the people thought we were coming to fight the UCK. But we were only preparing to defend ourselves if we had to withdraw. The Macedonians don't yet realize that this is not NATO's war."

So far, the only tangible military aid that the Macedonians can count on is the limited assistance (intelligence and vehicles) which they are receiving from the Serbs. "We are dealing with these same UCK in south Serbia, and therefore we have a common enemy," said a Yugoslav intelligence officer from Belgrade. "All of our indications are that the UCK will mount a major offensive on May 15, and we will do all we can to assist our Macedonian allies."

Captain Pollei confirmed that NATO had also been advised of the significance of this date and that the German contingent would accordingly be put on stand-by notice to evacuate Tetovo if necessary. However, with violence escalating over the past few days, the UCK may be compelled to launch their planned strike even sooner. For Macedonia, it already seems too late to prevent the next round of civil war in the Balkans.

TETOVO, MACEDONIA – 2 MAY 2001 (Evening)

During supper, a number of the hotel staff joined Friedhelm Peel and me. They were curious to hear what I thought about the current situation, and what the immediate future would hold. Most disagreed strongly with my opinion that further bloodshed could not be avoided. The consensus among them was that Macedonians were a peace-loving people, unlike the other Balkan cultures. "The Serbs and Croats brought the violence upon themselves," said Dimitar, a 36-year-old waiter. "We enjoy our lifestyle, our homes... We are not looking to destroy all of that in a war." The others at the table nodded their agreement.

SKOPJE, MACEDONIA – 3 MAY 2001 (Thursday morning)

I first learned of the ambush at Kumanovo on the Tetovo-Skopje bus. Most of the passengers travelling with me were teenagers, presumably heading back to school after the holiday. My seatmate, Dragan Mirev, introduced himself as a volunteer soldier. His colleagues in the Tetovo garrison had heard the reports over the army's radio-net, and he was well-informed about the incident.

It was just past daybreak, on a side road outside Kumanovo, when a Macedonian army patrol came under heavy fire. Standing in the open hatch of his armoured personnel carrier, a machinegunner was killed instantly when a rocket grenade brought the carrier to a halt. Inside the APC, the startled soldiers scrambled to pull the body of their dead comrade clear. One soldier pushed forward bravely to replace the dead man at the machinegun. Before he could cock and aim the weapon, he too was cut down by a fusillade of small-arms fire. Thyssen-Hermelin APCs are usually equipped with an armoured turret, but these hastily acquired vehicles were delivered without this vital protection.

Realizing the futility of trying to fight back blind from inside the carrier, the remainder of the Macedonian section dismounted through the rear cargo doors. Through fire and movement tactics, they were able to extricate themselves from the ambush site without further casualties.

The APC's driver was not so lucky. Although unhurt, he could not exit through the rear of the disabled vehicle, and the two dead bodies were proof that any attempt to clamber out over the APC's exposed topside would be suicidal. Abandoned by his comrades and unable to pull back, the terrified young soldier curled up and hid under the APC's steering wheel. Minutes later, UCK guerrillas swarmed over the carrier, pulled him out and took him prisoner. The survivors managed to radio for assistance, and two helicopter gunships set off from Skopje to pick them up.

Dragan Mirev was eager to discuss military issues with me after I told him that I was a former soldier. Speaking excellent English, he complained about the lack of faith his comrades had in their own chain of command. According to Mirev, this conflict was undeniably inter-ethnic in its origin, but the Macedonian government refused to admit this was the case. By leaving Albanian officers in key posts throughout the chain of command, the Macedonian troops had become distrustful of their orders. Anytime they suffered an embarrassing setback, the rank-and-file was quick to blame Albanian *quislings* (or fifth columnists).

When I began asking specific questions about the size and composition of his unit, Mirev became suspicious and ended our conversation.

My first objective when I arrived in Skopje was to officially register myself with the press agency. This turned out to be more difficult than I had presumed. Although technically a sub-section of the Ministry of Information, the foreign press office was located in a separate, hard to find location. My taxi driver was apologetic that he had to make three separate inquiries before he could find the correct address.

Atanas Georgievski, the bureaucrat responsible for issuing accreditation, had all my paperwork ready, but beyond that he was of little help. Unable to speak any English (or German), Georgievski simply shrugged his shoulders when I inquired about the day's developments. During the long drive from the bus station, I had learned from my taxi driver that the Macedonian government had issued a strong statement in response to the Kumanovo ambush. It was my understanding that official ultimatums had been issued to the UCK for the safe return of the Macedonian prisoner. In preparation for a military counter-strike, President Boris Trjkovski had ordered nine Albanian villages surrounding Kumanovo to be evacuated of civilians. Georgievski simply shrugged when I pressed him for details about the location of the villages and of the times of possible press conferences concerning this state of national emergency.

A helpful secretary, who spoke a little English, explained to me that there were no events scheduled for the media. In fact, other than a Greek television crew and myself, there were no other foreign journalists presently registered in Macedonia. Presuming that all would be quiet, the regular European correspondents had departed for the May Day holiday. Local Macedonian stringers were providing the only international coverage for the wire services.

Without CNN or BBC present, the flare-up of fighting in Macedonia was not considered news outside of the Balkans.

SKOPJE, MACEDONIA – 3 MAY 2001 (Thursday afternoon)

With the press agency and Ministry of Information unable to furnish me with anything new about the situation, I felt my best recourse would be to plug into the Macedonian media. I headed to the offices of Skynet Television, where Sonja Stefanovic introduced me to the channel's military reporter, Rade Lesko. A ex-soldier, Lesko had been covering the ethnic violence from the outset.

He informed me that Skynet was trying to send a camera crew into the disputed Kumanovo territory, but that the Ministry of Defense was strictly prohibiting all access into the region. With few official statements being issued – and few reporters on the scene – it was difficult to piece together a clear picture of just what was happening. The helicopter gunships were maintaining a continuous presence and, according to eyewitnesses, the Macedonian army was moving large columns of armoured vehicles and artillery to cordon off the Kumanovo area.

The Macedonian government's 6:00 p.m. deadline expired without the UCK releasing its prisoners and a new deadline set for the following morning. The Defense Ministry stated that there were too few hours of daylight left to launch a major offensive. Of particular concern was the high risk of collateral damage to the homes of the Albanians who had ignored the government's directive to abandon their villages.

It seemed that a major showdown between the Macedonian security forces and the UCK guerrillas was not only imminent, but unavoidable. I tried to arrange transport to Kumanovo but with the onset of darkness, the bus service had been cancelled, and the Albanian and Macedonian taxi drivers I approached were willing to risk the dangerous 35-kilometer drive.

Unable to proceed until daybreak, I found an Internet café and sent a detailed situation report to my office at *Esprit de Corps*. After a quick meal, I found lodgings at a cheap student hostel. Although I still had some travel funds, the overall situation was so fluid that I had no way of predicting exactly how long I had to budget for.

SKOPJE, MACEDONIA – 4 MAY 2001 (Friday morning)

I left the hostel very early, the sleepy reception clerk had not been able to provide me with an update on the situation. However, the fact that the buses were running again seemed to indicate that a major battle had not been fought during the night. The passengers aboard the 7:00 a.m. bus were primarily Macedonian high school students and elderly Albanian villagers.

As we passed by the Skopje aerodrome, two Mi-24 Hind helicopter gunships lifted off. They flew over the bus with a deafening roar, then headed north.

The reaction on the bus was animated. Boys shouted to each other and pressed their faces against the windows, craning their necks to get a better view of the aircraft. By contrast, the adults looked anxious, and several of the women began muttering what I presumed were prayers.

Both police and army units were out in force at the city limit checkpoints, but, curiously, nobody boarded our bus to check identification. The entire city of Kumanovo seemed to be abuzz with activity as we wound our way through crowded streets to the central terminal. While there was a great number of uniformed security force personnel about, most of the bystanders were nervous-looking civilians eagerly seeking out news of the latest developments. As there was no press center in Kumanovo, I reasoned that the best place for me to obtain an update on the situation would be at police headquarters. At the entrance, a section of heavily-armed policemen were manning a bunker and barricades had been erected on either side of the gate to obstruct vehicle traffic. As a steady stream of police arrived for duty in their civilian clothes, the armed guards stopped pedestrians to check identification cards.

The overall situation was tense, and the police were understandably jumpy. When I approached the detachment commander it was clearly evident that he did not want to have to bother with a foreign reporter. My officially-stamped accreditation papers made no difference to him. Pointing his Kalashnikov at my chest, he told me what could only be loosely translated as "fuck off!"

One of the incoming reservists had overheard my clumsy attempt to introduce myself in Macedonian, "*Ja sam Kanadski novinar*" [I am a Canadian journalist]. He must have outranked the gate detachment commander because when he barked out an order, the Kalashnikov was immediately lowered. Although I never did catch his name, he spoke good English and was keen to tell me that he had a brother in Toronto.

After I explained to him that I was trying to get an update on the crisis, he personally escorted me into the police compound. At the front desk, I noticed there were a few other foreigners waiting to speak to the police chief. My newfound "protector" introduced me to a harried sergeant and then excused himself to report for duty.

All of the foreigners were then ushered into an empty office on the second floor. Besides myself, there were a pair of International Red Cross (IRC) officials and a monitor from the Organization for Security and Co-operation in Europe (OSCE). They had all been in the Kumanovo region the previous evening. Olivier Chow was the senior IRC representative in Skopje and was a veteran of Cambodia and Kosovo. Hours earlier, he and his partner had been called out to provide medical assistance to Albanian civilian casualties caught in a fierce firefight, but were unable to do so in the absence of a cease-fire. "The Macedonian conscripts were too jumpy," said Chow. "They were shooting at every shadow." Finally, the word had been passed along that the IRC's presence was no longer considered urgent. Four Albanians had died of their wounds in the meantime, and there would be plenty of time for Chow to collect the bodies when the fighting subsided.

The OSCE monitor, an American, said that he had been more successful in performing a similar mission of mercy in another contested village.

When we finally met the police chief, the OSCE and IRC representatives voiced their objections to the presence of a reporter (me) in the room. They explained that this was because they would be providing the Macedonian authorities with confidential information, which could not be made public.

I had little choice but to return to the outer office and spend the next 90 minutes watching the feverish activity of the police mobilizing in the courtyard below. I noticed that there were quite a few Rambo types in the ranks sporting combat knives on their web belts and extra magazines taped to their Kalashnikovs. As veterans know, such theatrical accoutrements are purely for show and generally indicative of inexperienced troops.

When I met police chief Dragan Nestorovski, his patience was beginning to wear a little thin. He had been awake for most of the previous 36 hours and looked at least ten years older than his 46 years. Using a large wall map, he illustrated the deployment of his forces and the nine villages presently occupied by the UCK. He explained that sporadic fighting was continuing although the Macedonian government had once again delayed its planned counter-offensive. The UCK still showed no sign of complying with the demand to release the prisoners. Nestorovski could not provide the names of the soldiers who had been captured or killed in the previous morning's ambush. They had been part of the elite army unit, the Scorpions, and only the military public office in Skopje could provide such information. When a secretary informed Nestorovski of an incoming phone call, I was curtly dismissed from his office.

KUMANOVO, MACEDONIA – 4 MAY 2001 (Friday afternoon)

There were still reports of sporadic fighting in the outlying villages, but no evidence that the Macedonian government had unleashed an offensive. The massive military build-up continued unabated. Gunships were constantly visible maintaining patrols in the Kumanovo area, and around noon a battery of howitzers rumbled through the city, heading toward the western outskirts. With so much military traffic on the major north-south highway, I was concerned that my departure would be delayed.

The attendant at the bus depot informed me that the Yugoslavia-Macedonia border remained open – despite the proximity to UCK forces. However, the last bus for Belgrade would leave Kumanovo shortly before dark, at approximately 5:00 p.m.

Although the situation on the ground remained confused and extremely fluid, I felt that I had collected enough information to cobble together a short news report for the *Ottawa Citizen*. So long as the Macedonian army did not launch a major counterattack overnight, my longer story would hold till the following morning.

Much to the chagrin of a waiter, I commandeered a table on a restaurant's patio which overlooked the city's central square, and began to write.

There were no Internet cafés in Kumanovo, so before dashing off to catch my bus, I faxed my hand-written text from the post office.

Macedonian concessions not enough to stop KLA (Ottawa Citizen)
KUMANOVO, Macedonia – It has been less than two years since the small city of Kumanovo was thrust into the world spotlight in June 1999. For four tense days, it was here that NATO officials and Yugoslav generals negotiated

the details of the Kosovo Peace Agreement that ended the 78-day air campaign against Slobodan Milosovic. Kumanovo now looks as if it might become the flashpoint that will again ignite ethnic hatred and plunge the Balkans into another full-scale civil war.

On May 3, the Macedonian government invoked the strongest measures possible to contain a large-scale incursion by Albanian guerrillas. Nine villages in the hills surrounding Kumanovo were ordered to be evacuated, and military and police reservists were mobilized. Now Macedonia's recently acquired squadron of Mi-24 Hind helicopter gunships maintains constant patrols over the disputed territory.

The Macedonian clampdown came after a week of scattered Kosovo Liberation Army ambushes and widespread retaliatory civil violence against the ethnic-Albanian minority. Aided by the military resources of the UCK, various Albanian political parties have pressured the Macedonian government for either increased autonomy or independence, and have threatened to "use force if necessary."

The offensive conducted by the UCK in March around the city of Tetovo proved the Albanians have both the means and the will to support this threat.

In the early hours of May 3, a large force entered Macedonia from Kosovo, and at 5:40 a.m. ambushed a security patrol. Two Macedonian soldiers were killed and a third captured after a brief, one-sided firefight. The guerrillas also kidnapped two civilians – a Macedonian and a Serb.

The villagers in this region of Macedonia – which borders Kosovo and south Serbia – are almost entirely ethnic-Albanian and have supported the UCK insurrection. Following the ambush, the guerrillas simply disappeared into the population.

"It is like fighting an army of ghosts," said Dragan Nestorovski, Kumanovo's hard-pressed police chief. "They are using the Albanian civilians as a human shield and trying to provoke us into creating a collateral damage incident which they will exploit in the international media."

It was to prevent such an incident that the Macedonian government ordered the evacuation of the villagers.

Throughout the tense night of May 4, at least four civilians were killed in firefights between security forces and the UCK. At one point, a team of international monitors from the Organization for Security and Co-operation in Europe (OSCE) was called upon to enter the battle zone to rescue a pregnant woman requiring an emergency Caesarian section.

So far, in this escalating conflict, the Macedonian security forces have proven themselves inept. Macedonia's troops are currently equipped with a motley collection of obsolete arms and vehicles "donated" by Germany and Bulgaria. Leasing Ukrainian Hind helicopter gunships (six are now in service, with 12 more on the way) and employing Serbian mercenaries to bolster inexperienced troops are indicative of how desperate the Macedonian government is to reverse the present imbalance in military capability.

Also hampering its effectiveness is the fact that, although this conflict is ethnic-based, Albanian commanders remain an integral part of Macedonia's police and army units. And many of the front line troops believe their own Albanian commanders have been culpable in the recent wave of UCK ambushes.

"The UCK always seem to know exactly where we are going to be and when we will be most vulnerable," said Dragan Mirev, a 36-year-old sergeant with the elite Macedonian paramilitary unit, the Wolves.

Sergeant Mirev's unit is based in Tetovo, where eight of his comrades were ambushed and butchered by the UCK for trophies.

The police chief in Tetovo and many of the senior officers responsible for coordinating the Macedonian security forces are ethnic-Albanians, and following the recent setbacks, their troops are increasingly suspicious of them.

"It is no way (to fight) a war, when you can't rely upon either the loyalty of your officers or your comrades," said Sergeant Mirev. "When our soldiers go into the front lines, the Albanian conscripts are now in the habit of unfastening their chin-straps just to let the UCK snipers know that they are not Macedonians."

Senior officials are well aware of the security risk and widening rift within the ranks of the security forces, but the Macedonian government is still desperately trying to initiate a program of appeasement to satisfy the Albanians' demands for increased autonomy.

"To ethnically cleanse Albanians from top government jobs and the military would signal the collapse of our diplomatic efforts and make civil war an immediate reality," said police chief Nestorovski. "In the meantime, we are undermining our own ability to effectively suppress the UCK revolt before it gains momentum."

It appears Macedonian appeasement efforts are running out of time. Without a last-minute reversal or a large-scale intervention by NATO troops, the UCK offensive could begin as early as May 15.

"We expect the UCK to mount a simultaneous diversionary attack against our positions in south Serbia," said a Serbian army spokesman. "The main KLA attacks will occur in Macedonia – at Tetovo and Kumanovo."

In the wake of last Thursday's clampdown, there has been an influx of international media and official agencies into the Kumanovo region. After ten years of hard-learned experience in the former Yugoslavia, most of these civilian observers are well-equipped with clearly marked armoured Land Rovers and protective clothing. It seems the stage has been set and the countdown begun on the next round of violence in the Balkans.

SKOPJE – 4 MAY 2001 (Friday evening)

There were only six other passengers aboard the Belgrade-bound bus. On the short stretch from Kumanovo to the Yugoslav border, a helicopter gunship had reassuringly escorted us along an otherwise deserted highway.

A young, attractive female border guard came aboard at the checkpoint and began examining passports. Wearing her beret in a decidedly unmilitary fashion – well back on her head so as not to disturb her stylish hairdo – her pistol and holster looked brand new, and she wore her gun belt tight around her waist to accentuate her hourglass figure.

When she took my passport she asked curtly in English, "What are you doing in my country?" I hastily produced accreditation papers and told her that I was a journalist. "Why are you leaving now?" she asked. "The fighting is just starting." As I began to explain that I had connecting flights to catch and a prior commitment in the Middle East, she interjected, "No. I'll tell you why you are leaving: It is because you are afraid."

BELGRADE – 5 MAY 2001 (Saturday morning)

We had barely got five kilometers inside Yugoslavian territory when a loud tearing noise erupted from the engine compartment and the bus ground to a halt. Although a technophobe with no mechanical skills, I could tell from the amount of oil gushing up through the floorboards that something was seriously wrong with our vehicle.

The driver and conductor both pulled coveralls over their uniforms and, for the next hour and 45 minutes, gamely tried to repair the damage, to no avail.

With dusk approaching, being stranded in this disputed sector of the Presevo valley was not a healthy situation. Passing Serbian military patrols (the only other traffic on the road) had notified the authorities in Bujanovac, and a second bus was eventually sent to rescue us.

Before leaving Ottawa I had received an invitation to become a columnist for the *Halifax Herald*. Therefore, in addition to filing field reports for the *Ottawa Citizen*, I also had a commitment to submit a weekly editorial commentary. The focus of my "On Target" columns is aimed at an audience primarily concerned with Canadian defence issues. Although NATO did not yet have troops on the ground, the deteriorating situation in Macedonia made it seem inevitable that peacekeepers would soon be deployed. With my deadline looming, I spent the rest of the Skopje-Belgrade bus ride penning my first "On Target" editorial with the intent of putting this latest Balkan crisis in a Canadian context.

Back into the Balkans (Halifax Herald)

TETOVO, Macedonia – In October 1995 Prime Minister Jean Chrétien proclaimed that our over-rotated, under-equipped front line peacekeepers were to be withdrawn from the Balkans because they "needed to come home to rest and re-equip." It has been nearly four years since the first contingent of Canadian soldiers experienced the horrors of the civil war that ripped apart the former Yugoslavia in Croatia and Bosnia.

For our tiny (and still shrinking) armed forces, this long-standing large-scale commitment – nearly 3000 troops per six-month rotation – had meant the mobilization of reservists and the use of second-rate and outdated equipment. Top generals issued grave warnings about the army's inability to maintain such a workload, but politically, it was deemed necessary for Canada to show a continued resolve in maintaining European security.

It was for this same reason – the paying of our partnership dues to NATO – Canadian soldiers would not enjoy the rest and re-equipping promised them in 1995. Once the warring factions in Bosnia had signed the Dayton Accord in

September 1995, it was soon apparent that an international armed implementation force would be necessary to enforce the shaky cease-fire. The multinational and widely divergent composition of troops known as the United Nations' Protection Force (UNPROFOR) had proven itself to be an unwieldy military organization from the outset. So, with the encouragement of the United States', NATO agreed to implement the Bosnian peace plan.

Since Canada has no separately dedicated NATO or UN formation, it was from the same burnt-out manpower pool and rusted-out vehicle fleet that we cobbled together the battle group for NATO. For many soldiers, the change in roles literally meant simply switching their blue berets back to green, and re-painting their white UN vehicles in camouflage patterns. It was supposed to take NATO just one year to bring peace to Bosnia, but six years later it is still trying to do so – with no relief in sight.

Then came the 1999 Kosovo crisis. Once again the U.S. pressured NATO to become involved in the Balkans. This time a "humanitarian bombing" campaign was designed to pressure Serbian security forces into abandoning the province to the Kosovo Liberation Army.

Although many former military officers (including Major General Lewis MacKenzie) and diplomats (such as former ambassador James Bissett) warned the Canadian government to avoid taking sides in this latest civil war, Chrétien heeded the White House's call. During 78 days of airstrikes against Yugoslavia Canada provided CF-18s, which launched 10 per cent of NATO's bombing attacks, and our Army was asked to scrape together a 1200-man battle group to enforce the peace agreement.

Following NATO's occupation of Kosovo, Canadian soldiers found there was little peace to keep. The Yugoslav troops had withdrawn, but the murders, ambushes, ethnic cleansing, and kidnapping continued at an alarming rate. The UCK (who refused to be disbanded, as called for in the peace agreement) proved to be a constant source of frustration and embarrassment for NATO troops as the guerrillas embarked on a vicious campaign of revenge against the Serbs.

In November 1999, despite the level of violence which still existed, Chrétien advised our NATO allies that Canada would be pulling our troops out of Kosovo "as the situation is now stable." Obviously, other NATO leaders did not agree with Chrétien's assessment because, by the time the last of our troops left Kosovo in June 2000, the NATO contingent (KFOR) was being reinforced to a strength of 50,000 soldiers.

Despite the presence of this military might, the situation worsened as the UCK widened the circle of violence to include areas bordering Kosovo, inside south Serbia and Macedonia. There have been a number of armed clashes with Yugoslav security forces over the ensuing months, but the UCK has steadily increased its hold on this disputed territory. Until now, NATO has made angry noises but taken no real action to deter the UCK expansion.

However, as the Albanian guerrillas shift their focus to Macedonia, it will soon become impossible for the European Community and NATO not to intervene. Last week's escalation of hostilities and civil disobedience in Macedonia clearly indicates that a full-scale confrontation with the UCK is now only a matter of time.

If this formerly-unravaged corner of the Balkans does erupt into civil war, NATO will undoubtedly be forced to react and furnish some sort of an intervention force. Should this happen Canada will once again be called upon to "pay her dues," and our weary little army will somehow have to scrape up the required resources. Unlike Jean Chrétien, however, our peacekeeping veterans have long since come to understand the complexities and bitter ethnic hatred that exists in the Balkans. As one soldier told me following his first tour in Yugoslavia in 1992, "Our job's not done. I'll be back here – in fact, my son and grandsons will be back here if they join the army."

LEFT: *The so-called underground university in Tetovo is actually a five-storey landmark in this small Macedonian city. Built and operated by donations from the Albanian community, the South Eastern Europe University did not receive official funding. However, the campus is anything but "underground."*
(SCOTT TAYLOR)

TOP: *On June 29, 2001, protesters in Belgrade denounced Serbian President Zoran Djindjic's decision to extradite Slobodan Milosevic, in the dead of night, to The Hague War Crimes Tribunal. (KNIGA KOMMERZ)*

ABOVE: *Residents of Tetovo during a lull in the fighting. (JAMES PHILLIPS)*

OPPOSITE PAGE: *Shattered houses and vehicles mark the confrontation line. (SCOTT TAYLOR)*

chapter five:
TO A HEAD

BELGRADE – 3 AUGUST 2001 (Friday afternoon)

As the Austrian Airlines flight touched down at Belgrade airport, I was reminded of the plot for the movie *Groundhog Day*, when the character played by Bill Murray becomes trapped time and time again – interminably.

Once again I was arriving late on a Friday afternoon with little time to accomplish anything. During my two-month absence from the Balkans much had happened. My assignment was to write some contextual backgrounders on these events before the dust completely settled on their newsworthiness.

Although my flight arrived on schedule, this time my attempts to make final arrangements for interviews were hampered by the calendar. I soon learned that during the hot summer months Belgraders practically abandon the city for beaches and cooler climes. With government offices, schools, and all major industries shut down, it is estimated that less than 30 per cent of Belgrade's population remains at home.

My first objective was to assess the political fallout in Yugoslavia from the handover of Slobodan Milosevic to The Hague Tribunal. In June, this issue had been of major international media interest. The internal political power struggle between Serbian President Zoran Djindjic and Yugoslav President

Vojislav Kostunica had centred on the fate of the deposed dictator.

Kostunica remained adamant that Milosevic would be tried in Yugoslavia for the crimes he had allegedly committed against the Serbian people.

This stand was popular with the nationalists, many of them believing that the War Crimes tribunal is a tool of NATO. On the other side of the equation, Djindjic's supporters were lured by the promise of substantial foreign aid in exchange for their compliance with Milosevic's extradition. To affect this, an international donor's conference had been scheduled to take place in Zurich, Switzerland, at the end of June. With the talks faltering, the U.S. State Department threatened to pull out of the conference. Their message was clear: no Milosevic, no money.

On June 23, an emergency session of the Serbian parliament had voted to approve a decree that paved the way for Milosevic's handover. Three days later, over 10,000 Serbs took to the streets of Belgrade to protest "selling out" to Western demands, but Kostunica had calmed the crowds with assurances that Milosevic would remain in Yugoslavia.

On June 28, the Serbian national holiday Vidovdan, Djindjic acted in direct defiance of Kostunica's federal authority. Not knowing whether or not the Yugoslav Army would interfere to prevent Milosevic's removal, he and his officials executed an elaborate abduction plot.

With decoy cars dispatched to confuse pursuers, Milosevic was transported from the Belgrade prison to the Republika Srpska (Bosnia). Here, he was turned over to NATO authorities and then whisked away by helicopter to arraignment hearings at The Hague's International Court of Justice.

Upon learning of the handover, thousands took to the streets to vent their anger at being betrayed. Even the subsequent announcement that $1.3 billion in economic aid had been pledged at the Yugoslavia donor conference did little to diminish public outrage. However, given the annual beach-bound exodus, summer is historically not the season for angry mobs in Belgrade.

As I soon discovered, I would have my work cut out for me simply tracking down enough people to research and write my story.

BELGRADE – 4 AUGUST 2001 (Saturday morning)
I had been fortunate enough to arrange a breakfast meeting with S., the Yugoslav intelligence officer I had met in May, and he quickly brought me up to

date on the situation in south Serbia. In early July, Serbian security forces had re-entered Presevo valley's notorious Sector B, and 1600 UCK guerrillas had withdrawn without a fight. As Yugoslav army and police units rolled into the five-kilometer Ground Security Zone, the Albanians had either pulled back to their bases in Kosovo or headed south to join their comrades in Macedonia.

One of the casualties of the Sector B operation was the flamboyant Commandant Leshi who was struck down by a sniper's bullet on the main street of Malo Trnovac. No one knew for sure who had killed the guerrilla leader. Some speculated that the assassin was one of his own men who had felt betrayed by the decision to retreat without giving battle to the Serbs. Others, including Kosovar-Albanian media had suggested that Leshi was murdered by a Yugoslav police sniper. This suggestion greatly amused S. "If we had such elite operatives, who can lie in wait for days behind enemy lines, we never would have lost Kosovo," he said. Asked for his own theory on who killed Leshi, S. replied without hesitation. "The Americans. They saw him as a continued political liability. If he returned to Kosovo, they would be pressured to arrest him. Such a move would anger the UCK and thereby put American soldiers at risk of terrorist retaliation. This was much simpler."

While praising Nebojsa Covic, Yugoslavia's special envoy for south Serbia and Kosovo, S. believed that the Serbs' success in Sector B would only be temporary. "The re-entry of our forces was allowed by NATO in order to boost Covic's authority with the Serbian minority in Kosovo. Their intention is to ensure official co-operation in the upcoming November elections in Kosovo," he said. "Eventually our troops will be pulled back from the Presevo valley, possibly as a bargaining chip in the event of a negotiated future partition of Kosovo."

Despite S.'s guarded optimism for a long-range solution, the violence in south Serbia continues. That same morning, two Serbian policemen were murdered at a checkpoint in the village of Muhovac. The Albanian assailants were believed to be members of the now-deceased Commandant Leshi's guerrilla force. Although formally disbanded, the UCK in south Serbia has merely been re-organized under the control of Commandant Muhamed Xhemaili.

BELGRADE – 4 AUGUST 2001 (Saturday afternoon)
One of my few Serbian contacts who had not yet left Belgrade was former

ambassador Pavle Todorovic. I managed to reach him on the telephone as he and his wife Ljiljana were packing their car. Although he was planning to drive to a seaside resort in Montenegro later that afternoon, he agreed to do a quick interview.

As a former friend of Slobodan Milosevic, Todorovic had particularly strong views about his handover to The Hague. Unfortunately, since his recall from Canada, Dr. Todorovic no longer had any ties to the Yugoslav government. His comments were therefore unofficial – the perspective of a former diplomat and high-ranking Socialist party member.

BELGRADE – 4 AUGUST 2001 (Saturday evening)

My attempts to locate a Yugoslav government spokesman had proven futile. However, I had been able to meet with Jasna Jovanovic, a Serbian journalist who works the foreign section of the Belgrade daily newspaper *Glas*. In addition to details on current Yugoslav issues, Jovanovic provided me with some insight into the local media scene.

"Under the Milosevic regime there was the state television-radio [stations], and newspapers with numerous 'independent' agencies all funded by opposition political parties," she said. "People had a choice of stories, which they could choose to believe or not believe. Since Kostunica's DOS came to power in October, the media have been so euphoric at their new-found editorial freedom that they have chosen not to use it." As a result of the similar content, newspaper sales have slumped and many veteran reporters are scrambling just to hang on to their jobs.

However, the controversy over Milosevic's handover reverse the trend. For the first time, the media began to openly criticize the Kostunica and Djindjic governments. "We have been collectively negligent in not holding these politicians accountable," Jovanovic admitted.

I was also fortunate to track down Mile Perisic, Pavle Todorovic's replacement as Yugoslavia's ambassador to Canada. Although only officially sworn into his new post in early June, Perisic was temporarily back in Belgrade on official business. A former journalist, the fiftyish Perisic had been extremely active in Serbian politics prior to his diplomatic assignment. A founding member of Zoran Djindjic's Democratic Opposition of Sebia Party, the Ambassador also had close personal ties to Kostunica and long-time Albanian Kosovar leader

Ibrahim Rugova, of the Democratic League of Kosovo. During the Bosnian civil war, Perisic had served briefly as a senior advisor to Radovan Karadzic, the president of Republika Srpska.

When Perisic had first arrived in Canada, *Ottawa Citizen* editor Bruce Garvey and I had visited the embassy to interview him. Although it was still several weeks before Milosevic was to be extradited to The Hague, Perisic had predicted exactly how it would be happen. "Without warning, in the dead of night," he told us.

Today, Perisic's connections with the uppermost levels of the DOS party, were again evident when he casually Perisic informed me that he was late for a dinner appointment because he had spent the afternoon at Kostunica's office.

BELGRADE – 5 AUGUST 2001 (Sunday morning)

It had been a long evening with Ambassador Perisic – too much food and too much beer. I was admittedly somewhat the worse for wear when these excesses were added to delayed jet lag. Despite this self-induced handicap, I still had a deadline to meet. I spent the morning in my apartment at the Genex Kula drafting a situation report for the *Ottawa Citizen*.

The handover of Milosevic to Hague further destabilizes Yugoslavia.
(Ottawa Citizen)

BELGRADE, Yugoslavia – Still evident in Belgrade's downtown streets are broken glass and smashed kiosks, the result of three days of violent demonstrations against Slobodan Milosevic's handover to The Hague Tribunal. While the civil disturbances have been curtailed for now, the deep political fractures created by Milosevic's sudden – and unconstitutional – extradition have shattered public confidence in both the fledgling federal and Serbian republic governments.

The once-universal popularity of Yugoslav President Vojislav Kostunica has been severely undermined by the extradition which was conducted, against his wishes, by Zoran Djindjic, President of Serbia. This led to a serious division within the ruling Democratic Opposition of Serbia Party (DOS). "In a single power-grab, Djindjic has revealed Kostunica to be nothing more than an impotent figurehead," said Dr. Pavle Todorovic, the former Yugoslav ambassador to Canada.

The international community further diminished Kostunica's domestic authority by denying him access into Kosovo on June 28 to celebrate Vidovdan, the Serbian national holiday which commemorates the anniversary of the 1389 Battle of Kosovo and is celebrated by Serbs around the world. Moreover, the UN's refusal to grant President Kostunica entry into what is still nominally Yugoslavian sovereign territory, has sent a clear message that the province of Kosovo has been fundamentally lost to the Serbs.

"The people feel betrayed and they will undoubtedly vent their anger on the streets once the weather cools. This will definitely be a very hot autumn in terms of political upheaval in Yugoslavia," Dr. Todorovic predicted.

The public euphoria which accompanied Kostunica's dramatic ouster of Milosevic last October, has long since disappeared, and hopes for a rapid economic recovery have not been realized. The federal treasury remains in arrears (just last week, pensioners received their April cheques), inflation is skyrocketing, unemployment is rampant and the rapid privatization of industry has sparked massive strikes across the country.

With the federal government seriously weakened, separatist factions are gaining momentum and threatening to break apart what remains of Yugoslavia. An independence movement has once again emerged in the northern province of Vojvodina. Under the Milosevic regime, the province had been stripped of its autonomous status resulting in strong resentment towards the central government.

In recent weeks, Vojvodina separatists have stepped up their demands to be granted full republic status. Josef Kasa, president of the Hungarian Vojvodina Party, represents the 30 per cent ethnic Hungarian minority and has threatened to "call in international support if necessary." In an effort to appease Kasa, Zoran Djindjic has appointed him as the Deputy Prime Minister of Serbia. "Djindjic and his cabinet are trying very hard to promote the new Serbia as one of inclusion," said Mile Perisic, current Yugoslav ambassador to Canada and co-founder of Djindjic's party. "However, the separatist movement in Vojvodina is economically-driven, not ethnically-based, with the primary leader being Nenad Canak, a Serbian. This is what makes this present movement such a threat."

With much of south Serbia's industrial capacity destroyed by the 1999 NATO bombing campaign or bankrupted after ten years of international sanctions, the relatively stable agricultural economy of Vojvodina has been bearing a disproportionate share of the tax burden. "Under such circumstances it is very easy to generate popular support for independence with promises of prosperity," said Perisic. Presidents Kostunica and Djindjic have both agreed to officially address the Vojvodina issue when Parliament resumes in September.

The possible breakaway of the Republic of Montenegro from Yugoslavia also remains a real and pressing concern for President Kostunica. Although the results of this April's elections did not give separatist President Milo Djukanovic a clear-cut mandate to hold an immediate referendum on secession, the reality is that Montenegro retains only a tenuous link to the federal Yugoslav authorities. Encouraged by the West to cut ties with the Milosevic regime, Djukanovic effected virtual independence through the creation of a separate economic system, and by seeking membership in international organizations. Montenegro now even boasts a national airline.

One of the few areas of Montenegrin-Yugoslavian cooperation which remains is security. "Given the increasing Albanian terrorist offensives in Macedonia, Serbia and Montenegro have a vested interest in sealing the border with Kosovo," said a senior Yugoslav intelligence officer. "NATO has proven to be unwilling to disarm the Kosovo Liberation Army and unable to prevent it from offensive actions. Given the large ethnic Albanian minority which lives in Montenegro and south Serbia, the potential for the UCK to expand its operations into these regions is a risk which is too imminent to be ignored."

The 2nd Yugoslav Army, which is comprised largely of Montenegrins, currently patrols the UN-imposed Ground Security Zone along the border with Kosovo.

In May of this year, following a six-month armed standoff, the 3rd Yugoslav Army reoccupied the Ground Security Zone in south Serbia, which had been seized by Albanian Kosovar guerrillas. The Yugoslav military's return to this area was negotiated by Nebojsa Covic, President Kostunica's special envoy for south Serbia and Kosovo.

Over the past few months Covic's apparent success has gained him a measure of popularity throughout Yugoslavia and revived hopes among the Serbs who remain in Kosovo. However, a personal advisor to President Djindjic confirmed that the re-occupation of south Serbia is only a temporary morale-boost-ing measure "to encourage Serbian participation in this November's Kosovo elections." Under the terms of Covic's agreement with NATO, Serbian forces will withdraw from the disputed territory by the end of the year – this time permanently.

Also directly linked to Kosovo's upcoming elections is the release of $1.3 billion (U.S.) in economic aid which was pledged at the June international donor's conference. Originally, the provision of this vital financial support was contingent upon handing over Slobodan Milosevic to The Hague. "Now the West is reneging on their promises and withholding the money. None of the funds have been released," admitted a government spokesman who spoke on the condition of anonymity. "President Djindjic feels betrayed by the West. He risked his government's domestic political credibility to comply with the Milosevic extradition – and now they've added another hurdle."

Faced with political uncertainty, economic hardship, and numerous developing crises, government officials recognize the potential for widespread civil unrest in the coming months. "I believe that the majority of the population is tired of the constant turmoil," said Ambassador Perisic. "However, it is the militant minority that is still willing to fight that poses the problem."

Branko Porobic, a 44-year-old former army sergeant, is one activist who intends to continue demanding reforms. "I fought NATO as an air defence gunner for three months in Kosovo, I stormed Parliament last year to oust Milosevic, and I will keep fighting this new government until they put Serbia on the road to recovery," he said.

Echoing these sentiments, Katarina Njegovan, a 24-year-old philosophy student and veteran political activist, vowed that she and her fellow students would once again take to the streets this fall. "Traditionally, Serbs don't protest in the summer – it is a time for holidays and relaxation."

President Kostunica promised to hold new elections within a year of his taking power. Ms. Njegovan predicts that public pressure will force the ruling DOS party to keep their promise, "And then we will get rid of this government. They did their job in removing Milosevic. Now we have to find leaders who know how to run a country."

BELGRADE – 5 AUGUST 2001 (Sunday evening)
Having filed my update on Yugoslavia, I began making preparations for the

second phase of my trip – a return visit to Macedonia. Since leaving Kumanovo in early May, I had followed the media reports closely and kept in touch with my sources by e-mail.

It was of particular note to me that as the fighting in Macedonia intensified, NATO Secretary General George Robertson and EU President Javier Solano had both become increasingly pro-Albanian in their public statements. When the fighting erupted in March, they had denounced the Kosovo-based UCK as "terrorists." By early May, the terrorists had evolved into "extremists" and by July they were referred to as "guerrillas." The international media reports had followed a similar pattern, as all references to the Macedonians became prefixed with the word *Slav*. Commentators anxious to dumb-down the Macedonian crisis would connect it to the Kosovo conflict by linking orthodox Serbs and Macedonians through religion. It was readily apparent that the Macedonian government had already lost "the battle of the airwaves" and from most reports, their security forces had not been doing much better on the ground.

The expected May 15 UCK offensive did not materialize until mid-June. One cause for the delay was the necessity to remove Albanian commanders from their UN-sponsored posts within the Kosovo Protection Corps (KPC). As these officers also held senior appointments with the UCK guerrillas, it would have been embarrassing for all involved had they turned up dead or as prisoners of war during the fighting in Macedonia. When Agim Ceku, the KPC commander, himself an indicted war criminal, released 19 of his top officers, he claimed he did so "because of their illegal association with the UCK."

The Kosovo-based media had praised General Ceku for his actions and noted that the dismissal of his lieutenants was "proof" that the KPC was not co-opted by the UCK. Although the dismissed KPC officers admitted that they had provided weapons, supplies, and intelligence to the UCK guerrillas, no arrests were made. Instead they were set free to join their troops in Macedonia and Agim Ceku was able to hire another 19 of his cronies for UN-funded jobs.

When the offensive began, the UCK had quickly seized control of a number of villages in the Tetovo sector. As regular government security forces pulled back, many Macedonian civilians (who represent a small minority in this area) tried to defend their homes. As in earlier fighting, the Macedonian military's most effective weapon against the guerrillas was a small squadron of helicopter gunships.

At the end of June, the UCK mounted a major operation to seize the village of Aracinovo, on the outskirts of Skopje, and nearly 500 guerrillas occupied this predominantly Albanian village. The strategic importance of Aracinovo is that it is built on a ridge which dominates the Skopje airport. Because it was widely believed that the UCK forces had been supplied with anti-aircraft weapons, all commercial flights were immediately suspended.

Unfortunately for the UCK, helicopter gunships continued to fly and Macedonian security forces were able to contain the UCK within the village and cut them off from re-supply. Elite police units and the cream of the Macedonian army soon established a formidable cordon around Aracinovo. Residents of Skopje could hear the steady rumble of artillery and watch the low-level helicopter attacks.

Despite pleas by the Macedonian government for Albanians to evacuate the village, most remained. International agencies expressed their concerns over the growing incidence of collateral damage, and tremendous pressure was applied by the European Union to abort the Macedonian counteroffensive. Eventually, NATO officials and UCK commanders were able to negotiate a plan for their safe withdrawal from Aracinovo; threatened with punishing economic sanctions, the Macedonians had little choice but to accept.

Under the terms of the agreement, NATO troops would oversee the demilitarization of Aracinovo and transport the UCK fighters to internment camps in Kosovo. American troops from the 502 Infantry Division stationed in Kosovo were assigned this task. In Aracinovo they herded approximately 500 guerrillas aboard 15 buses.

Much to the chagrin of the Macedonian authorities, the Americans ignored the agreement and disembarked the UCK guerrillas – still armed – inside Macedonia near the ethnic Albanian stronghold of Radusa where they promptly resumed their attacks. The official story was that, en route to Kosovo, the convoy had been stopped by UCK tanks, and that the lightly equipped and heavily outnumbered escort had reluctantly released the UCK prisoners to avoid American casualties.

Macedonian intelligence knew this story was a fabrication for the simple reason that the UCK did not have tanks. It was also revealed that 16 American military advisors, all former senior U.S. Army officers working for MPRI, a company contracted to train the Albanian guerrillas, were among those that boarded the buses in Aracinovo.

When news broke of the Americans' duplicity, Macedonians rioted in the streets of Skopje. Mobs targeted the American embassy and McDonald's restaurants. After months of embarrassing defeats, the Macedonian army had been poised to deal the UCK its first major setback when the U.S. directly interfered to swing the balance. While U.S. military assistance to the UCK was officially denied, the same could no longer be said about the State Department's diplomatic position.

In early July, Macedonia's Prime Minister, Ljubo Georgievski, accused James Pardew, the newly appointed U.S. special envoy, of "forcing Macedonia to cave in to the demands of the Albanian guerrillas." Coincidentally, Pardew's resumé included a stint in 1993 as the senior intelligence officer responsible for covertly supplying Bosnian-Muslim forces with U.S. arms. It was also Georgievski's belief that the British and Americans had wrested control of the Balkan peace agenda from the French and Germans. Faced with negotiating with this powerful partnership, the Macedonian Prime Minister stated that the only threat he had not been presented with, so far, was "that NATO will conduct an air strike on us."

The Macedonians were also losing ground in the media war. In mid-July, as the fighting around Tetovo intensified, civilians began fleeing their homes. A trickle became a flood when the Macedonian security forces could no longer maintain a foothold in the Tetovo-Kosovo corridor, and the UCK began a wave of ethnic cleansing. On the night of July 15, local UCK commanders notified Macedonian inhabitants that they must flee their villages or face possible execution. Over the next five days, in a scene reminiscent of the previous decade's Balkan conflicts, tens of thousands of refugees packed up whatever they could and abandoned their homes. Unlike the much-televised plight of Albanians who fled Kosovo in 1999, the international media all but ignored the forced Macedonian exodus.

Some young Macedonian paramilitaries remained behind to fight one-sided battles against the UCK, most in the besieged village of Ratae. At the end of July, as the fighting continued and the refugee situation threatened to become a humanitarian crisis, NATO special envoy Peter Feith brokered a temporary cease-fire in Macedonia. The contested Tetovo-Kosovo corridor was to be demilitarized by both parties while Albanian and Macedonian political parties ironed out a more comprehensive long-term peace plan.

For the first time in months, international monitors were optimistic that a full-scale inter-ethnic civil war could be avoided. As my Skopje-bound bus departed from Belgrade, it seemed as though I'd mistimed my trip. Nevertheless, I hoped that the same attractive Macedonian guard who doubted my reason for leaving in May would again be on duty at the border.

SKOPJE – 6 AUGUST 2001 (Monday morning)

On this hot summer morning, the Macedonian capital certainly did not look like a city on the brink of civil war. Like the Serbs, most Macedonians were on vacation and had left the urban centers. However there was still a handful of bureaucrats working at the Foreign Affairs building and the Macedonian embassy in Ottawa had notified them of my arrival. Despite an extensive wish list and weeks of prior notice, I was told that most of my VIP interview requests had yet to be arranged.

My earliest appointment was with Vladimir Buchkovski, the recently appointed Defence Minister, but this was not scheduled to take place until Wednesday morning. I decided to obtain my press credentials from the Ministry of Information office and then grab a bus to Tetovo. At least I could visit the recent battlefields and try to locate my contacts there.

TETOVO – 6 AUGUST 2001 (Monday evening)

It was early evening and Friedhelm Peel was sitting outside the Hotel Electra drinking a beer when I arrived. "Hey, where have you been? You've missed all the fun!" he yelled. Over the course of our evening meal, Peel brought me up to date with the summer's excitement. He was very proud that even at the height of the fighting, construction at the South East Europe University (SEEU) continued. Even after UCK guerrillas shelled the site, Peel had not discharged his terrified workers. "It was just a few mortar shells," he explained. "The Albanians were trying to hit Macedonian artillery positions about three kilometers beyond our buildings."

Although local Albanian leaders still did not accept the SEEU and its appeasement program, Peel did not believe the UCK would deliberately attack the construction site. "We are paying their contractors too much money for them to seriously jeopardize this project," he said.

At dusk, with the police curfew already in effect, a dozen shadowy figures approached our table from the rear entrance of the Electra's banquet hall. They were mostly off-duty hotel staff and their acquaintances. I had met many of them during my previous visit and learned that many now possessed photocopied versions of my book *Inat: Images of Serbia and the Kosovo Conflict*.

Word had spread of my earlier predictions that the fighting would escalate and since that had become reality, it now seemed that I was regarded as some sort of Balkan War guru. This evening, they had come to the Electra to find out what would happen next.

I felt completely at a loss as they gathered around the table anticipating my words of wisdom. Rather than disappoint them completely, I muttered that, having only just arrived, I had yet to make a first-hand assessment. Any prediction I gave at this point would be based on media reports. "And who believes those foreign journalists?" I told them.

TETOVO – 7 AUGUST 2001 (Tuesday morning)

Armed with my official press accreditation, I set out early for the Macedonian army caserne. This time the guards were in a no-nonsense mood, and I noticed that all of the soldiers were now equipped with body-armour and modern assault rifles. More bunkers had been dug into the lawn surrounding the headquarters building, and a great number of armoured vehicles were parked inside the compound.

A young captain was summoned to the gate and instructed me to stand well away from the entrance while he went to telephone his superiors in Skopje. My request was to interview an officer who could give me an overview of the current military situation in Tetovo and, if possible, describe the previous month's fighting. It was also my hope that I would be granted permission to photograph some elements of the Macedonian security forces. The captain was polite, but he advised me that it would take some time to get through to the Defence ministry. He suggested that I return in an hour.

I would have gladly killed the time at a quiet outdoor café, but the same Macedonian civilian who had berated me as one of the "Western media prostitutes" a few months before just happened to be on hand. Overhearing the captain's comments, Aleksa apologized for his previous outburst and invited me to join him and his family for coffee while I waited. His frequent presence at the army caserne's front gate was explained by the fact that he lived directly across the road. Not really having much choice, I followed him to his apartment.

I was introduced to his wife and two teenage daughters, all of them eager to express sentiments similar to Aleksa's. Over the next 40 minutes they persistently interrupted each other to advise me what *skots* or assholes Western journalists are. (Although tempted, I did not dare reveal my first name to them.) As for their opinion of the *Shqiptares*, Slavica, the eldest daughter, was the most bellicose. In addition to educating me to the fact that Albanians live in walled houses "so they can have sex with their own family members," Slavica complained that Albanian men were "always staring at [her] *titske* [breasts]." Even with her parents nodding their grim approval, it was difficult for me not to laugh out loud. Slavica's *titske* were enormous. To make matters worse, she had packed them into a black under-wire bra clearly visible under a tight, low cut white T-shirt, thereby creating an impossible-to-ignore cleavage. Unable to come up with a suitable comment, I made my apologies and cut short my visit.

When I arrived at the caserne, the Macedonian army captain advised me that I was not to interview or photograph any soldiers during my stay. When I asked him how I was supposed to report "the other side" of the story, he replied, "You are the journalist. That's your job."

I returned to the Electra, changed into my gym gear and set off on a reconnaissance run. It was readily apparent that the Macedonian army had given up a lot of ground in Tetovo. Other than the caserne, there were only two manned *punkts,* or bunker complexes, inside the city limits. Beyond the central square there was no evidence of a Macedonian security presence. The police bunker astride the Kosovo road that I visited on my earlier trip had long since been overrun or abandoned.

In the northern and western suburbs I noticed several armed Albanians who were brazenly wearing their crested black UCK T-shirts at the outdoor cafés. By contrast, soldiers at the Macedonian *punkt* at the old soccer stadium were on high alert. The bunker itself was a sandbagged semicircular redoubt with observation and firing ports. There were land mines laid out in front of the defensive position, approximately 200 meters beyond several badly damaged houses. This was now the front line; the most exposed Macedonian outpost. My sudden appearance from the Albanian-controlled sector startled the garrison. A heavy-set sergeant emerged from the entrance to order me inside the bunker. After my passport and press pass were checked, everyone relaxed. The icebreaker, once again, had been my name – this time coupled with my jogging attire.

TETOVO – 7 AUGUST 2001 (Tuesday afternoon)

Knowing that the UCK was operating openly inside the city, I was anxious to make contact. Heading past the central square, I spotted a familiar face – the young Albanian chap I'd met at the Albanian Democratic Party offices.

He was carrying two heavy bags and struggling along in my direction. We exchanged greetings, and he asked me if there was any way in which he could be of help. His leader, Arben Djafferi, was in the southern city of Ohrid attending the peace negotiations, he told me, so he could not arrange an interview. However, he was eager to put me in touch with the UCK commanders. "I will take you to Slatina with me right now," he said, holding up his parcels. "I'm bringing some cigarettes and candy to the UCK fighters anyway."

After hailing a taxi with an Albanian driver, he used his cell phone to make preparations for our arrival in Slatina. The taxi had taken a detour past the old stadium, just beyond the view of the Macedonian army *punkt*. As we turned north, back onto the main road, I saw a large red and black Albanian eagle flag dangling from a cable. "This is the new border," my young Albanian guide said with evident pride. "The Macedonians don't dare come beyond this point." A short distance away was an unmanned checkpoint—with UCK spray-painted across the sandbags. "Before the demilitarization agreement brokered by Peter Feith, our soldier freely occupied these posts," he said. "They are still here—they are just not visible during the day."

When we arrived in Slatina, I was introduced to Blerim Jakupi, a 24-year-old schoolteacher who had been appointed as my guide. The DPA assistant departed in the taxi and headed further up into the mountains. Blerim explained to me that the UCK was headquartered just three kilometers away, around the village of Brezna. The guerrillas had been notified of my arrival and had agreed to be interviewed later that afternoon. In the meantime, Blerim wanted to show me the damage in Neopristina. The night before, the Macedonians had bombarded the village with artillery and tanks, he told me. If true, this would represent a serious violation of the cease-fire.

At Neopristina, we were greeted by a score of young Albanians in civilian clothing. Many of them spoke German, and they were anxious to describe the bombardment. Although their stories differed slightly, the consensus was that in two separate barrages over a period of three hours, the Macedonians had fired at least 70 shells into the village. Two civilians had been slightly hurt, and several homes had suffered damage. One farmer was still in shock as he pointed to his shrapnel-laced tractor and shattered windows. The sickly sweet smell of fresh manure, mixed with the acrid stench of cordite, hung over the village. After a decade of covering Balkan wars, it was an all too familiar smell.

The Albanians believed that a large number of the artillery shells had been duds. Whenever they located a protruding tail fin, they carefully circled it with rocks. Upon learning that I was ex-military, they took me to one of the duds, which had implanted itself next to a barn. They asked me how they could remove it. When I suddenly kicked it, several of them threw themselves to the ground, while others shouted in alarm.

When they regained their composure, I pointed to the splash surrounding the impact area, which indicated that the shell had already exploded. Judging from the tail fin, it was an 82 mm mortar (a relatively short-range weapon).

As irregular paramilitaries in the enclave at Ratae were the only troops within range to fire a round of that calibre, it seemed to indicate that Macedonian regular army units had not violated the cease-fire.

At a café in the center of Neopristina, we encountered an OSCE international monitoring team investigating the bombardment. Team leader Carl Underwood, an American Vietnam veteran, came over to introduce himself. According to Underwood, the Macedonians had been firing at Neopristina in retaliation for UCK attacks on a dam up a nearby creek that provides Ratae's water supply. When first asked about this, Albanian villagers had denied the allegation. They denied it again, even when standing by the dry creek bed. "It's annoying as hell when they just keep making up new lies," said Underwood as he headed back into the café to rejoin the investigation.

Back in Slatina, Jakupi and I had met with the local Albanian civilian authorities and tried to establish exactly what, if any, official jurisdiction they held.

The headman, or acting mayor, was a thickset man in his early forties who went by the anglicized name of Denny. Having spent a few months in the United States, Denny admitted that he had adopted his moniker from the popular restaurant chain.

Despite their best efforts to explain the new civilian administrative structure in this demilitarized zone, I could not, for the life of me, understand how the system worked. One point they made abundantly clear was that they did not have, nor would they accept any direction from the Skopje-based Macedonian government.

After approximately 30 minutes of conversation in the coffeehouse that doubled as the town hall, we were interrupted by a commotion outside. Five armed, uniformed UCK soldiers were crammed comically inside a tiny Yugo, which had sent up a cloud of dust when it braked to a halt. The driver and two guards hastily dismounted to take up protective firing positions as the others got out of the car. A crowd of schoolboys came racing over to the guerrillas, excitedly chanting "U-C-K, U-C-K!"

After I was introduced to Commanders Mouse and Jimmy, we all went back into the café so we could talk and be heard above the clamour of the kids.

After exchanging pleasantries – as well as a round of one-upmanship in the sharing of Balkan war-zone experiences – we had a very straightforward discussion. As I was an ex-military type, they talked openly about their forces. The previous night, Herr Peel had told me that American helicopters had been supplying arms to the nearby village of Sipkovica. Despite the use of a covering smoke screen, Macedonian security forces spotted two Chinooks transport helicopters. When the Macedonian media published photos of this not-so-covert aid to the Albanians, the Americans replied that the delivery was "vital humanitarian aid."

I asked Mouse and Jimmy about the American claim and they both laughed out loud. "What do you think?" asked Mouse. "This is summer in the Balkans, and every village has plenty of food stocks." Still laughing, he asked, "Did the Americans really say it was humanitarian aid?"

Commander Jimmy was more direct. "We don't have heavy artillery and the Macedonians do. Is it wrong for the Americans to even the playing field?"

I smiled and agreed. Denny shouted, "God Bless America—and Canada too!"

The UCK soldiers and commanders had agreed to pose for a few Rambo-like photos outside the café. However, the photo session was cut short by the arrival of my taxi driver. He told us breathlessly that the Macedonian Wolves had just launched an attack in the demilitarized zone. The UCK raced to their car and sped off to the renewed cheers of the Albanian schoolboys.

My driver regretfully informed me that he would have to take a more circuitous route back to Tetovo, but was insistent that he would not charge me extra.

SKOPJE – 8 AUGUST 2001 (Wednesday morning)

Despite the fact that the weather forecast called for the temperature to soar above 40 degrees Celsius, I was wearing a long-sleeved shirt and tie. I had an interview later in the morning with Macedonia's new defense minister, Vladimir Buchkovski, and I felt a certain amount of decorum was necessary.

Friedhelm Peel also had a meeting in Skopje so I hitched a ride with him to the capital. Arriving in the city centre before 9:30 a.m., we agreed to meet for a late supper back at the Hotel Electra. We had no idea that at that moment all hell was breaking loose on the stretch of road we had just travelled over.

The first inkling I had that something was wrong was the flurry of activity at the Macedonian Defense Ministry. A crowd had gathered in the guarded entranceway and were trying to get in, while on the other side of a barrier people were trying to reclaim their identification cards in order to get out.

It took me a while to work my way forward to a harassed military policeman at the reception window. As soon as I told him I was there to interview Minister Buchkovski, the young corporal put a finger to his temple and asked incredulously, "Are you *fucked*? Do you have any idea of what is going on?" When I tried to explain to him that I didn't, I was contemptuously dismissed.

A short, pot-bellied colonel at the rear of the queue had seen – and understood – the curt exchange. Politely, he explained to me that the UCK had just mounted a major offensive. The Tetovo-Skopje highway had been cut off and that many soldiers were killed in an ambush. Furthermore, there could be no interview with Buchkovski today because he was trapped in Tetovo. The helpful colonel did not know when or if there would be a press conference, as the information was too sketchy. He suggested that I go to the official press accreditation counter for an update on the situation.

As I walked to the nearby foreign media office, a flight of Mi-24 Hind heli-

TOP LEFT: *As the UCK offensive gained momentum, Macedonian paramilitary troops, such as the Lion pictured here, appeared in the front lines.* (SCOTT TAYLOR)

TOP RIGHT: *When the UCK launched a mortar barrage against Tetovo, the streets were hastily deserted.* (SCOTT TAYLOR)

ABOVE: *Under fire, wounded Macedonian police are medevaced from the Tetovo caserne.* (SCOTT TAYLOR)

Dark areas show higher elevation.   • — • Kosovo Macedonia border

TOP: *The wreckage of a Macedonian vehicle marks the grisly August 8 ambush site at Grupcin on the Skopje-Tetovo highway. Ten policemen were killed and 14 wounded in this UCK attack. (JAMES PHILLIPS)*

ABOVE: *Map showing the contested Kosovo-Macedonia border region. (KATHERINE TAYLOR)*

copters flew overhead towards the Tetovo highway. Unfortunately, Atanas Georgievski was the only person on duty in the office. He knew nothing of the UCK attack, and without a mutual language – he spoke only Macedonian and Greek, a decided drawback when dealing with the foreign media – we were reduced to communicating in sign language. In this manner, I learned that I was one of only five foreign journalists registered in Macedonia. The others were an American, two from a Dutch television crew and a reporter from Abu Dabai. As it seemed unlikely that the Macedonian military would hold a press conference, I contacted Rade Lesko at Skynet Television. He told me that ten soldiers had been killed and 14 wounded. A number of civilians had also been attacked along the 42 kilometres of highway that separate Tetovo and Skopje, and the Macedonian army had closed the road. "Until when?" I asked stupidly. "Until we win the battle, I would assume," Lesko answered. The ambush had taken place outside the village of Grupcin, approximately half-way between the two cities.

I had no way of knowing whether or not this was part of a sustained offensive by the UCK or an isolated attack. However, with most of my gear and travel documents still in Tetovo, I had to get back as quickly as possible.

I hailed a taxi and told the driver I wanted to go to Grupcin. He had been listening to his radio and told me it was not possible. "The road is closed," he said. I showed him my press pass and told him that as a foreign correspondent I had clearance to get through. He bought it, and we set off.

The bluff worked at the first police checkpoint as well. However at Saraj, a village on the western outskirts of Skopje, the Macedonian security forces were turning back all traffic, and there was a lineup of vehicles parked along the roadside. A crowd of curious drivers had gathered at the head of the column, anxious to obtain word of the battle's progress.

My driver was only too ready to obey the policeman at the barricade. As soon as he stopped and I stepped out of the car, he turned around and sped off back to Skopje – without waiting to be paid.

There were at least two dozen heavily armed security personnel at the Saraj roadblock, along with armoured personnel carriers and a sandbagged *punkt*, which appeared to be the headquarters. I was hoping to talk my way through by telling the commanding officer that it was important for a foreign journalist to be on the scene to confirm the UCK's ambush at Grupcin and present the "big picture."

A surly-looking policeman came towards me shouting "fuck off" or its Macedonian equivalent before I even had time to state my case. I therefore politely asked to see his superior.

Overhearing the conversation, a hatless policeman lounging in the shade nearby yelled out that he was in charge. After a few moments of talking to him, I realized my case was hopeless. Even when I asked for details of the ambush and the current situation, he just shrugged and said, "Ask the Defense ministry spokesman."

Admitting defeat, I turned to the policeman who had first approached me and said, "*Izvini* (I'm sorry)." As I picked up my briefcase, he suddenly lunged forward and struck me across the chest with his Kalashnikov. "*Ne ma izvini!*" he shouted. Surprised and knocked off balance, I was just regaining my composure when he struck me again, this time more forcefully, still shouting, "*Ne ma izvini!*"

As I walked back towards the line of parked cars, the police and the assembled onlookers were all laughing. I decided then and there that, whatever it took, I would get through to Tetovo.

KONDOVO – 8 AUGUST 2001 (Wednesday afternoon)

I climbed a hillside in order to get around the police checkpoint. Without a map, I reasoned that if I headed west, then south, I could get back onto the main highway at the bottom of the hill. I came across a rail line, which I wrongly assumed led to Grupcin and Tetovo. After walking nearly three kilometers, I learned of my mistake from a trio of young Albanian boys who were crossing the tracks on their way back from swimming. They had been quite startled by my sudden appearance. Drenched in sweat, dressed in a shirt and tie, and carrying a briefcase and camera bag, I must have been a very strange sight, indeed.

The boys were puzzled when I asked how far it was to the highway. My dead reckoning had been correct, but I had forgotten to factor in the curve of the Vardar River, which ran through the valley. To get to Grupcin, I would have to retrace my steps, almost all the way back to the police *punkt* in Saraj.

Footsore from walking in my leather dress shoes, I asked the boys if I could rent a bicycle. This request amused them and they ran off ahead of me to the village of Kondovo to see if they could find one.

News of the approaching stranger soon spread throughout this little Albanian village, and when I arrived in Kondovo, I was swarmed by curious children. An uncle of one of the boys I had met on the tracks joined the group and tried his best to dissuade me from making the trip. "There is much fighting in the valley; it is very dangerous right now," he said. "Join my family for lunch and we will arrange for a driver to take you to Tetovo via Kosovo tonight."

He told me that he could put me in touch with the local UCK commanders as they still had routes open. I really did not want to spend too much time with the UCK, especially with copies of my book in my briefcase – *Inat* had not been well received in Kosovo. Finally realizing that I was determined to get to Grupcin, he produced a battered old mountain bike. Using his tractor engine as a compressor, he re-inflated the rear tire and explained that only the front brake worked. After sharing a midday meal with his family, I changed from my sweat-soaked shirt and tie into the clean T-shirt they gave me and bade them farewell.

A number of young Albanians offered to guide me across the Vardar and when I started off, they ran along beside me. From the direction of Tetovo, the crump of far-off mortars could be clearly heard and columns of black smoke rose from the next valley. Macedonian fighter jets were visible overhead and helicopter gunships occasionally appeared above the ridgeline.

Things were really heating up. As we reached the banks of the Vardar, an American Twin Huey utility helicopter roared over us at treetop level. A grinning door-gunner gave us a thumbs-up and the kids cheered wildly. Startled at the appearance of a NATO aircraft so blatantly violating Macedonian air space, I asked out loud, "What the hell are the Yanks doing here?" One of the older boys looked at me sternly and said, "They're here to help us – or don't you think they should?" I noticed that the helicopter had veered west and was heading straight towards the Grupcin ambush site. Dodging the boy's question, I pointed at the now distant chopper and said, "At least with NATO up there, things should be a little safer."

There was a ford across the Vardar about a kilometer from the Macedonian police *punkt* at Saraj. Crossing the river, I knew that the police could see us. I just hoped that they would not be unduly alarmed by a bicyclist surrounded by a cluster of teenaged Albanians. I came out on the highway on a slight rise, just out of sight of the roadblock.

With my heavy briefcase clamped across the handlebars and my camera bag tightly slung across my back, I set off on the 25-kilometer ride to Grupcin. I have never been much of a cyclist and with my unbalanced baggage, I dared not lift a hand to wave goodbye to my Albanian escorts. Shouting thank you over my shoulder, I wobbled away.

It did not take long for the euphoria of having slipped past the police to evaporate. I was overcome by an overwhelming sense of anxiety and fear. As I climbed the first long slope on the eerily empty four-lane highway, I suddenly felt very much alone. I realized that nobody had any idea of my whereabouts and that I was riding a dilapidated bicycle into the middle of a combat zone. I convinced myself that I could not go back now, and that I would be able to visit the ambush site and make it all the way back to Tetovo before dusk.

The ride was proving to be much more strenuous than I had thought it would be. The bicycle had seen better days – a slight warp in the font wheel prevented me from picking up any speed, even on the downhill stretches. The seat was set too low and I could not peddle safely while standing for fear that my shoes would slip. My butt was also beginning to feel the effects of not having a ridden a bike for at least ten years.

I had not seen another living soul since I got back on the highway, and without a watch or map, it was difficult to measure my progress. Ahead, plumes of smoke were rising above the horizon and the dull thump of artillery was becoming louder. As my fears mounted, I began talking out loud to the bicycle, coaxing it along.

Two Hind gunships suddenly roared overhead less than 30 metres off the ground, the aircrew probably as startled at the sight of a lone cyclist as I was of them. About 800 meters ahead of me, they hovered directly over the highway and began firing rockets at an unseen UCK position. Startled by the blasts, I almost fell off the bicycle. Empty metal casings, each weighing approximately one kilogram, came plummeting down all over the highway and bounced off the asphalt with a curious metallic pinging sound. When I reached the spot where the gunships had fired, I stopped briefly to pick up one of the still-hot rocket tubes as a souvenir.

I was beginning to wonder if I had somehow passed Grupcin when, off to my right, I heard a muffled hiss, and turned to see a camouflaged figure on a grassy slope, pointing in my direction. Two other armed men joined him and took up firing positions. They were about 150 meters away, but they offered no formal challenge. I could not tell whether they were UCK or Macedonian security forces, but assumed that this was close to the ambush site, and with so much air activity about, the UCK would be long gone. I kept riding straight down the middle of the road, hoping that I looked more ridiculous than threatening. At any moment I expected to be either shot or at least challenged and stopped.

Just as I was beginning to believe that I was in the clear, I saw a pair of flashing headlights coming towards me in the oncoming lane. I assumed that the hidden gunmen had radioed for a mobile police unit to check me out. I was already thinking about how I could get rid of the bike and hitch a ride when the white Mercedes roared past me. The flashing lights were not a signal for me to stop, but to get the hell out of the way.

I passed the burnt-out hulk of a civilian Yugo, with the charred remains of the driver still inside, the flames flickering at the edge of a blackened field. A little farther on, I rode past an abandoned Macedonian army bunker. A few minutes later, I came upon four armoured personnel carriers in the middle of the road, their turrets constantly traversing in a threatening manner. Ahead of them were the shattered remains of two army vehicles, their blackened hulks still smoldering.

As I approached, a dismounted soldier spotted me and shouted an alarm. The turret of the rearmost APC swung around and the machinegun barrel was depressed until it centred squarely on my chest. I could not understand what the soldier said, but knew immediately that I was not welcomed here.

A sergeant gestured for me to raise my hands in the air. With my briefcase on the handlebar and only one brake handle, this proved to be rather difficult. About 20 meters away from him, I dismounted and walked toward him with my hands raised high. He was not only angry with me but also very edgy about the situation. Behind him, I could see body parts of Macedonian soldiers strewn across the road.

After examining my passport and press credentials, the sergeant shouted, "What the fuck are you doing here? The road is closed!" Realizing he meant to intimidate me, I instead shouted back my own question: "If the road is closed, then how did I get here?" Startled by my outburst, he calmed down a little and asked where I got on the highway. I told him past Saraj, and that I came here directly from Kondovo. Playing dumb, I asked, "Is there some sort of trouble ahead?"

He didn't wish to elaborate and kept telling me that I must go back, as this place was too dangerous. When I asked why the other Macedonian patrol had not stopped me, this news puzzled him. When I explained to him exactly where I had seen the figures on the hillside, it was apparent from his reaction that they must have been UCK.

Not only were he and his detachment stuck in the open in a killing ground, but now I had also brought the unwelcome news that the UCK had stepped in behind them. He became even more insistent that I leave the site immediately and ride all the way back to Skopje.

I knew that, physically, I could not manage it even if I had wanted to. My arse was killing me and I was so dehydrated that I was no longer sweating. Then I spotted three Albanian civilians – an old man and what appeared to be a young married couple – standing beside the road. I asked the sergeant why I could not simply stay with them. "Just forget that you ever saw these people," he snapped, and went over to the nearest APC to use the radio. A member of the Wolves special forces had overheard our conversation. Lowering his voice, he said, "Look, just get your bike and get out of sight. Go back a couple of kilometers and hide beside the road. We hope to have the road to Tetovo clear in a couple of hours."

As I started to ask another question, he cut me off. "Just get going before that terrified idiot kills you." I hurried back to my bicycle.

I decided to get off the highway and try to find a telephone to contact the *Ottawa Citizen*. I hoped to dictate a quick story, and at least let someone know where I was. I retraced my route back a couple of kilometers and turned onto a small farm track. The first house I approached appeared to be deserted. I called out, hoping to attract the owner's attention but the sudden roar of two gunships coming in low drowned me out. The helicopters passed directly overhead and began to plaster the next hillside, meaning the UCK forces had cut the road to Skopje. Getting no answer at the farmhouse, I pushed my bicycle up the steep path towards the hamlet I could see about a kilometer away.

I had barely gone 60 meters when two UCK soldiers emerged from the woods lining the track. To say that they startled me would be an understatement. One had a Kalashnikov, the other a pistol, and both were aimed directly at me. I dropped the bicycle and put up my hands. The one with the pistol hissed in German, "Get off the road you idiot. Do you want to get us all killed?"

I grabbed my briefcase and camera bag and plunged into a thicket with them. "Who are you and what the hell are you doing here?" he asked.

When I told him I was a Canadian journalist, his demeanor changed completely. Holstering his pistol, he smiled broadly and said, "Welcome my friend."

From our vantage point it was still possible to see the Macedonian armoured column at the ambush site. My new friend advised me that it was dangerous for me here, and he used his cell phone to call for a car and driver to take me further away from the highway.

Within minutes, a little red Yugo came racing down the farm track and braked beside us. Hiding the bicycle under some branches, I hurried over and got in. Our destination was the hamlet I had been heading towards, which I learned was Bojane.

In the central square, about a dozen cheerful Albanian men and teenage boys came over to greet me. I asked for some mineral water, which I drank thirstily, and then a telephone. Several of them produced their cellular phones, even after I told them that I wanted to put a call through to Canada.

I reached Bruce Garvey at the *Citizen* and brought him up to date. He had heard of the ambush on the wire service, then I informed him that I had been in the middle of the fighting. It was not a great phone connection, but I dictated the details as best I could. Garvey assured me he would be able to piece together a story from what I told him.

Not wanting to worry my family with my predicament, nor for them to learn of it in the morning paper, I asked Garvey to call my wife early the next morning in order to brace her. He wished me luck and I signed off.

During my phone call, several Albanians had crowded around, trying to follow my story. When I finished, one of the older men asked, "Why didn't you tell them about how our women and children are suffering?" When I replied that I hadn't seen any women or children, I immediately realized that I had taken his bait.

A few men escorted me to the basements of some of Bojane's larger houses. In each crowded cellar, there were approximately two dozen women and children sitting on mats around the floor, rocking back and forth and pretending to cry – from fear of the Macedonian police, I was told. I say *pretending* because the whole scene was so badly acted, it was embarrassing to be a part of. I knew that I was expected to express my shock and sympathy, but seeing the young girls laughing behind their hands at each other's phony tears made it impossible for me to feign compassion. When my guide asked if I would like to photograph this "suffering," I lied and said that I was out of film.

"They have been down in this shelter since the fighting in June," he told me. When I asked if all they did was sit and cry all day, every day, he replied with a straight face, "Yes."

As we were leaving, I glanced back and saw young children spilling out eagerly into the back garden, and teenage girls watching our passage from an upstairs window.

BOJANE – 8 AUGUST 2001 (Wednesday evening)

Dusk was fast approaching, and it would be too risky to ride the bike to Tetovo. The villagers said it was still too dangerous to drive and invited me to spend the night in Bojane. They would prove to be very gracious hosts.

When I asked if there was a restaurant in Bojane, there was a flurry of activity. A slight young man immediately headed into a nearby chicken coop from which he emerged triumphantly holding an old rooster by the legs. Crusted in sweat-salt and aching from my ride, I also inquired about a hot shower.

This could not be provided as Bojane's village water tank was dry. The Macedonians were to blame for this, I was told, as the water truck had refused to make its regular delivery after the ambush.

A wash basin was provided along with a bucket of cold water. I did my best to clean up, but I was hesitant to wash my feet in front of a crowd of Albanian onlookers. I finally couldn't resist the urge, so I sat down and removed my stinking shoes and socks. To my amazement, one of the Albanians knelt down and began pouring cold water on my feet. Embarrassed, I tried to pull away, only to have the bystanders insist that he be allowed to continue. For the next ten minutes, he bathed and massaged my feet with such care that I started to worry that this constituted some form of Albanian sexual foreplay.

As we waited for dinner, we crowded into a farmhouse to watch the evening news. The Grupcin ambush was the top story on all the local stations. I was amused to see that the "on-the-spot" reporters were in fact doing their stand-ups from the *punkt* at Saraj – 25 kilometers from the fighting.

We had just finished eating the tough old rooster when a car pulled into the farmyard. The pair of UCK from the farm track got out and were soon organizing the able-bodied men in the village into four-man detachments. A collection of pistols and rifles was distributed and a shift list made up. The Macedonian army had managed to re-open the highway and was now mount-ing a counteroffensive under the cover of darkness. The villagers were dis-persed to observation posts outside of Bojane to monitor the Macedonians' progress.

Virtually every Albanian had a cell phone and contact numbers for neigh-bouring villages. When the Macedonian armoured column began probing the hillside, its every move was tracked and reported by hundreds of civilian sup-porters of the UCK. Watching the Albanian network in action made me realize that the Macedonian army faced a formidable adversary.

Left alone in the farmhouse, I bedded down for the night. As I fell asleep, the James Bond film *The Man with the Golden Gun* was playing on the TV, occa-sionally interrupted by nearby bursts of machinegun fire.

BOJANE – 9 AUGUST 2001 (Thursday morning)

I awoke at first light and, despite aches and pains from my previous day's bicycle ride, was anxious to get back on the road. The Albanian sentries re-turned in shifts to have breakfast and report that all was quiet. I learned from the morning television news that the Tetovo-Skopje road was open once again. However, when the villagers tried to arrange a taxi to come for me from Tetovo, no driver was prepared to take the risk. I would have to continue the rest of the journey by bike.

I retrieved my bicycle from the thicket at the UCK outpost at the foot of the farm track and slowly started the final leg of my trip. Along the remaining 15 kilometers, I saw only a handful of civilian cars on the re-opened roadway, and all of them were travelling at top speed. At the ambush site, the Macedo-nian army units were nowhere to be seen. The victims' bodies had been re-moved but the hulks of their vehicles remained in the middle of the road.

A couple of kilometers further on, I passed a shot-up civilian bus that was still burning. What astounded me about this particular vehicle was that it had been attacked within full view of a German military base. Although they would have been within range – and able to witness the UCK attack against the unarmed passengers – these NATO troops did not have the mandate to intervene.

Finally arriving at the Hotel Electra, I met Friedhelm Peel and we shared a late breakfast. The Grupcin ambush had forced him to spend the night in Skopje. He admitted that his "adventures" at the Playboy Club did not compare with my own. After he set off for the university construction site, I set to work in the Electra's dining room, writing a backgrounder for the *Ottawa Citizen*. As I concentrated on my article, I was only vaguely aware of distant explosions.

Macedonia: The crisis continues (Ottawa Citizen)

TETOVO, Macedonia – As international envoys and Macedonian government officials attempted to hammer out a peace deal in the holiday resort of Ohrid, thereby clearing the way for the first NATO peacekeepers to deploy, fighting and violence continued unabated across the country. Yesterday, ethnic Albanian rebels (UCK) mounted a major offensive to cut the main highway between the capital of Skopje and Tetovo, the country's second-largest city. After suffering heavy casualties – ten dead and 14 wounded in an ambush – Macedonian security forces battled to regain control of this vital route. Helicopter gunships pounded rebel villages and armoured columns inched their way up steep mountain paths to engage the UCK guerrillas. A handful of smouldering vehicles bore stark testimony to these attacks.

Angered by news of the ambush, mobs of Macedonian citizens took to the streets to ransack ethnic Albanian shops in Skopje, which then prompted Albanians to unleash a fusillade of small-arms fire into the Macedonian suburbs of Tetovo.

"As the peace talks stalled, this cycle of hatred gained momentum and we are still plunging headfirst into civil war," said Vojce Stojkoski, a 47-year-old ethnic Bulgarian contractor based in Tetovo. "Even now that the politicians have signed an agreement, I don't believe either side can be prevented from continuing the violence."

When this conflict first erupted in March, the stated objective of the Albanian minority leaders was to achieve increased autonomy through revisions to the Macedonian constitution. However, after five months of successful military action, the Albanians have gained virtual control of 30 per cent of Macedonia's territory. Hard-line Albanian leaders were dealing from a position of strength at the Ohrid talks, and many of their followers feel that outright autonomy is still possible. Arta Gylanize, a 38-year-old political assistant with the Albanian Democratic Party, said she hoped her leader, Arben Djafferi, would refuse to sign the agreement. "This land was once all part of Greater Albania and we should not have to live under the Macedonians," said Gylanize.

With the Ohrid peace plan, the Macedonian government has conceded to nearly all of the major ethnic Albanian reforms, and this has caused severe resentment among the Slavic majority. The complex arrangement proposed to recognize Albanian as an official language in regions of Macedonia where they "constitute over 20 per cent of the population" has been denounced as "unworkable" in the local media. In response to the provision to recruit 1000 ethnic Albanian police, the Macedonian police reacted violently. Following a drunken rampage at a local pub in Tetovo, the police officers who caused the destruction were unrepentant. "How are we supposed to react to the news that we will be serving alongside the same criminals that we've been fighting for months?" asked Rade Jolevski, a 22-year-old police reservist in Tetovo. "How do we justify this to our dead comrades?"

President Boris Trjkovski is regarded as a moderate who has pursued a policy of appeasement, while Prime Minister Ljubo Georgievski, from the same ruling Unity Party, has emerged as a hard-line nationalist. Macedonian extremists have now organized a paramilitary movement called the Lions, and they are echoing Georgievski's call for a military victory prior to implementing any appeasement measures.

At the beginning of the hostilities, the Macedonian security forces were woefully ill-equipped. As a result, when the Albanian UCK guerrillas first encroached from Kosovo last March, they were hard-pressed to contain even this limited offensive.

From then on, the government has been hastily trying to bolster its fighting forces with modern weapons and foreign mercenaries. Despite pressure from the European Union to desist from such an arms build-up, the Macedonians have tried desperately to keep pace with the concurrent UCK mobilization. At present, the Macedonian military possesses a relatively powerful punch from leased attack helicopters, fighter jets, and new armoured vehicles. "The majority of these weapons were acquired in exchange for tomatoes and wine from the Ukraine," said Rade Lesko, a defense reporter with Skopje-based Skynet Television.

Over the past week, both Javier Solana and George Robertson, President of the EU and secretary general for NATO respectively, have made direct interventions to the Ukrainian government to cut off this flow of weapons and munitions. "It is unbelievable that they tried to keep us from arming our soldiers, and yet these same 'peace envoys' have not publicly admonished the United States for the blatant equipping of the UCK," said Lesko. The direct provision of military aid, advisors, and intelligence to the UCK has provoked a number of violent anti-U.S. riots here in Macedonia.

In late June, with the UCK guerrillas in the village of Aracinovo threatening to overrun Skopje's airport, the Macedonian security forces were able to employ their superior firepower to gain a rare victory. As they closed the noose around the UCK enclave, EU pressure allowed American troops to intercede and evacuate the guerrillas. When the UCK were later released, still armed and still inside Macedonia, the American embassy (and many other NATO country embassies) was stormed and vandalized.

The UCK is quick to acknowledge the U.S. military support it receives. Commander Mouse, a 47-year-old UCK officer in the Tetovo sector, shouted, "God Bless America and Canada too for what they have given us!" when I interviewed him. While he would not elaborate on Canada's contribution, Mouse confirmed that two U.S. Chinook heavy transport helicopters had delivered heavy mortars and munitions. "We have all the equipment and men we need to capture Skopje in 24 hours," said Commander Jimmy, a 22-year-old Albanian guerrilla who is already a veteran of Chechnya, Kosovo, and south Serbia. "Militarily, the Macedonians are no match for our soldiers."

As part of the Ohrid peace plan, NATO will deploy an advance party of 400 soldiers into Macedonia to disarm the UCK. A force of nearly 3000 NATO troops – including up to 200 Canadians – have already been assembled in Thessalonika, Greece, and are only awaiting a diplomatic agreement before moving in. Given the recent fighting, the UCK are very reluctant to comply with the immediate disarmament clause. "We will only handover our weapons when we are sure that NATO is prepared to protect us," said Commander

Jimmy. Under the present terms of the agreement, NATO forces will only be committed for a period of 30 days. As a result, the Albanians are unlikely to fully comply with the demilitarization of their troops.

For these guerrillas, any relinquishing of the territory they've captured will be a bitter pill to swallow. In the nearly 30 per cent of Macedonian territory under UCK control, these fighters are regarded as heroes by the local population. Virtually every able-bodied Albanian male voluntarily assists the UCK through the provision of logistic support and intelligence gathering.

Following yesterday's ambush on the Skopje-Tetovo highway, hundreds of Albanian civilians served as watchers in the woods to report, by cellphone, every movement of the Macedonian forces. The UCK is thus able to evade Macedonian traps. "It is like the U.S. Marines trying to fight the Vietnamese – only the Albanians have cellular phones," said Goran Stefanovic, a 36-year-old sergeant in the paramilitary Macedonian Wolves. "We can only try to defend those areas inhabited by a [Slavic] majority."

Morale has been plummeting throughout the front line Macedonian security forces, particularly here in the desperate Tetovo sector. The UCK still roam freely within the city at night and control the high ground during the day. The Macedonians rarely mount vehicle patrols and remain in their heavily sandbagged bunkers. The Macedonian minority population in the Tetovo region have been leaving their homes since the fighting flared up again in July, and it is now estimated that over 30,000 refugees have fled. Since the earlier firefights, the UCK has managed to cut off the main highway several times. Whenever the Tetovo-Skopje highway is declared secure another flood of Macedonians depart in search of refuge.

"The army is unable to protect us and the government seems to have given up on Tetovo," said Sasha Petrovska, a 26-year-old teacher. "Many of us have applied to the Canadian embassy in Skopje for refugee status, but they refuse to accept that anyone is a refugee except Albanians."

For those few non-Albanians who remain in Tetovo, each radio broadcast is eagerly anticipated for news of relief. "The best we can hope for is a quick signing of the peace deal, and that NATO arrives soon," said Ms. Petrovska.

TETOVO – 9 AUGUST 2001 (Thursday afternoon)
By the time I completed my report and filed it, the escalating fighting in Tetovo

was becoming worrisome. Throughout the morning, as the shelling had moved steadily closer, I had been interrupted several times by concerned hotel staff. They wanted to know if I was making plans to leave Tetovo while there was still time. Just before lunch, Friedhelm Peel had arrived to pack up a few things. He was very upset that his superiors in Germany had ordered him to abandon the university project "until calm can be restored." He offered to give me a lift to Skopje and I joked that I would stay where the action was because, unlike him, "I had *cojones*." Peel, with a typically narrow German sense of humor, didn't catch the joke. He protested that he did not wish to leave his post "but he must follow orders."

Around 2:00 p.m., Carl Underwood and his team of OSCE monitors arrived at the Electra for a midday meal. They were the only patrons in the restaurant and I gladly accepted their offer to join them. With classical music playing on the sound system and the heavy thud of artillery fire nearby, lunch seemed surreal.

Underwood boasted that, as an ex-U.S. Special Forces soldier, he had no intention of evacuating Tetovo. He had heard that the UCK was about to launch a big push to capture the city before the peace deal was signed. "I have no doubt in my mind who's going to win this fight," said Underwood. "That's why I rented an apartment in the Albanian sector of town."

His bravado was short-lived. When a heavy machinegun opened fire erupted just a few blocks away he rose from the table and said to his colleagues, "That's it boys. Let's get the hell out of here. From here on in, we can report from the German camp." As their white jeep pulled out of the parking lot, I suddenly realized I was the last foreigner left in Tetovo.

With no way out of the embattled city, I decided I should at least try to take a few pictures. I loaded up my 35 mm camera and headed towards the caserne. By listening to the calibre of the weapons in use, it was possible to follow the forward momentum of the UCK offensive. Throughout the early morning, the Macedonian artillery had been lobbing shells into outlying villages. Heavy machine guns and tank cannons had joined the fray once the UCK vanguard entered the western suburbs. Now, as I headed out from the Electra, the unmistakable chatter of Kalashnikov sub-machineguns could be heard above the din. The UCK had pressed to within 100 meters of the Macedonian *punkt* by the soccer stadium.

The normally congested central marketplace was now completely deserted. As I walked down the empty streets, I began to wonder if there was anyone left in Tetovo at all. From a doorway, where a half-dozen armed Macedonian civilians were huddled, I was challenged by a young man who asked, "*Ko si ti?* (Who are you?)" He seemed satisfied when I yelled back, "*Kanadski novinar.*"

I walked down the middle of the streets, hoping that my camera and "journo-jacket" would be enough to identify me as a non-combatant. The alternative was to creep along seeking cover, in which case I might be mistaken for a UCK by a jumpy conscript. When I was still 200 meters from the caserne, the front gate opened and an armoured personnel carrier came racing out of the compound. I pulled out my camera, hoping to get a picture as it drove by. The turret gunner, who had been aiming his machine gun at the contested high ground, spotted me and frantically traversed his weapon. With the machine gun pointing directly at me, I snapped a photo then hastily held both my arms high. The APC thundered past. The screams of a wounded soldier within could be heard above the roar of its motor.

The caserne's gate had been left wide open and I could not see any guards. When I approached to within 20 meters, a German-speaking sergeant called out to me from a sandbag bunker. "*Bitte kommen sie zuruck, momentan ist nicht so gute zeit* (Please come back, right now is not such a good time)." Inside the caserne, a number of machine guns were pounding back defiantly at the unseen UCK guerrillas. From the occasional *whump*, I assumed that the Macedonians had brought forward some tanks to bolster their defenses. I thought that a photo of a tank in action would make a great illustration, but there was no way I could get inside the compound. Small-arms fire was still intense around the stadium *punkt*, as I cautiously made my way forward to the Macedonian outposts.

I had not gone far when there was a tremendous explosion on the other side of a garden wall. It was so close that the concussion took the air out of my lungs. I ran around the corner expecting to photograph a tank, which I presumed had just fired directly over my head. Instead, I found a smoking crater in the middle of an empty alley. Air was still hissing out of the tires of a nearby jeep and a red Volkswagen Golf had been badly shredded by shrapnel.

It suddenly dawned on me that the *whumps* I was hearing were not Macedonian tanks firing up into the hills, but the UCK's heavy mortars firing down into the caserne.

No longer worried about appearances, I bolted back to the hotel.

During my absence, the last of the Electra's staff had headed home. The waiters had thoughtfully left me the keys and a short note: "See you tomorrow – maybe."

When I went to my room, I realized how genuinely concerned the staff was about my welfare. They had left me a bottle of white wine, two pork chops, some bread and a Kalashnikov rifle. The rifle was a thoughtful gesture, but it posed a bit of a moral dilemma for me. If I was found with a weapon, it would be difficult to invoke any kind of immunity. On the other hand, if I witnessed atrocities against civilians, it would be difficult for me to conscience inaction. I checked the action on the Kalashnikov, counted the spare rounds and locked it in Friedhelm Peel's room.

With keys to the entire hotel, I went into the office to place a telephone call to *Esprit de Corps*. Julie Simoneau, our office manager, had been scheduled to undergo spinal surgery earlier that day and I was anxious to learn of her condition. I also wanted to let one and all know that I was okay, and that I had survived the Grupcin incident. (My bicycle adventure story had run that morning on the *Citizen*'s front page.) As I was talking to senior editor Bill Twatio, who assured me that Julie was recovering well, a tremendous firefight erupted very close to the Electra. Unable to hear each other above the sound of the machine guns, we had to sign off.

In that murderous exchange, six Macedonian policemen were wounded at the *punkt* in the southwest suburbs. Armored personnel carriers were dispatched to the scene, and under the cover of a smoke screen and suppressive machine-gun fire, the Macedonians were able to evacuate them successfully.

Armed civilians from both ethnic camps joined the fray and neighbours were firing at each other all over the city. There were no longer any clear-cut front lines, but it was evident that the Albanians were gaining the upper hand.

As dusk fell, the Macedonian army pressed a relief column of armoured vehicles into the caserne. Hearing APCs rumble past the hotel, I went outside to watch. As I stepped out into the street, an Albanian gunman in the building opposite suddenly opened fire on the Macedonians.

Without slowing down, the APC turret gunners simply began spraying bullets in his general direction. Ricochets thudded into the wall above my head and I quickly retreated back inside. Returning to my room, I finished off the pork and wine the staff had left me, and then slept like a baby.

Tetovo, August 10, 2001 (Friday morning)

The day dawned so quietly that at first I believed the city must have fallen to the UCK. For the first time in a week, there was not even the distant sound of gunfire.

However, the animated discussion among breakfast patrons and the Electra staff who had returned during the night, confirmed that the Macedonians had held. I was informed that the bombardment had ended around 4:00 a.m. A government spokesman in Skopje described the Tetovo battle as a "light skirmish with one policeman wounded." As there had been no Macedonian journalists on hand to witness the fighting, no one challenged his statement.

Those who had remained in the city knew better. The actual number of casualties for the Macedonian security forces was eight dead and 35 wounded. Nobody could even estimate UCK or civilian losses. That morning the citizens of Tetovo felt a great deal of resentment towards their government.

"They sold us out, as part of the peace deal," said one angry resident. "Why didn't they send the helicopters to help our soldiers?"

A good question – and nobody had an answer

As the Macedonians were downplaying the previous day's fighting, the OSCE reported that the battle was still raging. Friedhelm Peel telephoned from Skopje to ask if I was safe.

When I described how quiet it was, he was astounded. "My superiors have just heard from the OSCE that a major counteroffensive is underway, and I've been ordered to remain away from Tetovo," he said. "Are you saying the OSCE report is *wrong*?"

I replied that, in this instance, the OSCE was actually a man named Carl Underwood. He and his team had been tucked away at the German camp throughout the fighting. I repeated that there hadn't been a shot fired in Tetovo in the past six hours. Twenty minutes later, an exasperated Peel called back to say that his bosses were not prepared to accept the word of a journalist over the assessment of a respected international agency.

With people back on the streets, sweeping up shell casings and reopening their market stalls, I took my camera and headed out to see the results of the fighting. The front gate at the caserne was now closed and the mood at the guardhouse was decidedly unreceptive. The stadium *punkt* was still manned, but I didn't get to within 50 meters of it before I heard a machinegun being cocked, and beat a hasty retreat.

On a side street I came across a heavily armed patrol of masked Wolves, which was stopping traffic and searching Albanian vehicles. The Wolves had used an APC to block the intersection and a number of taxi drivers were standing at gunpoint beside their cars. I thought this would make a dramatic photo, but the section commander disagreed. Spotting my camera, he screamed, "*Ne ma photo!*" One of his men whirled towards me, aiming and cocking his weapon in a single motion.

With arms stretched and the camera pointed skyward, I stammered, "*Izvini, Izvini,*" and backed away from the APC. The Wolf kept his rifle aimed directly at my chest until I had turned the corner, some 20 meters up the road.

TETOVO – 10 AUGUST 2001 (Friday afternoon)

From the stadium *punkt* I had seen that a number of houses up the hillside were still smouldering. I believed that these buildings had been targeted by the Macedonian artillery as suspected UCK positions, and went to investigate.

Unlike the city center, there was no one on the streets as I walked up the hill. At first, I heard the cries of children and the sound of radios playing behind the shuttered windows, but as I got closer to the shelled buildings, everything became eerily quiet. The only sound was the crackling of flames coming from blackened ground floor doorways and windows. Although a little spooked by the silence, I took some photographs.

I had just turned to head back into the city when I saw two armed UCK soldiers carrying a heavy box of ammunition into one of the damaged houses, about 30 meters away. Startled by my presence, they lowered the crate and one of them unslung his Kalashnikov and pointed it at me. I was holding my camera to the side and trying to back up to show that I meant no harm. He yelled at me in German to come forward.

Walking slowly towards them, I realized that the cross street at the intersection I was nearing ran straight down the hill to the Macedonian *punkt*. The Albanian warned me to be careful of sniper fire and, as I glimpsed a dead

TOP LEFT: *This passenger bus was another casualty of the August 8 Grupcin ambush. It was attacked in full view of a NATO camp 800 metres beyond. (JAMES PHILLIPS)*

TOP RIGHT: *Macedonian police units in the front lines around Ratae. (SCOTT TAYLOR)*

ABOVE: *Following the UCK summer offensives, the new Albanian-controlled "border" was brazenly marked by flags draped across the Tetovo-Kosovo highway. (JAMES PHILLIPS)*

TOP: *A Macedonian punkt as seen from the Albanian trench lines in southwestern Tetovo.* (*JAMES PHILLIPS*)

ABOVE: *These heavily-shelled houses concealed the UCK bunker complex overlooking the old stadium in Tetovo. Immediately after taking this photo the author was brought inside for questioning.* (*SCOTT TAYLOR*)

body lying in the gutter, I ran across the street at his urging. Several more UCK suddenly appeared, all of them extremely agitated by my presence. An officer explained that it was not possible for me to leave, as I "had seen too much."

I was led down into a bunker. The UCK soldiers stacked their rifles in neat rows by the doorway; hanging above them from hooks was a large collection of U.S.-made night vision goggles.

The size and construction of the bunker amazed me. It looked as if they had tunneled through to link up at least four basements. They had also dug out a secondary, bombproof shelter, complete with sandbags and reinforced beams. There were at least 40 UCK fighters crammed into the first room; some slept in hammocks, as others cleaned weapons or prepared meals. Food and ammunition were piled high in every corner. Everything, from fresh melons to rocket grenades, was stacked in separate, orderly piles.

Leaving me to wait in a small office, the UCK platoon commander called his superiors to report my presence. When he returned he was not at all friendly. I was informed that I would be taken to headquarters, and a mean-looking little guy came forward to escort me there.

Climbing into a battered Yugo, my guard placed his 40 mm grenade launcher in the back seat while the officer gave him instructions. Alone with the guard, I asked him if he spoke any English or German. He responded with a shake of his head, without saying a word.

As we pulled onto the road, he gunned the engine and began swerving. I presumed this was to distract the aim of any Macedonian police sniper, as we were still in range of the *punkt*.

Just beyond a barricade, which was draped with an Albanian flag that marked the "border," we overtook several heavily laden UCK troops who were moving forward towards Tetovo. They spoke briefly to my driver, who then turned abruptly off the main road into a district called Poroj.

We stopped at a house which was, I presumed, a battalion headquarters. In a front room, several high-ranking UCK officers were standing over a map table conducting an operations briefing. I don't speak Albanian, but having been a soldier, I understood from the blast my guard received from the commander that he had messed up in a big way. We backed out of the headquarters and hurried to the car. I figured that, among other things, I wasn't supposed to see that the UCK was using NATO maps to plan its attacks.

We drove at least another five kilometers beyond Tetovo and then wound our way up a steep mountain road to another village, where we stopped outside a large new house with an attached garage. A UCK platoon was lounging in a walled garden and, through the open garage door, I could see an impressive array of rocket launchers and heavy machineguns. Entering through the back door, we removed our shoes, as is customary in Muslim homes. I was escorted to a second-floor bedroom, and my guard locked me inside.

About an hour later four men entered the room and began to question me. One spoke excellent German and translated for the others. "You will be going to Kosovo to explain yourself," I was told. I knew that going to Kosovo would be dangerous, particularly as my identity would then become known to certain key figures in the UCK.

I decided to play stupid and told them that I would love to go to Kosovo, but first I must return to Tetovo to pack my things. After this was translated, I could tell that the brigade commander was convinced he'd snagged a simpleton.

Asked why I had been taking photos of their bunker, I replied that, having witnessed the shelling the day before, I presumed they were all dead. "I didn't think anyone could survive such a barrage," I told them.

The answer obviously appealed to the commander's martial pride and he gave instructions to return me to the Tetovo bunker where I had first been apprehended.

Downstairs, my shoes had disappeared. Looking around, I noticed a soldier, with his back to me, was wearing them. I tapped him on the shoulder and asked for them back. He seemed surprised and said something to his companions as he sheepishly took them off. The German-speaking translator, who was standing beside me, started to laugh and explained, "He said he didn't think you were going to need them anymore."

TETOVO – 11 AUGUST 2001 (Saturday morning)

Sporadic fighting had erupted during the night, but it had only been on exchange of small-arms fire. There had been no artillery or mortar fire, and the rumored Macedonian counterattack never materialized, even though paramilitary forces had been pouring into Tetovo steadily since Friday afternoon.

The kitchen at the Electra was a very busy place. Although the banquet hall was empty, the restaurant had been contracted to provide meals for 535 special forces policemen.

Bending the rules rather than disobeying an order, Herr Peel had returned to check on his abandoned construction site. In Skopje, he had been caught up in the rioting which followed the UCK offensive and further reports of the mistreatment of Macedonian civilians. Several road workers had been captured by the UCK and were severely beaten before being released. Skopje TV stations had then shown graphic footage of mutilated bodies – including images of the initials U-C-K carved into the workers' backs.

Albanian shops and American franchises were once again popular targets. Peel had been on the street when an angry mob closed in on McDonald's. "The crowd quickly lost their nerve when one security guard came out and fired a pistol in the air," he told me. "The Macedonians were anxious to vent their frustration, but nobody was about to get themselves killed."

Although all hell was still threatening to break loose in Macedonia, it was time for me to head home. I accepted a lift to Skopje with Friedhelm.

We packed up our kit – including the bicycle, which we would return to the Albanians in Kondovo when we drove through town – and said goodbye to the Electra staff. While traffic on the highway was light, every car we passed was packed full of grim-faced Macedonian refugees and their belongings.

SKOPJE – 11 AUGUST 2001 (Saturday afternoon)

Since my mid-afternoon arrival back in the capital, there had been a tremendous amount of air activity. Macedonian helicopters were making regular flights to the north, although their destination did not seem to be Tetovo. While I was checking in at the hotel, the clerks told me that land mines had claimed the lives of eight policemen around Kumanovo, and that there was a major offensive underway along the Kosovo border.

The helicopters were obviously providing support to this Macedonian Army operation, which was taking place around Radusa. The young hotel receptionist told me that the peace talks in Ohrid had broken down. European Union and NATO envoys were reportedly flying into Skopje to try and salvage the talks and pressure both parties into an eleventh-hour agreement.

Unable to contact a government spokesman for official comment, I filed a "colour" piece on the worsening crisis.

Macedonia: The last big push before the peace deal (Ottawa Citizen)
SKOPJE, Macedonia – The escalation in fighting over the past few days has threatened to blow apart a shaky peace deal that is still scheduled to be signed. Although Macedonian and Albanian political leaders have reached an agreement, the continued violence is pushing their country closer to a full-scale civil war.

The first priority for NATO and the international community will be to ascertain the revised balance in the military situation following the current fighting. "At a minimum, this will take three to four days and the first troop deployments by NATO would not begin for at least another week," said an OSCE spokesperson in Skopje. "During that period we can expect that extremists in both camps will attempt to improve their positions or settle a final score."

Since last Thursday, the ethnic Albanian guerrilla army (UCK) has been mounting a major offensive to capture Tetovo, forcing the Macedonian security forces to commit more and more troops just to maintain a tenuous foothold in the eastern suburbs. On several occasions, the UCK guerrillas pushed to within 100 meters of the last Macedonian compound, only to be repulsed by tanks and heavy artillery.

In heavily-fortified bunkers overlooking the Tetovo soccer stadium, hundreds of UCK guerrillas are prepared for the final push. Platoon commander 'Snake' Arifaq, a young Kosovar Albanian, expressed pride in the performance of his men during the fighting. "The Macedonian army has fired every weapon in their arsenal at us, but still our positions are intact," he said, brandishing an American-made 40 mm grenade launcher. His fellow soldiers were also well-equipped with an array of sophisticated weapons in preparation for a sustained offensive, and the UCK's well-constructed bunkers were piled high with munitions and food.

As for his men's compliance with the proposed peace deal, Snake was angry about the disarmament terms. "This country is my country, Kosovo is my country, and Albania is my country – that is what we are fighting for!" he exclaimed.

In an effort to achieve a measure of military balance, Macedonian security forces have also been mounting operations in the Tetovo-Kosovo corridor. This area was the scene of heavy fighting in July and, under the terms of a cease-

fire brokered by NATO envoy Peter Feith, the region was to have been demilitarized by both factions. However, since Saturday, the Macedonians have
launched a number of attacks here, aimed at cutting off UCK supplies and
reinforcements. In the town of Radusa – a major staging area for the UCK –
Macedonian troops achieved some initial success, but a sudden counterattack
left them encircled. Just 15 kilometers from Radusa, residents of Skopje witnessed a steady stream of Mi-24 Hind helicopter gunships flying back and
forth from this fierce battle.

In Tetovo itself, during lulls in the UCK's attacks, the Macedonians are
making a determined effort to re-establish some control within the central district. Special Macedonian units – the Wolves and a paramilitary force known
as the Lions – have been making their presence felt. The heavily armed, masked
security troops have been making daylight incursions into the city to conduct
sudden vehicle searches. The presence on Tetovo streets of the ultra-national-
ist Lions has added a frightening new dimension to the burgeoning civil war.
"If the UCK want to use terror to force Macedonians from their homes, then
we shall reciprocate," promised Captain Zelen Chovek. "If the Albanians try
to take Tetovo, we will make them pay a terrible price."

Tens of thousands of Macedonians have already fled their homes in the
Tetovo-Kosovo region, which is now controlled by the UCK. "We can never go
back now," said Julia Josifoska, a 32-year-old nurse from the village of Tearce.
"It will be impossible to live with the Albanians after what has happened."

The refugee crisis in Macedonia has reached epic proportions. Out of a
population of just two million, an estimated 132,000 people have been displaced from their homes. Most of the Macedonians have fled to urban centers
like Skopje, while a large number of Albanians have fled north into Kosovo.

When intense fighting broke out last Thursday, foreign aid workers and
international observers were also evacuated from Tetovo. Since that time it
has been difficult for the agencies to establish a clear picture of what is actually happening.

SKOPJE – 12 AUGUST 2001 (Sunday afternoon)

As I prepared to catch my bus back to Belgrade, the news reports were still
sketchy. Apparently, the Macedonian army had suffered a serious setback during the Radusa operation. Rumour had it that the Macedonian helicopter gun-

ships were only conducting intimidation flights and not firing their weapons. As a result, the UCK had become much bolder. The restrictive rules of engagement for the helicopters were a direct result of European Union and NATO pressure at the Ohrid negotiations. Without the choppers' support, the ground force in Radusa had been compelled to retreat and abandon several armoured vehicles.

Further west, the Macedonians had launched an attack against suspected UCK positions in the village of Ljuboten. The house-to-house sweep had left six Albanians dead and a number of buildings destroyed. Albanian leaders claimed that the Ljuboten raid was simply retaliation against innocent civilians. Allegations of torture and murder were leveled at the Macedonians, and the presence of the UCK in Ljuboten was vehemently denied by the Albanians. Newly appointed Minister of the Interior Ljubomir Boskovski, considered to be a Macedonian hard-liner, was personally accused of launching the attack.

When the U.S.-based Human Rights Watch issued an indictment of Boskovski and his police force, the minister was quick to denounce his accusers. Labeling Human Rights Watch as "an international mercenary organization," Boskovski said, "They accuse me of being present [in Ljuboten] and watching when civilians were murdered. That is a monstrous accusation."

The reassuring news, as far as I was concerned, was that there had been little fighting in the Kumanovo district and that the border with Yugoslavia remained open.

BELGRADE – 13-16 AUGUST 2001 (Monday to Thursday)

I arrived in Belgrade on Monday morning in time to hear news of the Ohrid peace plan. At the last possible moment, the Macedonian parliament had made concessions and the agreement was signed. The international media then focused on the deployment of NATO peacekeepers. I was disappointed that such complex issues were being condensed into a few simple sentences, and that the pundits' optimistic predictions did not reflect the situation on the ground.

On August 16, just three days after peace had been declared, Corporal Sasha Sokolov was gunned down near Tetovo's stadium *punkt*. The 27-year-old policeman was a member of an elite tactical squad. Sokolov and his partner had stopped an Albanian car at the checkpoint, but when both of the occupants bolted rather than produce identification cards, Sokolov immediately gave chase. A trained sniper, the Macedonian policeman could have shot the fleeing Albanians. But as they were unarmed, he instead followed the pair into a nearby house, where a trap was sprung. At point blank range, a third Albanian opened fire with a Kalashnikov, killing Sokolov instantly.

A veteran of the earlier fighting in Kumanovo and Aracinovo, Sasha Sokolov had, until recently, been at home in Skopje, on leave before being recalled to active duty after his comrades were killed at the ambush in Grupcin. Sokolov had been one of the reinforcements brought in to stabilize the Macedonian lines during the UCK offensive against Tetovo on the night of August 9. With so many of his friends killed or wounded in action, Sasha had been angered at the Macedonian government's decision to sign the peace deal. In particular, the idea of granting immunity to the UCK guerrillas did not sit well with him. When news first broke about the Ohrid agreement, he had telephoned his mother to express his bitterness.

"So many of our young men believed they were protecting Macedonia, and now our government is treating their killers like heroes," he had complained to her. "How can murderers not be brought to justice?"

Now his grieving family is left to ask the same question.

Before starting out for the Belgrade airport, I wrote and filed my next "On Target" for the *Halifax Herald*. As I predicted, Canada was now officially involved in this latest round of Balkan violence.

Macedonia: West was no help to beleaguered government (Halifax Herald)
SKOPJE, Macedonia – On August 13, international envoys and government officials in Macedonia hammered out a last-minute peace accord. However, this eleventh-hour attempt to avoid yet another Balkan civil war may yet prove to be a case of too little, too late as the fighting here continues to escalate. Under the terms of the agreement, once a cease-fire can be established, a NATO force of some 3000 peacekeepers, including up to 200 Canadian soldiers, will be deployed into Macedonia. The major task of these NATO troops will be the disarming of the ethnic Albanian guerrillas (UCK) who have successfully established control over nearly 30 per cent of Macedonia's territory. For the battered Macedonian security forces that have fought the UCK over the past six months, the arrival of the NATO force will be a bitter pill to swallow.

"If NATO hadn't been arming and equipping the UCK in Kosovo, there would be no need for them to disarm these guerrillas now in Macedonia," said Goran Stefanovic, a sergeant with the elite Macedonian police unit, the Wolves.

At the diplomatic level, the provision of military aid to the UCK has been vehemently denied, but on the ground in Macedonia, there is no ignoring the massive amount of materiel and expertise supplied by NATO to the guerrillas.

The U.S. also frequently uses their tactical helicopters to gather intelligence inside Macedonia, without authorization from the Macedonian government. The sight of the U.S. choppers prompts ethnic Albanian villagers to cheer wildly, waving their arms to encourage "their air force."

The prevailing Albanian attitude toward NATO is tangibly displayed at the UCK brigade headquarters, just outside Tetovo. Here the security platoon wear T-shirts emblazoned with a Nike logo and the phrase, "NATO Air – Just do it!"

On the other side of this conflict, the woefully-equipped Macedonians have been hard-pressed to field a credible fighting force. Over the past six months, however, there has been a steady infusion of modern weaponry (and mercenary advisors) into Macedonia, with most of this international support coming from the Ukraine.

At the height of last week's fighting, both George Robertson and Javier Solana made personal entreaties to the Ukraine to cut off military aid. Given such interference, it is little wonder that the Macedonian majority has staged violent anti-NATO riots, attacking embassies and McDonald's restaurants.

In the past, Canadian soldiers serving as peacekeepers in the Balkans have won a reputation from all factions for their fairness and impartiality. However, after the 1999 bombing campaign against Yugoslavia and now through NATO's provision of illicit aid to the UCK, trust is steadily being eroded. When, or if, Canadian troops deploy into war-torn Macedonia, it will no doubt dishearten them to learn that the death and destruction which they encounter was aided and abetted by their own government.

ABOVE: *As the fighting continued, the front line Macedonian army and police units were better trained and equipped. By mid-August helmets and body armour had been issued to most of their combat troops. (SCOTT TAYLOR)*

TOP LEFT: *After the Ohrid peace agreement was signed, many Macedonian refugees returned to their villages – only to find that their homes had been destroyed by UCK guerrillas.* (JAMES PHILLIPS)

TOP RIGHT: *As NATO peacekeepers deployed into Macedonia, this Orthodox church in Lesok was destroyed by retreating UCK forces.* (JAMES PHILLIPS)

ABOVE: *Abandoned UCK trenches in southern Tetovo.* (JAMES PHILLIPS)

OPPOSITE PAGE: *Canadian armoured vehicles deploy into Skopje as part of the NATO intervention force* Essential Harvest. (SCOTT TAYLOR)

chapter six:
ESSENTIAL HARVEST

SKOPJE – 27 SEPTEMBER 2001 (Thursday afternoon)

The August deployment of NATO peacekeepers had briefly focused international media attention on this latest Balkan crisis until the terror attacks of September 11 blew everything else onto the back pages. Even with a sizeable Canadian contingent participating in *Operation Essential Harvest*, there had been little coverage in Canada. With their 30-day mission just concluded, I was hoping to interview some of the troops before they left Skopje. As their home base is Canadian Forces Base Petawawa, located about 200 kilometres from Ottawa, a story would have enough local interest to run in the *Ottawa Citizen*.

In addition to covering Canada's NATO contribution, I intended to conduct a series of interviews for "Situation Report," a weekly show about international military affairs and conflict analysis I host on E-press, a web-based news site. A technophobe, I was a bit leary about taking their expensive digital camera into the field for the first time, particularly as all the segments to date had been taped in an Ottawa studio by E-press technicians.

Another cause for concern was an e-mail I had received a few days earlier from Blerim Jakupi, the guide in Slatina who had introduced me to the UCK commanders. He informed me that the Albanians were not pleased with my reports and had singled out an E-press interview that I had done with James Bissett, Canada's former ambassador to Yugoslavia. "If Albanians could see this they would be very disappointed – really!" Jakupi wrote. "First, Bissett knows nothing about the Albanian question, or maybe he knows everything but he is afraid to offend his Slav friends? The other thing is that... I think Bissett is sick mentally and should visit an institution..."

His e-mail's last line contained a thinly veiled threat: "Take care and say hello to your family from me and, if you come to Macedonia again, I'd like you to stop by my village." I had never mentioned my wife and son to Jakupi.

Although I had made arrangements through Trajan Tregovski, a Toronto acquaintance, to stay with his in-laws in a village near Skopje, as a precautionary measure I decided not to advertise my whereabouts by registering at a hotel. Vlatko Kocev, Trajan's 22-year-old nephew, had offered to translate and drive me around during my visit.

Vlatko and his girlfriend were waiting for me outside the baggage claim exit at the airport. Although we had never met, I couldn't miss them: they were holding up an oversized photo of me. After introducing ourselves, I explained to Vlatko that I had very little time and that I wanted to file the Halifax column I had written on the plane, register my press accreditation with both the Foreign Ministry and NATO, and talk to the Canadian troops, all by the end of the day. Vlatko replied that all of that must wait because his grandparents had prepared a special lunch for me.

I had been in the Balkans often enough to know that I couldn't win this exchange. On the way to lunch we stopped at the Kocev family's tire shop, from where I faxed my story to Canada.

NATO playing favourites in treatment of indicted war criminal (Halifax Herald)

SKOPJE, Macedonia – With some 200 Canadian troops now on the ground in Macedonia (as part of NATO's latest intervention force), it's time somebody started seriously questioning Canada's long-range Balkan policy. Throughout the domino decade of bloody civil wars that accompanied the disintegration of Yugoslavia, Canadian soldiers have been on continuous deployment to the region: originally serving as UN peacekeepers, this designation would later be changed to NATO peacemakers, and by the time of the Kosovo crisis, Canada's military would become a belligerent in this complex conflict. Despite our changing role, one constant has been that the reality experienced by our front line soldiers is rarely reflected in Western (i.e.: U.S. State Department-inspired) media reports on the ongoing Yugoslavian tragedy.

The most vivid example of this occurred during NATO's 78-day air campaign against Yugoslavia in 1999. As cockney spokesman Jamie Shea took to the airwaves to demonize the Serbian people and justify NATO's attacks, respected officers such as Major General Lewis MacKenzie and Colonel Don Ethell spoke out publicly to denounce Canada's participation in the bombing. Having witnessed first-hand the multi-factional hatred and violence that pervade the Balkans, Canadian soldiers are unwilling to assign blame or take sides in this brutal civil war. However, driven by U.S. interests and a jingoistic media, NATO leaders have not been so hesitant to play favorites.

This current crisis in Macedonia began last March when Albanian guerrillas staged attacks from inside NATO-occupied Kosovo. The weapons carried by the Albanians were the same ones NATO was to have collected from the Kosovo Liberation Army (known as the UCK) back in 1999. Over the past two years, with a powerful occupation force which numbered upwards of 40,000 personnel, NATO has been unwilling or unable to disarm the UCK. Only when the fighting spread into Macedonia, and the UCK seized 30 per cent of its territory, did NATO decide to intervene.

The Canadian combat group, which had been hastily dispatched from service in *Operation Palladium* in Bosnia to participate in the Macedonia mission, is equipped with new Coyote reconnaissance vehicles. These state of the art armoured personnel carriers have been praised by NATO spokesmen for "providing a vital asset in monitoring the flow of illegal arms across the Macedonia-Kosovo border."

Disgruntled Macedonian citizens are quite correct in asking why, if such a surveillance capability existed within NATO's arsenal, wasn't it employed to *prevent* the Albanians from entering Macedonia in the first place?

NATO could also be questioned as to why it was reluctant to arrest the UCK's military figurehead, General Agim Ceku, an indicted war criminal. Many Canadian peacekeepers had witnessed the atrocities committed by Ceku's troops in Croatia in 1993 and 1994 and it was largely on the strength of their testimony that The Hague Tribunal issued a sealed indictment.

Agim Ceku, an Albanian Kosovar by birth, began his military career as an officer in the federal Yugoslav National Army (JNA), but switched loyalties to the Croatian independence movement when Yugoslavia began to break up in 1991. In 1993, as a colonel in the Croatian army, he commanded the notorious operations in the Medak Pocket.

It was here that the men of the Second Battalion, Princess Patricia's Canadian Light Infantry came face to face with the savagery which Ceku was capable of, when over 200 Serbian inhabitants in the Pocket were slaughtered, some of them burned alive. The traumatized troops buried the grisly remains and were encouraged to collect all possible evidence "in order to bring the perpetrators to justice."

In 1995, Ceku, by then a general, was still at large and was responsible for shelling Serbian refugee columns and targeting the UN "safe" city of Knin during the Croatian offensive known as *Operation Storm*.

A few months after the *Storm* atrocities, Canada's own Louise Arbour began making a name for herself as the chief prosecutor for The Hague War Crimes Tribunal. Dismissing the evidence of Canadian troops, she and her lawyers chose to pursue more politically prominent suspects, and nothing was done to bring Ceku to justice.

In January 1999, the world's attention shifted to war-ravaged Kosovo. With the blessing of the U.S. State Department, Agim Ceku took his retirement (at age 37) from the Croatian army and was appointed supreme commander of the Kosovo Liberation Army (UCK).

During the air campaign against Yugoslavia, Ceku was portrayed as a loyal ally and was frequently present at NATO briefings with top generals such as Wesley Clark and Michael Jackson.

Under the terms of the 1999 Kosovo peace agreement, Ceku's Albanian guerrillas were to be disarmed and re-constituted into a UN-sponsored (non-military) disaster relief organization known as the Kosovo Protection Corps (KPC). However, as recent events have shown, Ceku's men gave up neither their weapons nor their quest for a Greater Albania.

Although maintaining an arm's length posture towards his former comrades, Agim Ceku is worshipped as a saviour by both the UCK guerrillas and the Albanian minority in Macedonia.

As this indicted war criminal continues to enjoy his freedom, bask in public acclaim, and collect a UN paycheque, Canadian soldiers are risking their lives to disarm his UCK force in Macedonia.

All in the name of peace and justice.

SKOPJE – 28 SEPTEMBER 2001 (Friday morning)

My hosts, Vladimir and Setka Kocevski, were a wonderful couple in their mid-seventies. Although they spoke no English, we quickly found a way to communicate. If I acknowledged that I was *gladden* (hungry), Setka would feed me. If I said that I was *sit* (full), she pretended not to understand and kept the food coming. Vladimir had a similar comprehension problem on the subject of *rakija* (brandy). "*Da mollim* (Yes please)," meant a tall glass full, while "*Ne hvala* (No thanks)," produced a small shot. An emphatic "*Absolut ne ma, ja radim* (Absolutely not, I'm working)," would send him looking for a bottle of wine.

Their village was a 20-minute drive from central Skopje. Vlatko had recruited his friend Tomce to drive. Tomce was a personable little guy who spoke no English, but immediately took it upon himself to point out the subtle differences between Macedonian and Serbian vulgarities. Under the guise of teaching me, he proceeded to comment on the attributes of every female we passed.

Our first stop was at the Macedonian Foreign Ministry, and this time almost everything had been organized for me in advance. Maja Apostolova in the America's Office had contacted a number of key politicians and academics who agreed to be interviewed.

I realized how flexible my schedule would have to be when Maja put down the telephone and told me that Stefan Pendarovski "will see you right now." Pendarovski had been a spokesman for the Macedonian Defense Minister, but was currently a special advisor on matters of national security to President Boris Trjkovski. As such, he was a great source, but I wished that I'd had more time to prepare not only my questions, but also my camera equipment.

While I was interviewing Pendarovski, Tomce was to locate the Canadian camp. As some of the NATO contingents had already left, I had feared that I would arrive only to find it empty. To my relief, the converted warehouse that served as their operating base was still full of Canadian soldiers preparing for the long trip home. I was detained at the front gate for nearly an hour while a nervous public affairs officer obtained clearance from National Defence Headquarters in Ottawa.

Once this hurdle was overcome, Major Roger Cotton, the commanding officer of the Battle Group, proved to be very open and hospitable. I was given direct access to the soldiers who had taken part in all aspects of *Operation Essential Harvest*. Their candid comments were a stark contrast to NATO's spin on the just-concluded mission.

Macedonia still on the brink of civil war (Ottawa Citizen)

SKOPJE, Macedonia – Canadian soldiers directly involved in disarming Albanian guerrillas report that the weapons which they collected were in fact "useless junk." Under the terms of the mid-August peace initiatives, the recently formed National Liberation Army (UCK) was to voluntarily disband and surrender their arms to NATO troops. In exchange, the Macedonian government was to amend its constitution to grant the Albanian minority increased rights and freedoms. At the September 26 deadline, NATO Secretary-General George Robertson declared the mission a success despite the facts that the proposed constitutional amendments seem unlikely to receive parliamentary approval and that the UCK's front line weaponry remains unaccounted for.

"Of the hundreds of weapons which we collected from the UCK headquarters in Sipkovica, I don't believe a single one was serviceable," reported Private Thomasz Plocica. "The oldest rifle dated back to 1849." Plocica is a member of 8 Platoon, Royal Canadian Regiment which assisted British Ghurkas on the September 21 Sipkovica operation.

The official NATO claim is that a total of 3875 weapons were collected from the UCK during the three phases of *Operation Essential Harvest*. According to Private Plocica these figures include "rifles which were held together with coat hangers and machine guns so rusted that they could not be transported safely, so they had to be blown up in location." Of the 397,625 land mines, rounds of ammunition and explosive devices claimed to have been collected by NATO, "not a single bullet was evident at the Sipkovica site."

To declare the mission a success, NATO would have to look at the situation in the narrowest possible military terms. As outlined in the peace agreement, NATO was to have collected 3500 weapons from the UCK. The records show that 3875 guns and rifles were voluntarily surrendered. Despite the impressive numbers, no one involved in *Essential Harvest* actually believes that the UCK in Macedonia has been disarmed.

At the height of the fighting, European Union monitors estimated the UCK's strength at approximately 7000 to 8000 troops with an arsenal of about 20,000 modern weapons, ranging from side arms to large-calibre mortars.

At a September 27 press conference, Ali Ahmeti, the head of UCK in Macedonia, announced that his forces were officially disbanded. He noted that any future violations of the cease-fire would therefore have to be blamed on the newly-formed Albanian National Army (ANA).

The Albanians are not the only ones who appear to be fully prepared to resume the factional fighting which has flared up repeatedly since last February. Macedonian nationalist hard-liners have also organized a number of paramilitary units, which operate outside the government's control.

On September 15, Canadian soldiers witnessed a large-scale violation of the cease-fire in the heavily contested Tetovo valley. "The Macedonians launched a series of rocket-propelled grenades at the Albanian-held village of Semsovo," reported Warrant Officer John Barr. Barr's men and other detachments of the Royal Canadian Dragoons that were stationed in observation posts around Tetovo were able to pinpoint the perpetrators. British SAS teams, acting on this intelligence, entered the village of Ratae and discovered that it contained an impressive array of arms.

"The Macedonians had so many of these powerful RPGs that they were using them in order to conserve their rifle ammunition," said Barr.

The Macedonian government initially disputed the NATO report, but the evidence produced by the Canadians forced it to concede that violations had been committed. As a result, the paramilitary Lions, which had garrisoned Ratae, were replaced with regular Macedonian army units. This action earned the Canadian Battle Group, and in particular their Coyote reconnaissance vehicles, high praise from NATO officials.

For the most part, though, the mountainous terrain of northern Macedonia proved to be a tough challenge for the Coyote's array of sophisticated surveillance equipment. "Because we use a line-of-sight radar, we can't see over hills, and the heavy woods also prevented us from tracking much of the [UCK] activity," said Sergeant Thomas Livingston. "All in all, our Coyotes were not as effective as we had hoped."

Defence Minister Art Eggleton has frequently suggested that the Coyotes are one of the military assets that Canada could provide to the U.S. in the war against terrorism. "Obviously our Minister is either unfamiliar with the Coyote's capabilities, or he hasn't looked at a topographical map of Afghanistan," said one trooper, on the condition of anonymity.

Major Roger Cotton, the officer commanding A Squadron, Royal Canadian Dragoons, denounced earlier reports that the Canadians' high tech Coyotes had been a specifically requested NATO asset for the Macedonian mission. "When we first arrived here [from duties in Bosnia], the Squadron was assigned convoy escort duties," said Cotton. "It took several days of advertising our capabilities [to NATO superiors] before we were assigned an appropriate reconnaissance role."

The September 11 terrorist attacks against America also had a direct and dramatic impact on the Canadian Battle Group in Macedonia. After the attacks on the World Trade Center and the Pentagon, Major Cotton demanded – and received – a satellite TV from NATO headquarters. "It was important for the troops to follow this event closely, as it developed," said Cotton. "It affected everyone deeply and we also needed to know if the incident would impact on us operationally." Throughout the tour, the Canadians spent most of their time on observation duty inside the Albanian-controlled sectors. As no one could predict what the reaction to the attacks would be among the Muslim UCK guerrillas, "the entire force went to an increased state of readiness," recalled Major Cotton.

The 200 Canadian soldiers who took part in *Operation Essential Harvest* left their camp in Skopje last Saturday and are expected back at CFB Petawawa (via Bosnia) sometime this week. Replacing the original 3500 NATO troops, which deployed to Macedonia last month, will be a reduced force of 700, code-named Task Force Fox. Many of the British units, including a large contingent of SAS commandos, have already left the Balkans for the Persian Gulf and Afghanistan.

Canada will leave one officer behind in Skopje – a public affairs spokesman – but no decision has yet been made on further participation in Macedonia. "I believe there *may* be a few staff officers sent over, but right now nobody knows for sure," said Major Chris Lemay.

Under Task Force Fox, NATO's new mandate is not to enforce peace, but simply to protect international observers. The proposed three-month timetable seems to indicate that even NATO officials doubt the limited success of

Essential Harvest.

In essence, the 700 troops committed to this mission will simply provide an extraction force to rescue civilian European Union monitors in the event that fighting resumes.

With the proposed constitutional changes unlikely to receive parliamentary approval and with both factions still well-armed, it seems that Macedonia is slipping towards an all-out war. For Canada's part, our over-stretched military, which had to rob troops from Bosnia in order to ante up for *Essential Harvest*, will not be a major player in the new peace process.

TETOVO – 1 OCTOBER 2001 (Monday evening)

Yesterday, I had taken advantage of a quiet afternoon to rest and catch up on my writing. The weather was unseasonably warm, and the Kocevski family had gathered for a feast. After too much wine and food at last night's festivities, I set up some interviews for later in the week and caught a bus to Tetovo.

Although I had not planned to stay overnight, my old friends at the Electra talked me into it. Friedhelm Peel was still there and explained that, even with NATO troops on the streets, the city remained tense. Many of the Macedonians who had fled the fighting had returned to the region – much to the resentment of the Albanians. The Macedonian police *punkts* were still fired upon regularly by elements of the officially disbanded UCK.

Goran, the paramilitary Wolf I had met last May, had heard of my arrival and was very keen to assist me. There had been some fighting in Ratae that evening, and Goran confirmed that the Lions had returned after the NATO mission had ended. Being a close friend of the Lions' commander, Goran thought he could arrange a meeting for me. The Macedonian enclave of Ratae was virtually cut off by the Albanians, but during daylight hours it was considered safe enough to visit.

RATAE – 2 OCTOBER 2001 (Tuesday afternoon)

It took Goran some time to convince Rade, the Lion commander, to allow me into Ratae. We met at an outdoor café in Tetovo, with Rade and his bodyguards wearing civilian clothes.

The Lions were suspicious of Western journalists and Rade was reluctant to grant my request. But Goran persisted, a taxi was called for me and a compromise was reached whereby I could not meet with, or report on, the presence of the Lions, however I could interview the regular Macedonian security forces stationed there.

My Ratae contact was Captain Marjan Ugrev, the 24-year-old acting battalion commander of the elite unit, the Scorpions. Ugrev's heavy armoured vehicles were dug into sandbagged embrasures all around Ratae – turning the village into an armed camp. In addition to the Scorpions, the Macedonian police had a number of tactical squads reinforcing the garrison. Although I wasn't supposed to notice, the Lions were also very active in Ratae.

Ugrev was surprisingly open about the strength of his forces and their disposition. During our conversation, two Landrovers adorned with machine-guns roared up like something out of the old television series "Desert Rats." A British Special Air Services (SAS) officer hopped out of one of the vehicles and immediately ordered a hitherto relaxed Ugrev, who had met me wearing a uniform shirt and gym shorts, into the café. Humiliated, Ugrev apologized to me and slowly made his way inside.

I took this opportunity to snap pictures of the other SAS troopers. The extremely photo-shy commandos assumed that I was a Macedonian and began exchanging derogatory comments about me among themselves. When I identified myself as a Canadian, they asked, "What are you doing mixed up with this lot? Shouldn't you be on the other side of the lines?" I made a vague reply about seeing both sides, and the need to remain objective.

Although they had only been in Macedonia for a month, they were anxious to "get out of this shit-hole and get off to the real war in Afghanistan." Many of their mates had already left for Pakistan directly from Skopje, and they were eager to turn over their responsibilities here to incoming German troops and join the rest of their unit.

Walking around Ratae's outer defenses, I was disappointed that my photography had been restricted to generic landscapes. Although I was allowed to enter the bunkers, I could not take photographs or video the soldiers or their weapons. At one bunker, I was debating whether or not to take a chance and film a short segment when a sentry shouted "UCK!" A solitary figure appeared in a clearing approximately 500 meters away, then disappeared before the police could open fire.

A sergeant shouted orders and a section of men scrambled to lock-and-load their weapons and don helmets. They fanned out from the bunker to conduct a search and sweep of the area where the UCK guerrilla had been spotted.

I grabbed my video camera and followed them. We covered about 400 meters of open ground – expecting at any moment to come under fire. It wasn't until the Macedonians reached the cover of a railway embankment that the sergeant noticed me. For a brief moment, I thought he was going to kill me. Fortunately, he calmed down after the operation had ended without their locating the Albanian; he and his men were also eager to see themselves in action. Back at the bunker, I drained my batteries replaying footage through the video monitor. The sergeant laughed uproariously when he saw himself point his gun at me and the film went out of focus as I dove to the ground.

SKOPJE – 3 OCTOBER 2001 (Wednesday afternoon)

I returned to Skopje for a meeting with Vladimir Buchkovski, the Macedonian Defense minister. Regarded as pro-appeasement, Buchkovski was one of the few Macedonian politicians who was well-thought-of by the ethnic Albanian minority. Given his portfolio, many Macedonians, including soldiers, were suspicious of him and his popularity with "the enemy." Although not a military man, he questioned the tactics of his predecessor, and suggested that the operation at Aracinovo had been "heavy-handed, in that armour and artillery were used."

Young Vlatko had offered to work the video camera and had quietly kept his counsel during the interview. However, as soon as we left Buchkovski's office, he gave vent to his frustrations. "It is because of pacifists like him that we are losing this war," he complained.

We drove directly to a press conference held by Ljubce Boskovski, the Macedonian Minister of the Interior. As director of police forces, Boskovski's portfolio overlapped the Defense minister's responsibility in the countering of UCK terrorists.

Unlike Buchkovski, he believed in taking a strong stand against the Albanian extremists and was quite popular with hard-line Macedonians. Boskovski announced that elite police units were going to start re-entering villages formerly controlled by the UCK. It was a significant statement, as it ran counter to the directives being issued by NATO officials. (Vlatko was immediately impressed by the tough-talking Boskovski.)

Foreign media had not attended Boskovski's press conference, nor had NATO been informed of the change in Macedonian tactics. At the press center, I heard a NATO public affairs officer screaming on the telephone, "Who the fuck does Boskovski think he is?"

Macedonians to mount major security operation (Halifax Herald)
SKOPJE, Macedonia – Just one week after NATO completed its initial 30-day intervention mission in Ratae the Macedonian Minister of the Interior announced plans to mount a major security sweep of the territory previously controlled by Albanian (UCK) guerrillas. Macedonian helicopter gunships were airborne for the first time since the Ohrid peace agreement was signed in mid-August. Columns of Macedonian police armoured vehicles and truckloads of combat-ready infantry also began making a show of force, apparently intended to test the UCK's commitment to disband their military forces.

Under the terms of the Ohrid cease-fire, NATO deployed troops into the disputed regions of Macedonia to collect weapons, which were to be surrendered voluntarily by the UCK.

However, at the conclusion of NATO's *Essential Harvest* operation, the warring factions in this tiny republic remain poised to resume their bitter conflict. The UCK's front line weapons remain unsurrendered and intact, and their units have been reformed under the new name of the Albanian National Army (ANA).

Macedonian security forces appeared anxious to either provoke an armed clash or force the guerrillas into hiding. At an October 3 press conference Ljubomir Boskovski, the Macedonian Minister of the Interior, decreed that his police forces "will begin to re-establish control over Albanian-minority villages."

Although the UCK checkpoints are presently unmanned, Albanian flags still fly defiantly along the demilitarized zone. With sporadic fighting a daily occurrence, no one can predict what response Minister Boskovski's aggressive new policy will get from the Albanians.

With their force presently in the middle of both a personnel rotation and mandate shift, NATO officials were caught unaware by this sudden, large-scale Macedonian operation. The troops from *Essential Harvest* have already begun to leave the region, and the incoming force – Task Force *Fox* – has yet to become fully operational.

Boskovski stated that the security sweep will be conducted primarily by elite police counter terrorist units and tactical border guard units. The Macedonian army, under the jurisdiction of Defense Minister Vladimir Buchkovski, will provide only logistical support. Should the fighting escalate, the Defense minister made it clear that his forces are better prepared now to deal with the Albanian guerrillas.

"We have made a strenuous effort to transform the army, particularly in the arming and equipping of counter-terrorist units," said Buchkovski. "We have set ourselves a December deadline to be able to defend Macedonia's borders."

During the relative respite created by NATO's presence, the Macedonian military has purchased 31 modern T-72 tanks and upgraded much of their obsolete hardware.

In addition, private funds, primarily donated by Macedonian nationalists living abroad, have equipped a number of paramilitary units.

In the still-surrounded northern enclave of Ratae, Macedonian army units serve alongside the Lions. "These paramilitaries are not under my control, but we welcome their assistance," said Captain Marjan Ugrev, battalion commander of the army's Scorpion commandos.

Foreign observers fear that hard-line nationalist units, like the Lions, may soon return to the Albanian-controlled regions in support of the current Macedonian security offensive.

"With nearly 15,000 Albanian weapons still unaccounted for and the Macedonians seeking revenge, it is a volatile situation," said one OSCE monitor.

SKOPJE – 4 OCTOBER 2001 (Thursday morning)

It was not until late last evening that Vlatko had been able to determine from where Boskovski planned to launch his police sweep. He had been informed that a media pool would accompany a police column into the Albanian village of Grusinci at around 9:00 a.m. This village was close to Skopje, just above Aracinovo, and had remained under UCK control since the July offensives. As I had previously arranged to meet Petar Goshev, a prominent Macedonian politician, we decided to head for Grusinci on our own. It was well after 10:00

a.m. before we finished taping the Goshev interview and were able to set off.

We had seen columns of troops moving out of Skopje all morning while helicopter gunships flew above the city. Unable to cover everything at once, I had teamed up with James Phillips, an American photojournalist based in Skopje. The 54-year-old Phillips had covered the Kosovo crisis and fallen in love with Macedonia. When the current crisis developed, he rented an apartment in the old part of the city and began to pump out information on his Web site (www.warREPORTS.com). Without official notice of the Macedonian police's intentions, Phillips headed off towards the Tetovo sector while I checked out the situation in Grusinci.

Vlatko had persuaded Tomce to drive us. We sped through Aracinovo and arrived at the Macedonian police bunker at the Grusinci turnoff shortly before noon. The police asked us why the media was heading through this sector, as several reporters and television crews had passed through at 9:00 a.m., as planned.

We drove the remaining two kilometers into Grusinci expecting to find a horde of journalists recording the triumphant return of the Macedonian police forces. What we found instead was an empty Albanian village. Although the streets were deserted, our progress was closely followed from behind shuttered windows. Everywhere, the Albanian eagle and the letters UCK had been spray-painted on walls. When we stopped, a pair of Albanians immediately stepped out of a house to ask us who we were. I told them that we were a Canadian TV crew, and Vlatko and Tomce nodded their heads vigorously in agreement. One of the Albanians asked, "Where are the Macedonians? Where is the media?" Apparently there had been a last-minute change in plans, and the Macedonians had not come to Grusinci after all. Realizing that we were alone and not the vanguard of a larger convoy, more and more Albanian men began to emerge from their homes. Vlatko and Tomce were terrified that they would be identified as Macedonians. I continued to speak in English while Vlatko and Tomce chain-smoked and pretended to understand.

I asked the headman how they had learned that the police intended to reoccupy the village. "We were notified this morning when a British SAS patrol came to warn the UCK," he replied. "You mean there are UCK in Grusinci?" I asked. "Can we speak to them?"

Vlatko's eyes almost popped out of his head. He was visibly relieved when the headman said, "Not in the village; the UCK have a camp in the hills where the SAS met with them." It was interesting to learn that the British were aware of secret hideouts for a guerrilla force they were publicly claiming to have disarmed.

We shot some background video footage of kids playing in the streets and then casually packed up and left Grusinci. We had barely cleared the village when Tomce suddenly went berserk, screaming something to the effect that I had almost gotten us all killed.

He had just calmed down when I received a call on my cellphone from Phillips. He told me that he had spent the morning chasing Macedonian army trucks, and that a major operation had not been mounted in the Tetovo corridor. It appeared that NATO or the EU had been able to exert enough pressure to force Boskovski to back off.

From Grusinci, we drove to the Macedonian police's training depot near the Skopje airport. As part of the Ohrid peace plan, 500 ethnic Albanian police were to be recruited and trained by NATO instructors. The plan was contentious and had caused quite a bit of resentment in the ranks of the Macedonian police. I had been advised by media contacts that permission to visit the NATO training site could only be granted by the U.S. ambassador and that, until now, no one had been allowed in.

Rather than waste time going through official channels, I decided to drive straight through and hope for the best. At the front gate, I was surprised when a lanky Albanian recruit stepped forward and lifted the barrier without asking for identification. Vlatko and I got out of the car and walked into the training compound unchallenged.

Outside the headquarters building, a half-dozen portly American police instructors were sitting on the front steps drinking cans of Budweiser. When I held up my NATO press card and explained why I was there, they angrily ordered me off the premises, and summoned the Albanian recruit at the gate who admitted he had mistaken me for an American instructor. While Vlatko tried to clear up the confusion about our entry, I kept the Americans talking.

And talk they did when I mentioned the September 11 terrorist attacks. One hefty cop who hailed from Brooklyn said, "American blood might be red, but our hearts are Red, White and Blue – put that in your paper." I thought this was 'over-the-top' patriotism, but dutifully scribbled it down.

I was able to learn that the whole Albanian training program was being run by the Americans. This group of instructors was originally based in Kosovo, where they had been recycling UCK guerrillas into the UN-sponsored Kosovo Police Force (KPF). They acknowledged that many of the current Albanian recruits in the Macedonian training program were former UCK. "That's why people like your *boy* here don't like us much," the Brooklyn cop said, pointing at Vlatko, who bristled but offered no response. I told them that I would contact the U.S. embassy and be back as soon as I had official clearance. Truth was, I couldn't be bothered.

* * * * * * * * * *

SKOPJE – 19 NOVEMBER 2001 (MONDAY EVENING)
This was my first stop on yet another whirlwind Balkan tour.

After leaving Macedonia in October, I had spent Thanksgiving in Belgrade before heading home. My stay in Canada was brief – less than four weeks – before I returned to Yugoslavia. A Serbian edition of *Inat* had just been published in Belgrade and I would promoting that book while researching this one. I also intended to cover the November 17 Kosovo elections for the *Ottawa Citizen*. However, the U.S.'s war on terror was well underway and the media remained focused on Afghanistan. Without any surprise results or violence at the polling stations, I hadn't bothered to file a story on Kosovo.

I had kept in contact with James Phillips through e-mails, and had arranged to stay with him. Not only was his apartment more central than the Kocevski's village home, but as a journalist, Phillips himself could provide me with a steady stream of information.

It was a cold, blustery night and a snowfall had delayed the arrival of the Belgrade bus by nearly 30 minutes. James Phillips and his driver were waiting for me at the bus station. Balkan priorities being what they are, pleasure preceded business and we headed out for an evening of dining and drinking at the *Dva Jelena* (Two Deer) restaurant. Mickey, James' driver, ordered a bottle of mastika, the traditional Macedonian liqueur. I had never tried mastika before. It turned out to be one hell of an introduction.

TETOVO – 21 NOVEMBER 2001 (Wednesday morning)
Tuesday had pretty much been a write-off. I awoke with a monumental hango-

ver that I wasn't able to shake until evening when the Kocevski family invited me to dinner. As usual, hospitality was not to be denied. Despite the cumulative toll on my constitution, I had to be up early to catch a bus to Tetovo. The South East Europe University was officially opening, and I had promised my old friend, Freidhelm Peel, that I would be there. It was to be a high-profile event. Rumour had it that President Boris Trjkovski would be on hand to cut the ribbon.

Security was extremely tight and guests had to pass through several police checkpoints. Senior Macedonian and ethnic Albanian politicians rubbed shoulders with local businessmen and foreign delegates.

Although not seated with the VIPs on stage, Friedhelm Peel was singled out for praise by the head of the foundation that had sponsored the university's construction. It had been quite an achievement, but as a symbol of Albanian-Macedonian cooperation, one had to wonder if the SEEU wasn't a case of too little, too late.

The Macedonian army was on full alert during the opening ceremony, and NATO troops maintained a security screen. President Trjkovski's appearance was cancelled at the last minute out of concern for his safety.

The university's rector announced that over 1000 students had registered for classes – less than 50 per cent of the school's capacity.

TETOVO – 20 NOVEMBER 2001 (Wednesday evening)

I had intended to stop at the Hotel Electra only to say hello to the staff. Within minutes of my arrival, however, I was paged to the telephone to take a call from N., the deputy director of Macedonian intelligence. I had met N. the previous month and had been intrigued by his appearance. In his three-piece suit, with gold pocket watch with chain and a shoulder-holstered, snub-nosed, .30 calibre revolver, he had the look of the quintessential 1930s Hollywood G-man. Since then, he had become a valuable source of information.

He insisted that I remain in Tetovo and join him and his colleagues for dinner. He told me a major operation was underway to unearth a mass grave and that he could provide me with additional details.

I had already heard about a dig at Trebos and knew things had not gone well for the Macedonian police. Re-entering the Albanian-controlled area in a surprise security sweep, seven UCK commanders had been arrested, which incensed the Albanians. Within hours, the UCK had grabbed hundreds of Macedonians as hostages from all over the Tetovo valley.

U.S. special envoy James Pardew successfully negotiated the release of the Macedonians in exchange for the independent confirmation that the UCK commandos were unharmed. The situation appeared to have been resolved, but that night a large force of UCK had ambushed a police convoy just outside of Trebos. Rocket-propelled grenades had disabled the lead police vehicle and the badly outnumbered Macedonians had been pinned down. Three police were killed and the same number wounded before NATO troops arrived to negotiate the withdrawal of the surviving Macedonians.

Pardew had been adamant that the release of the Macedonian hostages was contingent upon the police ending their operations around Trebos. When Minister of the Interior Ljubce Boskovski refused to issue orders to do so, N. and his colleagues believed that Pardew had passed along this information to the UCK. "How else could the Albanians have known to launch such a major ambush?" N. asked. Although he offered no proof, it indicated the level of mistrust that existed between NATO and Boskovski's police force.

Midway through our meal of fresh mountain trout (allegedly caught in the Albanian-controlled sector), the cellphones of all nine police officers present rang simultaneously. Two explosions had just been reported in central Tetovo, outside the offices of the European Union monitors. Asked if they had any suspects, N. replied, "The *Shqiptares*! Who else?" The table erupted in laughter.

TREBOS – 22 NOVEMBER 2001 (Thursday morning)

N. made arrangements for me to visit the exhumation site, but nobody had figured out how I was to get there. It was not as simple as one might assume. Although Trebos is only four kilometers from Tetovo, Macedonian taxi drivers would not drive into the Albanian sector and Albanian drivers were afraid to cross the Macedonian police checkpoint. Finally, an Albanian agreed to take me by a route that circumvented the police and entered Trebos from the far side. The driver did not wish to give his name, but was quite talkative about the recent fighting in the area. He said he gladly gave "gifts" to the UCK to help finance their war effort, but that he had never taken up arms.

When he continued to use the moniker UCK, I asked him if he didn't mean the ANA (National Liberation Army) or ONA (Albanian Liberation Army). He laughed and said, "The only people who use those names are NATO and you, the media. Have you ever seen ANA or ONA spray painted on walls or on our soldiers' crests?" The answer, of course, was no.

At Trebos, a roadblock barred the way to the site. Two EU monitors were standing nearby, beside a German army truck. Behind them, about a dozen young, muscular Albanian men wearing black UCK T-shirts were milling around an obviously newly-constructed bunker. Barely 400 meters down the road, Macedonian armoured vehicles were clearly visible.

One of the tough-looking Albanians strode toward me and asked me what I wanted. When I told him I wanted to see the mass grave site, he blocked my way and said, "No one goes down that road." I ignored him and addressed one of the EU monitors standing at the barricade. I told him that I had official clearance and that I presumed the EU would monitor my safe passage. "You better listen to them," he replied, nodding his head toward the Albanians in the bunker. I asked him to exert his authority on my behalf. "Are you kidding?" he answered. "I can't even get my own truck through here."

The Albanian was able to follow the conversation and knew I was not rallying much support. Coming closer, he said menacingly, "If you go down that road, the Macedonians will kill you and blame the UCK. If necessary, *we* will kill you to prevent that from happening." I could not debate this Balkan logic.

When I returned to Tetovo, N. called to inform me that a visit to the Trebos site would no longer be possible. Carla del Ponte, The Hague Tribunal's chief prosecutor, had flown into Skopje that morning, and while I was detained at the Albanian barricade, had held a press conference at the airport "forbidding" any journalist from visiting the alleged mass grave. On the plus side, N. advised me that I had been granted an interview that evening with the man at the center of the events, Minister of the Interior Ljubce Boskovski.

U.S. foreign policy contributing to instability in Balkans (Halifax Herald)
TETOVO, Macedonia – Over the past few weeks a number of dramatic events have taken place in the Balkans, highlighting the continued instability within both Serbia and Kosovo.

In addition, despite the presence of NATO troops and international monitors, the tiny Republic of Macedonia continues to hover on the brink of an all-out civil war. While it certainly cannot be cited as the root cause of the present ethnic strife, America's altered foreign policy in response to the terrorist attacks of September 11 has undoubtedly heightened tensions here and further destabilized the region.

With President George W. Bush anxious to keep Arab allies on-side in his coalition against terrorism, it has become a U.S. State Department imperative not to appear anti-Muslim. To this end, many U.S. politicians have been trumpeting their past efforts to aid the Bosnian Muslims and Albanians in the Balkans militarily. The Hague Tribunal, in response to this U.S. political pressure, has accordingly stepped up its efforts to bring in Serbian commanders accused of alleged war crimes against Bosnian Muslims.

In Belgrade, Serbian President Zoran Djindjic (the man who turned over Slobodan Milosevic to The Hague) has been anxious to cooperate with the West in this regard. For Djindjic, such appeasement is viewed as an economic necessity for the recovery of his war-ravaged republic.

However, not all Serbs share Djindjic's vision. In early November, when the Red Beret police unit was tricked into turning over two suspects to The Hague, the rest of this elite force took to the streets in protest. Squads of armed, masked policemen used their armoured vehicles to block major highways throughout Serbia as they demanded the resignation of the Minister of the Interior.

While a bloody confrontation was narrowly avoided through peaceful negotiations, the Red Berets remain a defiant and formidable nationalist threat to Djindjic's already unpopular coalition government.

The November 17 elections in Kosovo were relatively uneventful, but extremely significant. As expected, the overwhelming Albanian majority dominated the voting, and Ibrahim Rugova, the moderate leader of the Democratic League of Kosovo, won a clear-cut victory over his more extremist rivals. With the large-scale participation of Kosovo Serbs (40,000 still reside in NATO-protected enclaves while 160,000 refugees are now living in Serbia), the UN authorities could consider the election results a best-case scenario. In a separate deal signed in Belgrade earlier this month, the UN decreed that no matter what the outcome, there could be no immediate move to declare Kosovo independent.

In the meantime, the UN will continue to administer this region as a protectorate and Kosovo will technically remain a part of Yugoslavia. What remains to be seen is how patient the Albanian Kosovars will be in waiting to be granted their independence. The UN had promised to create a utopian multi-ethnic Kosovo, but all of the officials directly involved realized that this was a pipe dream. The ANA, formerly the Kosovo Liberation Army (UCK), remains an extremely powerful and belligerent force in the region, and it has been exercising an increased independence from NATO's control.

Nowhere is this more evident than in the embattled valleys of northern Macedonia.

There were a number of violent clashes last week between ethnic Albanian guerrillas and Macedonian security forces all across the Tetovo valley. These skirmishes, combined with the near-collapse of the parliamentary coalition formed to govern Macedonia, have once again thrust this tiny Balkan republic to the edge of all-out civil war.

The Ohrid peace plan should have been well on its way to implementation. However, for those closely monitoring the situation here, Macedonia remains a lit powder keg. Despite a nifty little name change from UCK to ANA (Albanian National Army), the guerrillas remain active and have retained their army. And now that one of the four major political parties has withdrawn from the governing coalition, the just-approved constitutional amendments seem unlikely to be implemented.

Despite the presence of a large contingent of international observers and a NATO protection force, fighting has continued almost daily throughout north western Macedonia.

Over the past few months, there has been a desperate attempt by Ljubce Boskovski, Macedonian Minister of the Interior, to reform and re-equip his police units. New weapons, armoured vehicles, improved training and the official recruitment of former paramilitary units have helped to shift the balance of military force away from the UCK. In addition, of all the current Macedonian political leaders, Boskovski is undoubtedly the most powerful of the hard-line nationalists. His growing popularity among the Macedonian majority comes as a direct result of his anti-appeasement policy towards Albanian terrorists.

For NATO and European Union officials, Boskovski's consistent lack of compliance with their demands has posed a constant threat to the peace proc-

ess. For Albanian political leaders, he remains their most formidable opponent. Anxious to prove that NATO's disarming of the UCK was merely a public relations sham, Boskovski staged a number of police offensives into the
territory controlled by the guerrillas. As expected, the Albanians responded to
Boskovski's provocation with a series of deadly ambushes, clearly indcating
that the guerrillas are still heavily-armed.

In spite of repeated requests for him to delay his operation to exhume a
mass grave near the village of Trebos, Boskovski has persisted. Even after three
police officers were killed and the Albanians seized hundreds of civilian hostages, Boskovski refused to stop the digging. So far, Macedonian authorities
have recovered the bones of at least two of six local villagers allegedly murdered by the UCK during its offensives in June.

However, instead of citing the Albanians for their non-compliance, embarrassed NATO monitors and, in particular, U.S. special envoy James Pardew
have increasingly singled out Boskovski for their wrath. Although numerous
official protests have been lodged against him to date, the 42-year-old Boskovski
remains wholly unrepentant.

Last month, when the crisis management team (consisting of a wide array
of domestic and international agencies) complained that the police were not
being cooperative enough, Boskovski withdrew from the team. In an attempt
to rein him in, Carla del Ponte, the chief prosecutor at The Hague War Crimes
Tribunal, hinted that he might soon be indicted.

On November 21, del Ponte flew to Skopje to deliver her warning personally, but in an interview later that day, Boskovski remained undeterred. "Carla
del Ponte's visit here [in Macedonia] was without foundation and without
any authority," he said. "The Hague Tribunal is losing its credibility. It is a
court that should not exist because it is driven purely by a political agenda
and is not concerned with the pursuit of justice."

Although Boskovski admits that there have already been several attempts
on his life, he refuses to acquiesce to the repeated Albanian demands for his
resignation. "This is Macedonia and we must collectively defend our pride; it
is our destiny," he said.

Despite this bravado, Boskovski may soon fall victim to his own political
party comrades. As a member of the Macedonian Unity Party (VMRO), he has
thus far enjoyed the support of both President Boris Trjkovski and Prime Min-

ister Ljubo Georgievski. However, with the recent withdrawal of the Macedonian Social Democrats, if VMRO is to successfully retain the remaining coalition partners it may eventually require the removal of Boskovski.

Should this happen, Boskovski is unlikely to remain a bystander for long, as the Macedonian national elections are scheduled for early in 2002, although European Union officials are desperately trying to delay the voting until June. In the meantime, Boskovski's police force remains fiercely loyal to him. As the violence continues and the ethnic divide widens, nationalist hard-liners like Ljubce Boskovski are likely to overtake their more moderate counterparts at the polls.

If this should happen, the terms of the current peace plan will be revoked and civil war in Macedonia will be unavoidable.

BELGRADE – 26 NOVEMBER 2001 (Monday morning)

For the past two-and-a-half months, the Balkans has been the Forgotten Front in terms of media coverage. The U.S.-led war on terrorism had stolen all of the headlines, and once the campaign in Afghanistan began, all else was ignored.

To be published, any news story had to have some hook or relevance to the events of September 11 or to the hunt for Osama bin Laden. Prior to leaving Canada, Bruce Garvey at the *Ottawa Citizen* had been realistic about finding space in the paper for any of my Balkan stories. "If it's connected to Osama bin Laden – no problem," he told me.

Having already written about the presence of Mujahadeen fighters in Bosnia, Kosovo and Macedonia, I felt it would not be too difficult to compile a comprehensive backgrounder on Muslim extremists in the Balkans.

During my recent trips I had met Captain S. of the Yugoslav intelligence service, N. and his agents in Macedonia, and Miroslav Lazanski, a well-known Belgrade-based military reporter. They had helped me gather evidence, including photos and videos, which proved that there was a link between the Al-Qaeda and Albanian terrorist organizations.

Bin Laden's Balkan Connections (Ottawa Citizen)

BELGRADE, Yugoslavia – With the swift collapse of the Taliban regime, the U.S.-led military campaign in Afghanistan has been reduced to an Osama bin Laden manhunt-cum-mop-up of the Al-Qaeda network. As American jets pounded the cave entrances around Tora Bora, Special Forces teams were closing in on the last redoubts of Taliban fanatics. Following the quick success in Afghanistan, President George W. Bush warned Americans to prepare for a wider war aimed at punishing those nations that harbour terrorists. Although there was no proven link between Iraq and the anthrax scare, in recent speeches Bush repeatedly singled out Saddam Hussein as an enemy of the U.S. threats were also leveled at the governments of Sudan, Libya, Syria and at the leaders of Palestinian extremist groups.

While it is believed that Saudi-born Osama bin Laden is still in Afghanistan, U.S. intelligence agencies cannot be sure of his exact whereabouts. What is known is that his extensive Al-Qaeda terrorist organization still has cells operating around the world.

As the U.S. dragnet is cast ever wider, it can only be a matter of time before the counter-terrorist effort revisits the Balkans. Over the past decade, Mujahadeen fighters – and in particular bin Laden's followers – have practiced their brand of terror in Croatia, Bosnia, and Kosovo are currently believed to be participating in Macedonia's civil unrest.

On November 20, while the Taliban was still offering organized resistance and extremists from around the world were volunteering to join their ranks, Pakistani police apprehended five Muslim fighters carrying Macedonian passports at the Afghan border.

For Macedonian intelligence officials, the arrests were further proof that the Mujahadeen formed the veteran core of the ethnic Albanian army known as the UCK. Since March of this year, the UCK had mounted very successful guerrilla offensive Macedonian security forces have maintained since the outbreak of hostilities that up to 150 Mujahadeen were active in the UCK ranks.

N., the deputy director of Macedonian Intelligence, confirmed that following the September 11 terrorist attacks his agency has "supplied a substantive dossier to the CIA," outlining bin Laden's Balkan activities. The information forwarded to the American Central Intelligence Agency included eyewitness accounts offered by Macedonian civilians who had been held hostage by Mujahadeen, along with incriminating photographs and videos, which security forces captured from the UCK.

Macedonian Minister of the Interior Ljubce Boskovski was eager for his forces to return into the areas presently controlled by the Albanian guerrillas in order to uncover additional evidence. Since mid-November 13, Macedonian police have been exhuming a mass grave near the ethnic Albanian village of Trebos. N. believes Mujahadeen fighters were responsible for the Trebos massacre "because of the manner in which the bodies were cut up and scattered."

N. also suspects that Mujahadeen fanatics staged an ambush against security forces last April. In this incident, eight policemen were shot outside the village of Vejce, and their bodies dismembered for grisly trophies. The Macedonian authorities are not the only ones to affix the blame for the Vejce ambush on the Mujahadeen.

During the summer offensive around Tetovo, guerrillas admitted they had gained combat experience in previous Balkan conflicts. These Albanians acknowledged the involvement of Arab and Afghan volunteers in training members of the UCK.

When the UCK insurrection began in March, the Macedonian government hastily acquired a fleet of six Ukrainian helicopter gunships to provide their troops with tactical air support. "Shortly after that, our pilots reported being tracked by sophisticated U.S.-made Stinger anti-aircraft missiles," said N. "We have been informed that the UCK received these Stingers from their Mujahadeen connections in Afghanistan."

American advisors and covert military aid have also contributed to the UCK's combat effectiveness, but since September 11 the Macedonians have noted a shift in U.S. foreign policy. "The CIA has been much more receptive to our reports about the Al-Qaeda," N. said. "Particularly after they discovered that one of the suicide hijackers had been active in both Kosovo and Macedonia."

Given their common goal of neutralizing Albanian terrorists, Macedonian police have been working closely with their Yugoslav counterparts. More importantly, as part of the U.S.-led global initiative to combat terrorism, the Federal Republic of Yugoslavia has been reinstated in Interpol – after a ten-year banishment. As a result, intelligence officers from the Yugoslav Army have been able to supply their international colleagues with a wealth of information about Mujahadeen activity in Bosnia and Kosovo. Yugoslav Intelligence believes that at least 50 of the 150 Mujahadeen that fought in Kosovo are still active members of the UCK.

Interpol had been tracking the Al-Qaeda's Balkan activities for some time. On October 23 this year, it released a preliminary report outlining bin Laden's personal links to the Albanian Mafia. In this report, Interpol alleged that a senior Al-Qaeda member had been the commander of an elite UCK unit in Kosovo during the fighting in 1999.

While U.S. President Bill Clinton's administration was the driving force in garnering NATO support for the UCK, numerous media reports clearly showed that the CIA had been well aware of bin Laden's Albanian links prior to NATO's intervention in Kosovo.

On January 17, 1999, the international press was filled with news of an alleged massacre of 45 Albanian Kosovars in the village of Racak. Clinton seized upon this particular incident (later disproved by UN pathologists as an Albanian hoax) to proclaim that the West could no longer overlook "Serbian atrocities." With Clinton's statement, NATO was irrevocably launched a confrontation with Yugoslavia.

Although lost in the American hype, Greek media outlets that same day were detailing the Taliban's presence in Albania at the invitation of ex-President Sali Berisa and former head of Intelligence Bashkim Gazidede. According to *The Tribune*, an Athens daily newspaper, Albanian security official Fatos Klozi confirmed that "bin Laden was one of those who had organized and sent groups to fight in Kosovo. There were Egyptians, Saudis, Algerians, Tunisians, Sudanese and Kuwaitis from different organizations among the [UCK] mercenaries."

Ten days later, on January 27, 1999, the Arab-language news service Al Hayat reported that an Albanian commander in Kosovo, code-named Monia, was directly connected to Osama bin Laden. The Al Hayat piece also proudly proclaimed that "at least 100 Muslim Mujahadeen" were serving with Monia's force in Kosovo.

The *Washington Post* reported in August 1998 that the CIA was not only aware of bin Laden's association with the Albanian regime, but that U.S. operatives had been prominent in the arrest of four Al-Qaeda agents in Tirana, Albania. American State Department officials later speculated that the bombings of their embassies in Kenya and Tanzania might have been bin Laden's revenge for the Tirana arrests.

The Al-Qaeda suspects detained by the CIA in Albania had been operating the Islamic Revival Foundation, "a charitable organization that official sources say provided a useful cover for the [suspects'] efforts on behalf of bin Laden," the *Post* reported.

In February 1998, the U.S. State Department removed the UCK from its list of terrorist organizations. However later that year, the CIA and its Albanian SHIK intelligence counterpart co-operated to successfully shut down a Mujahadeen cell operating in conjunction with the Albanians in Kosovo.

Some of the most revealing links surfaced in December 1998 when Al-Qaeda agent Sheik Abdel-Kader was arrested in Tirana for the murder of his Albanian translator. During his trial, Abdel-Kader confessed to being a senior commander in bin Laden's network, and claimed he had recruited a force of some 300 Mujahadeen to fight in Kosovo. European media covering the trial reported Abdul-Kader's revelation that Osama bin Laden – although a wanted terrorist – had travelled freely to Tirana in 1994 and again in 1998 to meet with senior Albanian officials. Abdel-Kader also testified that, when Sali Berisa's regime collapsed into anarchy in 1997, state armouries and government offices were looted. Many of the 10,000 heavy weapons and 100,000 passports that went missing conveniently fell into the hands of the Al-Qaeda.

Osama bin Laden – stripped of his Saudi citizenship in 1994 – is alleged to have retained the Bosnian passport he was issued in Vienna in 1993. The granting of official travel documents to bin Laden was first reported on September 24, 1999 by *Dani*, a Bosnian Muslim weekly newspaper. The rationale behind bestowing citizenship on a wanted terrorist was that Bosnian President Alija Izetbegovic had been thankful for the Mujahadeen's contribution to the creation of a Balkan "fundamentalist Islamic Republic."

Dani also reported that Al-Qaeda terrorist Mehrez Aodouni had been arrested in Istanbul while carrying a Bosnian passport. Like bin Laden, his citizenship had been granted "because he was a member of the Bosnia-Herzegovina army."

Canadian soldiers serving with the United Nations Protection Force (UNPROFOR) were among the first to report the presence of Mujahadeen in the ranks of the Bosnian Muslims, as early as 1992.

The edition of the Asian *Wall Street Journal* reported that, in 1993, bin Laden appointed Al Zawahiri, the Al-Qaeda's second-in-command, to direct all his operations in the Balkans.

While no exact numbers exist, it is estimated that between 1500 and 3500 Arab volunteers participated in the Bosnian civil war. Their main area of operation was in the region of Zenica, with most of them serving in the 7th Brigade of General Sakib Mahmuljin's 3rd Corps, nicknamed the Guerrillas. Identified by red and green Rambo bandannas emblazoned with the crest "Our Road is Jihad," this unit earned a reputation for brutality.

On June 27, 1993, the *Sunday Times* reported that Bosnian Muslim officers had reservations about the Mujahadeen volunteers. Colonel Stjepan Siber, then-deputy commander of the Bosnia-Herzegovina army, admitted to the *Times* that "It was a mistake to let [the Mujahadeen] in here... They commit most of the atrocities and work against the interests of the Muslim people. They have been killing, looting and burning."

According to reports, it was the Mujahadeen who were serving with General Nasir Oric in the Muslim enclave of Srebrenica and who committed some of the most barbaric atrocities of the war. Beheadings of Serbian civilians were commonplace, and in some villages the Mujahadeen would dynamite homes with the inhabitants trapped inside.

No attempt was made to hide such atrocities. In fact, General Oric would often address the media at the site of a massacre. On one such occasion, while standing in front of Mujahadeen brandishing human head trophies, Oric pointed to a flaming ruin and proudly told reporters, "We blew those Serbs to the moon."

Alija Izetbegovic was proud to display the fighting prowess of his Mujahadeen volunteers. Following a successful attack against Serbian positions around Vozuce on September 10, 1995, the Bosnian President held a televised medal presentation parade. The Mujahadeen who had provided the vanguard of the assault force, were awarded 11 decorations for valour, including the Golden Crescent, Bosnia's highest honour.

Yugoslav Intelligence estimates that over 1500 Bosnian citizenships were granted to Mujahadeen and Al-Qaeda fighters following the Dayton Peace Accord in 1995. Most of those soldiers are believed to have settled in the Zenica region.

According to Miroslav Lazanski, author of the new book *Osama bin Laden Against America*, the Al-Qaeda still maintain two operational bases in Bosnia. One of these contains only the best fighters and is commanded by an Algerian,

Abu Al Mali.

Following the September 11 attacks, FBI and CIA agents uncovered evidence that two of the suicide hijackers had come from this Bosnian camp. Abu Mali was subsequently arrested while travelling to Istanbul on a Bosnian passport.

It is evident from recent events that the U.S. military is well aware of the continued Mujahadeen presence in the Balkans. General Myers visited NATO troops stationed in Bosnia in late November 2001 to warn them against a possible Al-Qaeda retaliation attack. In addition, on December 4, the White House added two Albanian terrorist groups operating in Macedonia and Kosovo to their list of outlawed organizations.

President George W. Bush's campaign against Osama bin Laden's terrorists has come full circle to confront the Clinton administration's dubious Balkan legacy.

ABOVE: *This Macedonian police checkpoint on the Tetovo-Kosovo highway had been captured by Albanian guerrillas and then abandoned following the Ohrid peace agreement. Similar reminders of the previous fighting remain visible throughout the Tetovo valley. (JAMES PHILLIPS)*

TOP LEFT: *In mid-September 2001, Macedonian villagers in the Tetovo valley attempted to block the withdrawal of army units. They did not believe NATO observers could protect them.* (*JAMES PHILLIPS*)

TOP RIGHT: *British SAS troops inspect the Macedonian enclave of Ratae.* (*SCOTT TAYLOR*)

ABOVE: *As part of the Ohrid peace initiative, Macedonian civilians return to their empty village – past an abandoned UCK checkpoint.* (*JAMES PHILLIPS*)

OPPOSITE PAGE: *After the NATO mission Essential Harvest, tensions remained high in northern Macedonia. Towns like Ratae remained virtual armed camps.* (*JAMES PHILLIPS*)

chapter seven:
WHAT LIES AHEAD

While the terror attacks of September 11 may not have changed the world, they undoubtedly shifted America's foreign policy in the Balkans. Past acceptance of, and even cooperation with, Muslim extremists has been swiftly curtailed. On January 16, American authorities announced that they had arrested six Algerian Al-Qaeda members in Sarajevo. British and American intelligence believed that they had been planning to attack NATO military installations inside Bosnia.

The suspected terrorists had fought in Bosnia during the civil war, and all had been granted Bosnian citizenship as a reward. In the early nineties, the U.S., Britain and, to a lesser extent, the German secret service had collaborated with these same Mujahadeen to assist the Bosnian Muslim army of Alija Izetbegovic.

Over the past four years, this collaboration included supplying arms and military materiel to the Albanian UCK guerrillas in Kosovo and Macedonia. Until now, NATO troops deployed in these regions had turned a blind eye to UCK activities. Since the occupation of Kosovo in June 1999, it is estimated that nearly 1000 Serbs have been killed or gone missing as a result of UCK terrorism. The few remaining Serbs in Albanian-dominated sectors live in

NATO-protected enclaves.

Nevertheless, on Sunday January 6, 2002, 36-year-old shopkeeper Dragolub Marvkovic was blown to pieces by a booby trap. It was the local UCK commander's way of "celebrating" the Serbian Orthodox Christmas. Vojislav Kostunica's condemnation of the UCK attack only underscored the political impotence of the Yugoslav president.

Despite Yugoslavia's cooperation with the West in handing over Milosevic and participating in the Kosovo elections, promised financial aid has yet to materialize. Most of the $1.3 billion (U.S.) pledged at the June 2001 donor's conference has yet to be paid, including Canada's $28 million.

Serbia has faced an extremely harsh winter. With many of the country's power plants still out of commission as a result of the NATO bombing, heating bills have been astronomical. In some cases, exceeding pension cheques by a factor of ten. Many families are unable to pay the charges. In this winter of discontent, Kostunica's popularity plummetted.

When Kostunica swept to power in October 2000, he had promised to hold another set of elections within a year. When the 5 October deadline passed, he pushed the date ahead to 23 December, the anniversary of DOS's consolidation of power. This date also passed without an election being called, further undermining DOS's credibility.

Of course, with Montenegro's President Milo Djukanovic refusing to enter negotiations with Kostunica and his Serbian counterpart, Zoran Djindjic, it remains unclear exactly what constitutes the Federal Republic of Yugoslavia. Djukanovic has refused to return to the federal fold even though he does not have enough popular support to win a referendum on separation.

The European Union continues to send mixed messages to the Montenegrins. In January, Javier Solana, the president of the EU, urged Milo Djukanovic to remain a part of the Yugoslav Federation during a conference in Brussels. However, the EU missed an opportunity to drive Montenegro back into the Federal Republic, at least economically, when it converted to the Euro dollar on January 1. Two years earlier, Dijukanovic had broken ties with the Yugoslav monetary system when he adopted the Deutsch mark as Montenegro's official currency. As a result, Montenegro now had no functioning monetary system. However, rather than forcing Montenegro back onto the Yugoslav dinar, the EU – under pressure from Washington – granted

Montenegro the right to circulate the Euro; the only non-EU country (other than the protectorate of Kosovo) so privileged.

The wild card in Montenegro remains the substantial Albanian minority. With a 50/50 split between Montenegrin federalists and separatists, the Albanians have the sway vote, should they choose to participate. Many analysts predict that continued instability in Montenegro will provide fertile ground for future UCK expansion as they continue to work towards a "Greater Albania."

Although many NATO officials, journalists and international monitors will officially deny knowledge of the Greater Albania concept, the UCK leadership has never hidden its true intentions. Maps produced in 1997 by the Albanian Political Emigration are carried by most UCK fighters. These maps tangibly illustrate the Albanians' historical claims to nearly 90,000 square kilometres in the Balkans, including not only Kosovo, but also territory currently recognized as part of Greece, Macedonia, Bosnia, Serbia and Montenegro. In November 2001, just days after the Kosovo election, Albanian political and military leaders met in Prizren to establish a comprehensive blueprint for the collective future of the eight million Balkan Albanians.

NATO officials understood how provocative this meeting would be to neighbouring states, but made no attempt to stop it. Newly-elected Kosovo leader Ibrahim Rugova chose not to attend, but indicted war criminal and Kosovo Protection Corps commander Agim Ceku was one of the keynote speakers.

As the Albanians boldly set out a strategy for the future, UCK commanders, in the short-term, still have their sights set on the dismemberment of Macedonia. Despite the concessions made by the Macedonians as part of the Ohrid Peace Agreement, the Albanians remain poised to resume a major offensive in the regions surrounding the Tetovo valley and Kumanovo. On January 10, 2002 the Albanian leaders in Macedonia issued a press release announcing their intention to "reorganize and re-activate" the National Liberation Army. The NLA is the rebel force that was voluntarily disbanded during NATO's *Essential Harvest* operation in September 2001.

The NLA has accused the Macedonian government of ignoring the peace accord. "Just as the Slav Macedonians do not feel any commitment to the Ohrid agreement we, the members of the NLA, as of today are forced to declare that we have no commitment toward the agreement whatsoever. We have proved that we can fight for our rights," a spokesperson said.

While everyone is bracing for an Albanian offensive following the melting of the winter snows, what remains unclear is whether the U.S. will continue to support the guerrillas.

There is little likelihood that the Americans and their NATO allies will risk retaliatory attacks by directly engaging the UCK. However, it is possible that greater efforts will be made to seal the Kosovo border in cooperation with the Macedonian military.

Secretary of State Colin Powell has indicated that the U.S. will scale back its military presence in the Balkans. But it will not be easy for the Americans to disengage themselves from the mess they have created without setting off another round of factional violence. In fact, it may prove impossible.

LEFT: *This map constitutes the "Greater Albania" concept which the extremists among the Kosovar fighters still believe they are striving for. It was drawn by* Albanian Political Emigration *and first published in the book* Kosovo Origins, *by Hugo Roth. This 90,000-square-kilometre region incorporates land currently recognized as Greece, Macedonia, Bosnia, Serbia and Montenegro.*

SLOBODAN MILOSEVIC
Former President of Yugoslavia. Rode a wave of resurgent Serbian nationalism into power in 1987, leading to eight bloody years of civil war and a decade of economic sanctions. The 1999 NATO air campaign temporarily solidified Milosevic's shaky leadership, but in October 2000 he was deposed in a civil uprising. Arrested and turned over to The Hague War Crimes Tribunal in June 2001. Remains the Leader of the Yugoslav Socialist Party.

VOJISLAV KOSTUNICA
Current President of Yugoslavia. Originally seen as being untainted by scandal and corruption, he easily swept Milosevic out of power in 2000. His approval rating soared above 90 per cent. However, the next 18 months saw Serbia's economic recovery stall and Montenegro's refusal to re-enter the Federal fold. Prior to the November 2001 Kosovo elections, Kostunica was able to negotiate a temporary reprieve from the UN regarding Kosovo's independence.

ZORAN DJINDJIC
President of Serbia. A founding member of the Democratic Opposition of Serbia (DOS). Considered unelectable at the Federal Yugoslav level. As the power behind the throne, he rode Kostunica's unprecendented popularity to a DOS victory in Serbia. Acting independently, he was responsible for Milosevic's arrest and extradition to The Hague. His "economics first" policy is viewed by many Serbs as "selling out" to Western interests.

UNCIVIL WAR: THE PLAYERS AND EVENTS

JUNE 10, 1999 – Four days of talks in the northern Macedonian town of Kumanovo, results in an announcement by a Yugoslav Army delegation and UN representatives that they have reached an agreement on the future of Kosovo. The 78-day bombing campaign ends. Yugoslav authorities estimate 1800 soldiers and civilians were killed and another 2000 permanently disabled. 120,000 refugees from Kosovo join the nearly 650,000 others already in Serbia. Damage to the Yugoslav infrastructure is estimated at $10 billion (US).

JUNE 12, 1999 – Yugoslav forces begin to leave Kosovo largely intact. Russian troops occupy Slatina Airport, in Pristina, as 5000 NATO peacekeepers fan out across the

province. The peacekeeping force, known as KFOR, will eventually number 40,000 troops.

SEPTEMBER 21, 1999 – KFOR and the KLA sign an agreement turning the KLA into a 5000-strong civilian armed force called the Kosovo Protection Force (KPC), paid for by the UN. Yugoslavia angrily condemns the agreement as "it legitimizes the action of terrorist bands and the criminal KLA in the guise of forming a civilian force." The agreement is seen as a further violation of its sovereignty and territorial integrity as guaranteed by UN Security Council Resolution 1244, which also called for KLA disarmament.

SEPTEMBER 23, 1999 – The

Bosnian Muslim weekly *Dani* reports that Osama bin Laden was issued a Bosnian passport in Vienna in 1993. Further south, Albanian authorities have yet to account for 100,000 blank passports that vanished, along with thousands of weapons, during civil disturbances in Tirana, Albania, in 1999.

SEPTEMBER 24, 2000 – Vojislav Kostunica wins a first-round upset with 52 per cent of the vote in Yugoslav elections. U.S. officials applaud Montenegro's decision to boycott the elections. A second round of presidential elections is scheduled for October 8.

SEPTEMBER 28, 2000 – Zoran Djindjic, chairman of the Demo-

NEBOJSA COVIC (forefront)
Yugoslav special envoy to Kosovo and south Serbia. Rose to prominence when Albanian terrorists occupied territory inside south Serbia in the winter of 2000, proving him to be a masterful negotiator. By the summer of 2001, Serbian forces had re-entered the occupied territories and NATO reduced the demilitarized GSZ around Kosovo to one kilometre. Campaigned successfully among the Serbian Kosovar communists for their co-operation in the 2001 elections.

IBRAHIM RUGOVA
Leader of Kosovo's ruling Democratic League of Kosovo. Although regarded as a moderate, remains dedicated to the cause of Albanian independence. Having won a strong majority in the Kosovo elections, he must continue to work with NATO and UN overseers as he establishes his government. While disappointed by the UN's deal with Yugoslavia to postpone Kosovo's Independence, Rugova recognizes the importance of cooperation with his "masters."

HASHIM THACI
Political leader of the Kosovo Liberation Army. The 41-year-old politician is regarded as a violent extremist, and was the driving force behind the UCK's guerrilla war. Despite the popularity of his UCK fighters following their NATO-assisted victory over the Serbs in 1999, Thaci has been unable to convert this sentiment into votes. However, despite running second to Rugova in popularity, U.S. pressure awarded him the position of Prime Minister in Kosovo.

cratic Opposition of Serbia (DOS), calls for a general strike for October 2 in order to force Milosevic's regime to recognize the election results.

SEPTEMBER 29, 2000 – 7500 miners stage a sit-down strike at the Kolubara coal mine complex, 100 kilometres south of Belgrade. 4,500 other miners join them two days later. Citizens from all over Serbia begin to converge on Belgrade.

OCTOBER 5, 2000 – The DOS calls for citizens to gather in front of the Federal Assembly building to protest the first round of the elections. The Parliament is stormed around 4:00 p.m. and part of it set afire. RTS, the state television station, is forced off the air. Police join the demonstrators. Newly-elected President of the Federal Republic of Yugoslavia Vojislav Kostunica addresses the crowd. Hundreds of thousands spend the night in the streets of Belgrade, celebrating their victory.

OCTOBER 7, 2000 – Kostunica is sworn in as the fourth president of the Federal Republic of Yugoslavia (Serbia and Montenegro).

DECEMBER 20, 2000 – UN Security Council condemns violence by Albanians in south Serbia. Yugoslav authorities report that "ethnic Albanian extremists" have carried out more than 400 armed attacks in the zone since June 10, 1999, killing 11 Serbian policemen and eight civilians.

FEBRUARY 13, 2001 – A violent battle erupts between the Yugoslav Army and the self-proclaimed Liberation Army of Presovo, Medvedja and Bujanovac (UCPMB) near the villages of Bukovac and Gornje Shoshaje in southern Serbia. The same day, peacekeepers in Kosovo come under attack after a busload of Serbs they are escorting runs into an ambush that kills one passenger and injures two near the town of Grilica. Angry Serbs mob the local headquarters of KFOR and the United Nations police in Strpce. At Mitrovica, Serbs kill eight Albanians and force others to flee their homes.

FEBRUARY 16, 2001 - A bus travelling on the Nis-Gracanica line is blown up by a remote-controlled device near the village of Livadice,

AGIM CEKU

Commander of the Kosovo Protection Corps. A former career officer in the Yugoslav National Army. Resigned his post during the breakup of Yugoslavia. Implicated in some of the worst atrocities commited during the civil war. Cited by Canadian commanders as a war criminal, but was hand-picked by NATO commanders to take over the UCK in January 1999, despite a sealed indictment from The Hague.

ARBEN DJAFFERI

Leader of the Albanian Democratic Party (DPA) (Macedonia). His party is considered to be the most moderate of the ethnic Albanian parties in Macedonia. When fighting began in February 2001, Djafferi denounced violence as a means to achieve Albanian goals. However, DPA retained a powerful voice in the Macedonian parliament, and their demands for increased human rights mirrored those of the more extremist elements.

IMER IMERI

Leader of the Democratic Prosperity Party (DPP) (Macedonia). Considered the front man for the UCK guerrillas, Imeri believed that violence was necessary to force home the Albanian demands. Although the DPP continued to have substantial representation at the parliamentary peace talks, Imeri himself was superceded as the voice of the UCK by more extremist defectors from his party who have since created their own political parties.

killing seven Serbs and wounding forty others. KFOR helicopters evacute the injured to a British military hospital near Kosovo Polje.

FEBRUARY 23, 2001 – Macedonian and Yugoslav ministers of Foreign Affairs meet with Process for Co-operation in Eastern Europe (SECP) member countries in Skopje to formalize the border between the two countries. They announce that the common goal for countries in the region is integration in the European Union.

MARCH 23, 2001 – On the eve of renewed fighting, President George W. Bush observes that "Macedonia is a close friend and a partner country of NATO, and a successful example of a democratic, multi-ethnic state in the

Balkans." However, U.S. actions would not match these words.

MARCH 30, 2001 – National Liberation Army (NLA) is formed following fighting in the Tanusevci region of Macedonia. Using the same Albanian-language acronym as the disbanded Kosovo Liberation Army (*Ushtria Clirimtare Kombetare -* UCK), its core membership consists of local Albanians. A political directorate headed by Ali Ahmeti demands revisions to the Macedonian constitution and guarantees for the Albanian minority.

MARCH 31, 2001 – The London *Sunday Times* reports that "hundreds of Kosovo Protection Corps (KPC) reservists were called up by their Albanian commander, Agim Ceku, in early March… and are

now re-emerging in Macedonia."

* * * * * * *

Former President Slobodan Milosevic is arrested after a 26-hour standoff at his home. He is taken to prison in Belgrade for questioning on corruption charges. Milosevic is arrested just hours before a deadline set by the U.S. which would quality Yugoslavia to receive foreign aid and to have economic sanctions removed.

APRIL 3, 2001 - U.S. Secretary of State Colin Powell promises $50 million in aid to Yugoslavia if Milosevic is arrested and turned over to The Hague. Yugoslavia hopes to raise $1.3 billion in international aid to repair damage to the country's infrastructure, sustained during NATO's bombing campaign.

ALI AHMETI

Commander of the National Liberation Army (UCK) (Macedonia). Following the September 2000 NATO intervention, he proclaimed that his UCK guerrillas were disarmed and disbanded. However, sporadic fighting continued and the UCK retained control of a large portion of Macedonian territory. As part of the proposed peace plan, he and his commanders are to be granted amnesty. Until then, Ahmeti remains holed up in the UCK mountain stronghold of Sipkovica.

BORIS TRJKOVSKI

President of Macedonia. Labelled a Macedonian nationalist by the Western media, he has been the champion of appeasement programs. As the Albanian guerrillas mounted their offensives, Trjkovski vacillated between strong military response and submission to international pressure. Hard-line Macedonians disapproved of this "gunpoint pacifism." Even within his VMRO party there is more division than their name (unity) would suggest.

LJUBO GEORGIEVSKI

Prime Minister of Macedonia. The number-two man in VMRO, he has often contradicted President Trjkovski. During the August offensives, Georgievski stated that no peace deal could be signed "as long as the guns were firing." In the end, the escalation of guerrilla attacks and international pressure forced Macedonians to accept the Ohrid peace agreement. Many Macedonians distrust Georgievski, believing he has been secretly collaborating with Djafferi.

APRIL 29, 2001 – Pro-independence parties win a slim majority in general elections in Montenegro.

JUNE 26, 2001 – 10,000 demonstrators march through Belgrade to protest the handover of Milosevic to the War Crimes Tribunal.

JUNE 28, 2001 – Milosevic is taken from Belgrade's central prison, sent to Bosnia by helicopter, and extradited to The Hague. He is charged with murder, deportation and persecution on political, racial and ethnic grounds. In the end, Western money sealed Slobodan Milosevic's fate, *Time* magazine reported. "The power of economic sanctions was underlined by the fact that Milosevic was first arrested to meet a deadline set by the U.S. Congress, and then

was extradited to coincide with a donor conference at which Western assistance was to be conditional on Belgrade's cooperation with The Hague Tribunal."

JULY, 2001 – Summer offensives by the UCK seize roughly 30 per cent of Macedonian territory. At Aracinovo, Macedonian security forces contain a large UCK force, but U.S. intervention prevents a complete Albanian defeat.

AUGUST 6, 2001 – Two members of the Serbian Interior Ministry are killed and two wounded in an attack by Albanian terrorists on a police station in the village of Mujhovac in south Serbia. The attack is attributed to the UCPMB and the fighters of a radical group led by Muhamed Xhemaili. Serbian

Deputy Prime Minister Nebojsa Covic visits the site as the U.S. embassy in Belgrade denounces the attack as "counterproductive because it is a threat to a process which has recently begun in southern Serbia; the process of reconciliation and rebuilding of confidence."

AUGUST 8-10, 2001 – The UCK's largest offensive almost succeeds in the capture of Tetovo. Peace talks are stepped up.

AUGUST 13, 2001 - Macedonian government and Albanian guerrillas sign a peace deal. NATO troops, including 200 troops from 2PPCLI, are deployed as part of *Operation Essential Harvest* with a mandate to disarm the Albanians.

LJUBOMIR BOSKOVSKI
Minister of the Interior (Macedonia). With his own police empire he is one of the most powerful political figures in Macedonia. His open defiance of NATO and strong anti-appeasement policies have earned wide-spread admiration. Despite early setbacks at the hands of the UCK guerrillas, Boskovski's police are now better-equipped and motivated. Viewed by Macedonian nationalists as their last hope, he is seen by European and Albanian leaders as an impediment to the ongoing peace process.

VLADIMIR BUCHKOVSKI
Appointed to the Macedonian Defence portfolio during crisis in July 2001, he preached a policy of restraint to his troops. Openly criticized his predecessor for using heavy-handed tactics during the shelling of Aracinovo, and soon became popular among the Albanians. However, as the UCK successes mounted, morale suffered. Many professionals quit the army to rejoin Boskovski's police units. A member of the Social Democrats, he lost his cabinet post in November 2001.

LORD GEORGE ROBERTSON
NATO Secretary-General. Britain's Minister of Defence during the Kosovo crisis, he embodied a jingoistic partisanship towards the Kosovar Albanians. That stance was altered slightly when the UCK entered south Serbia in 2000. Robertson issued mild rebuffs to his former allies while urging the Serbs not to retaliate. When the UCK switched its focus he warned the Macedonian government not to employ their helicopters against the rebels.

AUGUST 30, 2001 – The War Crimes Tribunal in The Hague files genocide charges against Milosevic. The following day he tries, unsuccessfully, to have the charges dropped.

SEPTEMBER 14, 2001 – Montenegro's pro-independence president, Milo Djukanovic, pulls out of talks on the future of the Yugoslav Federation. The Montenegrin government has not recognized Yugoslav institutions since then-president Milosevic forced through constitutional amendments in 1999 that it regards as illegal.

SEPTEMBER 26, 2001 – NATO concludes weapons collection operation in Macedonia. 3875 weapons are collected and trucked to

Greece for destruction. Many Macedonians claim that the Albanians are hiding weapons and that the peace accord rewarded "Albanian aggression." Parliament is reluctant to pass reforms. Operation *Essential Harvest* ends in Macedonia. Task Force *Fox*, under German command, is established to "provide a secure environment for the monitors of the international community."

OCTOBER 11, 2001 – An amnesty is declared for disarmed guerrillas in Macedonia.

OCTOBER 23, 2001 – Interpol claims that Albanian terrorists are linked to Osama bin Laden. A report indicates that one of bin Laden's military commanders was appointed to head an elite unit of

the KLA during the Kosovo crisis in 1999. The KLA, according to the report, maintains close links to Albanian criminal gangs which control 70 per cent of the drug trade in Austria, Germany, and the Scandanavian countries. Osama bin Laden is reported to have visited the Balkans three times between 1994 and 1996.

OCTOBER 29, 2001 – Stating that he is proud of what he achieved in his 13 years as President, Milosevic refuses to cooperate with UN War Crimes Tribunal which he describes as an illegal institution under the UN Charter.

NOVEMBER 17, 2001 – Elections are held in Kosovo for an interim government while the international community grapples with the future

JAVIER SOLANO
President of the European Union.
During the 78-day bombardment of
Yugoslavia, he was the secretary-
general of NATO. Although
overshadowed by more bellicose
counterparts, Solana nevertheless
supported the intervention.
Throughout the Macedonian crisis,
he worked closely with his NATO
successor, George Robertson, to
pressure the Macedonians into
accepting a peace deal. Solana
instructed the Ukraine to suspend
its arms shipments. As a result, at
the height of the UCK offensives in
August, the Macedonians could not
employ their helicopter gunships
for lack of ammunition and parts.

CARLA DEL PONTE
Chief prosecutor, The Hague War
Crimes Tribunal. In November
2001, Del Ponte flew into Skopje,
Macedonia to announce her
intention to "investigate and
prosecute" war crimes committed
during the previous summer's
ethnic clashes. Made it clear she
would review crimes committed
"by both sides" in the conflict.
However, she singled out Minister
of the Interior Lubjce Boskovski
and his police force for alleged
atrocity against Albanian civilians
in Ljuboten. She barred reporters
from visiting a mass grave
exhumation of Macedonian
civilians in the village of Trebos.

JAMES PARDEW
U.S. special envoy – Macedonia.
Former U.S. Intelligence officer
responsible for supporting Bosnian
Muslims in 1993, Pardew is viewed
as a strong Albanian supporter,
rather than an honest broker in the
Macedonian peace process.
Several times during the crisis
Pardew was able to exert
tremendous pressure on the
Macedonian government –
particularly in forcing them to abort
an offensive in Aracinovo. When
the UCK ambushed a Macedonian
police patrol outside Trebos in
November 2001, Pardew was
accused by Macedonian
intelligence of having tipped off the
Albanian guerrillas.

status of the province. The Yugoslav government announces that it is prepared to support Serb participation in the elections, provided that the necessary conditions are met. These include providing security guarantees to Serbs, creating safe conditions for the return of Serb refugees, tracing missing persons, and cooperating closely with the Yugoslav and Serb authorities. Seats are set aside for the Serbian minority, and the Ashkali, Roma, and Egyptian communities. Under pressure from the United States Rugova's rival, Hasim Thaci, was appointed as Kosovo's Prime Minister.

NOVEMBER 26, 2001 – Kosovo's Central Election Commission approves the final results of the Assembly elections. Ibrahim Rugova's Democratic League of Kosovo (LDK) wins 45.6 per cent of the popular vote to take 47 seats in the Assembly and form a minority government.

DECEMBER 15, 2001 – NATO peacekeepers in Kosovo detain several persons after searching the offices of an American-based Islamic charity suspected of supporting international terrorism.

JANUARY 1, 2002 – When the EU converts their currency to the new Euro, special permission is granted to Montenegro and Kosovo to officially use this new currency – contrary to the EU's position on Montenegro remaining a part of the federal Republic of Yugoslavia.

JANUARY 11, 2002 – The disbanded National Liberation Army (NLA) in Macedonia announces that it is "reorganizing and reactivating" its units and accuses the Macedonian government of ignoring the peace accord that would grant the ethnic Albanian minority a greater role in the police, parliament and education systems and

GEORGE W. BUSH
President of the United States. During the November 2000 post-election confusion a large force of Albanian guerrillas entered south Serbia from Kosovo. That these UCK units had passed undetected through the American sector led to speculation that NATO had cooperated with the Albanians. While campaigning, Bush had hinted at withdrawing U.S. forces from the region. However, a bold powerplay by Clinton's departing regime guaranteed that he could not easily extricate NATO from the Balkans. After the events of September 11, Bush has once again been forced to rethink U.S. foreign policy in the region.

BILL CLINTON
Former U.S. President. Under his administration, the U.S. greatly expanded its involvement in the Balkans. Siding with the Bosnians and Albanian Kosovars, America provided covert military support to Muslim extremist guerrillas. After the CIA had uncovered links to bin Laden's Al-Qaeda network in Albania, Clinton continued to assist the KLA. In order to justify NATO's intervention in Kosovo, Clinton's advisors were prepared to overlook the KLA's close links to international Muslim extremist organizations. NATO's failure to disarm the KLA in 1999 paved the way for incursions into Macedonia.

COLIN POWELL
U.S. Secretary of State. Inheriting a tangled mess from his predecessor, Madeleine Albright, Powell has been making efforts to reduce American presence in the Balkans. However, Bosnia and Kosovo cannot be abandoned without setting off a new round of civil wars. The presence of NATO troops in the regions may have provided short-term suppression of ethnic hostilities, but without massive economic redevelopment, there can be no long-term relief. Powell must also begin to mend fences with Yugoslavia, and this can only be done by clarifying U.S. policy towards Montenegrin independence.

expand the official use of the Albanian language. Ethnic Albanians account for nearly a third of Macedonia's population of two million.

JANUARY 16, 2002 – Ukraine announces plans to set up a plant in Macedonia to service and modernize Macedonia's armed forces. Kiev halted arms shipments under pressure from the West during last year's guerrilla conflict. Croatians mark ten years of independence. Former German Foreign Minister Hans Dietrich Genscher, the driving force behind international recognition of Croatia, arrives in Zagreb to mark the anniversary.

JANUARY 17, 2002 – In an open letter of protest, the Episcopal Councils of the Serbian Orthodox Church in the United States and Canada denounces the failure of NATO and the UN to take decisive action against terrorism and violence in Kosovo. Since NATO troops entered the province on June 12, 1999, 1000 Serbs have been killed and over 1200 abducted. The Serbian language is completely banned in public life and cultural monuments, and 110 churches and monasteries have been destroyed.

JANUARY 19, 2002 – American forces arrest six Algerians in Sarajevo linked to Osama bin Laden and the Al-Qaeda, and transport them to Guantanamo Bay, Cuba. Allegedly, the Algerians were planning to attack NATO bases at Tuzla and Srebrenica. All had come to Bosnia in the early nineties to fight alongside Bosnian Muslims and had been rewarded with Bosnian citizenship.

Compiled by Dr. Bill Twatio

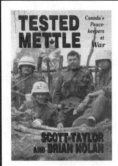